California
Economic
Growth

2004 Edition

CENTER FOR CONTINUING STUDY OF THE CALIFORNIA ECONOMY

California Economic Growth—2004 Edition was prepared as part of the research program of the Center for Continuing Study of the California Economy (CCSCE). Stephen Levy, Senior Economist, directed this project and was the report's principal author. Linda Bresnan prepared and edited the report and, with Nancy Levy, handled the report production. CCSCE appreciates the valuable assistance of Robert K. Arnold in providing conceptual guidance to the *California Economic Growth* series.

CCSCE staff specializes in analysis and long-term projections of economic and demographic variables in California and subareas of the state. *California Economic Growth—2004 Edition* is the product of an internally financed, ongoing program of CCSCE to provide business and government decision makers with an independent assessment of the future growth of California and subareas of the state.

Other publication in the CCSCE annual report series: *California County Projections*.

Table of Contents

INTRODUCTION

INTRODUCTION

California Economic Growth has been the cornerstone of the CCSCE publication series. It is the report in which CCSCE outlines its analysis of the state's economy and alerts subscribers to the early signs of future trends.

Even though a modest recovery is now underway, these are very difficult times in the national and state economy. Moreover, the polarization and partisanship that is affecting so many parts of our lives has also reached economists. We hope that our independent voice remains helpful to readers.

The main focus of the 2004 edition is on two issues: 1) helping readers think through the current economic problems to see how they affect (or don't affect) long-term economic prospects and challenges for California's regions, and
2) **introducing a new set of job projections** based on the new NAICS industry classifications under which all job data is now reported.

The estimates and projections of California's economic characteristics published in this report are part of an ongoing research program of the Center for Continuing Study of the California Economy (CCSCE). Except where noted, all the detailed estimates and projections in this report were prepared by CCSCE.

Our work benefited greatly from the continuing assistance of many dedicated people working for local, state and federal agencies involved in data collection and analysis. CCSCE wishes to acknowledge the special assistance of the following persons:

Howard Roth, Chief Economist of the California Department of Finance; Mary Heim of the Demographic Research Unit of the California Department of Finance; Jeff Reynolds and Joe Fitz of the California Board of Equalization; Ben Bartolotto, Research Director of the Construction Industry Research Board; Elizabeth Hill and Brad Williams of the Legislative Analyst's Office; and the entire staffs of the U.S. Bureau of Labor Statistics, the California Employment Development Department, and the California Department of Finance, who have responded graciously to numerous requests for data and assistance.

CCSCE also wishes to acknowledge the ongoing support of the many private and public sector clients and our loyal subscribers who have affirmed the value of having an independent perspective on the California economy.

MAJOR ECONOMIC REGIONS
OF CALIFORNIA

1. LOS ANGELES BASIN
2. SAN FRANCISCO BAY AREA
3. SAN DIEGO REGION
4. SACRAMENTO REGION
5. SAN JOAQUIN VALLEY
6. REST OF STATE

About California

California is the world's sixth largest economic power with a Gross State Product that exceeds $1.4 trillion. With 36 million residents and nearly 12 million households California is by far the nation's largest state market. Major regions of the state – the Los Angeles Basin, San Francisco Bay Area, Sacramento, San Diego and the San Joaquin Valley – are among the nation's largest regional market areas.

The need for credible information about California is well recognized. Private investors worldwide are constantly comparing California's economic environment to other locations. Financial institutions must assess the security of public and private debt and investments in the state. Public agencies must plan to meet the public service demands of 600,000 new residents each year.

Many of the nation's future challenges will first be met in California: maintaining competitiveness in high technology industries, capitalizing on the state's ethnic diversity, integrating the Internet into our businesses and homes, expanding into Asian markets and combining environmental protection with economic growth. What happens in California will influence national policy in these and other areas.

ABOUT CCSCE

The Center for Continuing Study of the California Economy (CCSCE) has become the recognized source of independent information about long term trends in California. CCSCE was founded as an independent, private economic research organization specializing in the analysis and study of California. CCSCE focuses on long term economic and demographic trends in the state and its major economic regions.

CCSCE works with private companies and public institutions that require an explanation and analysis of the growth process as well as detailed quantitative projections. CCSCE has developed a proprietary model to project long term economic trends in California based on a detailed analysis of the prospects of California industries within the framework of national and global trends.

CCSCE uses its findings to help decision makers in both the private and public sector make long term strategic plans regarding business decisions and public policy.

CCSCE was established in 1969 by Robert K. Arnold and Stephen Levy. It has been a source of reliable information on California for investors, businesses, and public agencies for over a quarter of a century.

EXECUTIVE SUMMARY

EXECUTIVE SUMMARY

Economic growth and prosperity in California is linked to national economic trends. In the short-term, California's job and income growth is shaped by how well the national economy is doing. In the long-term, national trends in jobs, population and income provide the context in which growth projections are determined for California and its major regions.

Long-Term U.S. Growth Projections (Chapter 4)

Moderate projected growth in population and jobs, combined with strong growth in productivity, provide the national economic context for assessing California's economic growth prospects.

- Population growth of 27 million is projected for 2002-2012. This includes approximately 10 million immigrants from foreign countries.

- More than 2/3 of the added population (18.5 million) will be aged 55 and above.

- Job growth of nearly 21 million is projected between the recession-depressed levels of 2002 and 2012.

- Productivity growth of 2.4% per year is anticipated. This is higher than anticipated a year ago, but still lower than the growth that has been experienced since 1996.

- Real GDP is projected to increase by 3.5% per year.

- National job growth is concentrated in sectors where California firms have above-average shares of national jobs and production.

- For every 50 job openings created by growth, there will be nearly 100 job openings created by retirements and occupational changes by workers.

The California Economy to 2012 (Chapter 5)

California's long-term job growth is determined by three factors: 1) the amount of national job growth, 2) which industries are projected to have above-average growth, and 3) the attractiveness of California as a location for entrepreneurs and workers in industries that sell to national and world markets. Firms that sell to national and world markets constitute what economists call California's *economic base*. Because these firms have a choice in where to locate new facilities, they are important for assessing the state's growth prospects.

Four major sectors account for the majority of projected U.S. basic industry job growth: 1) Professional and Business Services, 2) Information, 3) Tourism and Entertainment, and 4) Wholesale Trade and Transportation. These industries have significant choices in where to locate facilities and where to concentrate job growth. **In each of these sectors, California accounts for an above-average share of national jobs:**

- In 2003 California accounted for 11.3% of total U.S. jobs, but had 13.7% of Professional and Business Services jobs. These include industries such as computer and management services, architectural and research and development services and national and regional headquarters offices.

- California accounted for 12.6% of Information Services jobs. These include software publishing and Internet-related services.

- California accounted for 14.2% of Tourism and Entertainment jobs. These include motion picture production, amusement facilities and hotels.

- California accounted for 11.4% of Wholesale Trade and Transportation jobs, many of which are related to foreign trade. **The state's share of U.S. foreign trade has been rising since 1990.** California handles 17% of the nation's foreign trade volume.

As a result, California is projected to have an above-average **and modestly increasing** share of jobs in the national economic base.

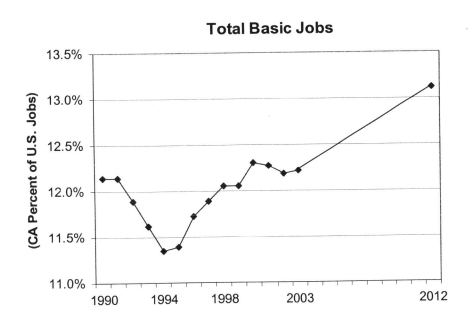

Total Basic Jobs

The two major manufacturing sectors in California's economic base—High Tech Manufacturing and Diversified Manufacturing—are still important in assessing the prospects for economic growth in California. **This is true even though neither sector is projected to add many jobs at the national or state level.** Manufacturing, especially High Tech Manufacturing is projected to have rising levels of production and sales. It is also expected to account for some of the job growth in Professional and Business Services and Wholesale Trade.

High Tech Manufacturing includes computer and electronic products, aerospace and pharmaceuticals. It is projected to have the highest growth in output of all basic industry sectors in the nation. Since the drop in its share of aerospace-related jobs in the early 1990s, California has accounted for a relatively constant 20% of the nation's high tech manufacturing jobs and an even higher share of high tech sales.

Most other manufacturing industries are included in CCSCE's Diversified Manufacturing sector. Although these industries are projected to have modest job and income growth nationally, the sector is large in California. It is critically important, especially in Southern California.

Despite the barrage of headlines about manufacturing firms leaving California, the state has recorded a slowly rising share of the nation's Diversified Manufacturing jobs. That modest share gain is expected to continue to 2012. After three disappointing years, exports of manufactured goods produced in California are up at double-digit rates in 2004.

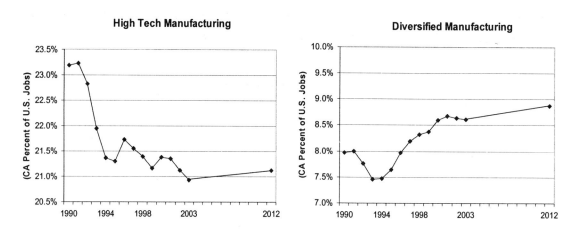

California is projected to add 3.5 million jobs between 2003 and 2012. Based on the job growth projected in the state's economic base, California will slightly outpace the nation in job growth. Job levels are projected to increase by 2.2% per year in California, compared with the projected 1.6% annual increase in the nation. The state's projected growth rate "advantage" is similar what happened between 1994 and 2003. At that time, state job levels increased by 1.7% per year, compared to national levels that increased by 1.3% per year.

California and United States
Total Jobs
1979-2012
(Thousands)

| | 1979 | 1994 | 2000 | 2003 | 2012 | Average Annual Growth Rate | |
						1994-2003	2003-2012
California	10,932.0	13,813.1	16,232.9	16,140.5	19,629.5	1.7%	2.2%
United States	101,401.5	127,235.7	144,132.4	142,336.9	163,756.8	1.3%	1.6%
CA % of U.S.	10.8%	10.9%	11.3%	11.3%	12.0%		

California economic growth rates outpace the nation during periods of strong economic growth, but California does no better than the nation in periods of economic slowdown. Job levels fell in California in the early '90s as the state's recession lasted much longer than the nation's. During the recent recession, the state and the nation had similar job losses.

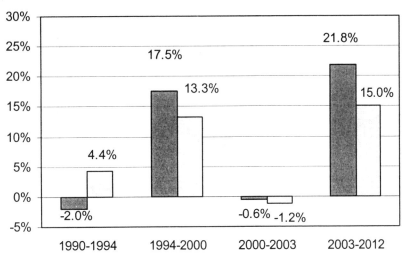

Past and Future Job Growth
California

Foreign trade and venture capital funding are additional areas critical to assessing California's economic prospects.

The volume of foreign trade is expected to grow much more rapidly than the overall national economy, with Pacific Rim trade growing even faster. California is the major collection and distribution center for trade going to and from China (which is the nation's fastest-growing trade partner) and other Pacific Rim countries. California accounts for 17% of the nation's foreign trade and, as described in Chapter 3, has reversed the downward trend in the state's trade share.

California firms receive more than 40% of the nation's venture capital funding. The state's **share of venture capital funding** reached a record high in 2003. Funding levels plummeted after the Internet bubble burst, and they are only now beginning to slowly rise again. An upsurge in venture capital funding will lay the foundation for future job growth in Silicon Valley and throughout the state.

Major Growth Trends

California's population is projected to increase by 4.9 million for the 2003-2012 decade or approximately 540,000 per year. Population growth has been larger than that since 2000 so CCSCE's projections anticipate an actual slowing in the annual growth for the rest of the decade.

California Major Growth Trends 2000-2012 (Thousands)				2003-2012 Percent Change	
	2000	**2003**	**2012**	**California**	**U.S.**
Total Jobs	16,232.9	16,140.5	19,659.5	21.8%	15.0%
Population	34,040.0	35,934.0	40,800.0	13.5%	8.2%
Households	11,502.9	12,015.8	13,738.2	14.3%	9.1%
Income (Billions, 2003$)	$1,202.4	$1,197.6	$1,746.1	45.8%	40.0%

Projections: CCSCE, Households for 2003 as of January 1, 2004

Household growth and housing production have moved upward since 2000. Housing permit levels are expected to reach 200,000 in 2004. Low interest rates and decisions by developers and communities to build housing on sites previously zoned for nonresidential uses are helping to push housing construction levels upward toward projected demand levels.

CCSCE projects that household growth could range from 1.5 million for the 2003–2012 period to more than 1.9 million. The amount of growth will depend on 1) the level of mortgage rates, 2) the amount of land that is rezoned to housing from nonresidential uses, and 3) how much the state is able to change state-local fiscal relationships to provide incentives for housing. Housing affordability has become a major concern, as discussed throughout this report.

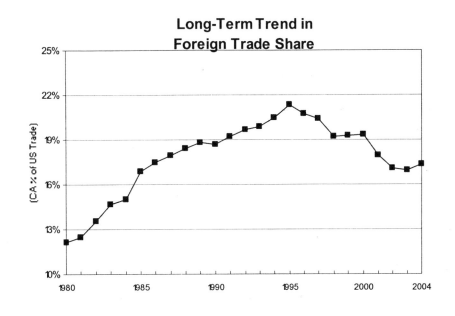

Long-Term Trend in Foreign Trade Share

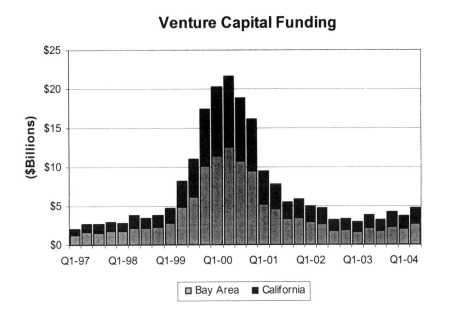

Venture Capital Funding

Strong productivity growth will support rising levels of real income in the state and nation. Total personal income in the state is projected to rise by 4.3% per year above the rate of inflation. Total income (in 2003$) will rise by nearly $550 billion or 45.8% between 2003 and 2012.

Per capita income in California is projected to increase 2.8% per year faster than the rate of inflation. In 2003, per capita income in California ($33,326) was 5.4% above the national average. By 2012, per capita income is projected to reach $42,796 (in 2003$), or 4.6% above the national average.

The Regional Economic Outlook (Chapters 7-12)

This section summarizes the economic outlook for California's major economic regions.

California and Economic Regions Total Jobs 1994-2010 (Thousands)					Average Annual Growth		
	1994	2000	2003	2012	1994-2000	2000-2003	2003-2012
Los Angeles Basin	6,457.1	7,389.1	7,460.0	8,976.2	155.3	23.7	168.5
San Francisco Bay Area	3,186.7	3,847.0	3,523.4	4,383.4	110.1	-107.9	95.6
San Diego Region	1,072.9	1,317.2	1,366.8	1,716.1	40.7	16.5	38.8
Sacramento Region	759.0	921.1	966.3	1,190.9	27.0	15.1	25.0
San Joaquin Valley	1,144.0	1,300.4	1,336.5	1,586.2	26.1	12.0	27.7
Rest of State	1,193.4	1,458.1	1,487.6	1,806.7	44.1	9.8	35.5
California	**13,813.1**	**16,232.9**	**16,140.5**	**19,659.5**	**403.3**	**-30.8**	**391.0**

Sources: 1990, 2000 and 2003 — BLS, EDD, CCSCE; 2012 — United States: BLS; CCSCE; California and regions: CCSCE

- The Los Angeles Basin is participating in the current economic slowdown, but it has not suffered the significant job losses experienced in the Bay Area or in the Basin a decade ago.

- The Basin is projected to add 1.5 million jobs between 2003 and 2012. The average annual increase of 168,300 jobs is slightly above the annual gains experienced in the 1994–2000 period. Basin jobs are expected to grow by 20.3%, close to the state average.

The Basin economy will benefit from growth in foreign trade, motion pictures, tourism, diversified manufacturing and professional services. The strong projected growth in foreign trade is expected to add jobs if the region maintains the aggressive expansion of port-related infrastructure. Housing costs and supply and regional infrastructure shortages are the most serious economic challenges facing the region.

- The Bay Area is currently the state's weakest regional economy, after being a star performer between 1994 and 2000. Tech losses, accentuated by a large drop in exports, continue to create significant job declines. **The Bay Area has accounted for more than the state's total job losses since 2000. By contrast, all other regions have added some jobs and have outpaced the national growth rate.**

  The Bay Area economy is projected to recover, with new gains in tech-related professional services, exports and start-ups reversing recent job losses. While the region should experience significant growth from 2003 forward, the region's job growth rate from 2000 forward will be the lowest in California— barely matching the national average.

- San Diego began a strong economic recovery in 1994 and has experienced continuing job growth through the recent recession. The region is expected to be one of the state's leaders in job growth in the decade ahead. It is expected to have a 25.6% job increase from 2003 through 2012—38,700 added jobs per year.

  The region's economic strength comes from proximity to Mexico (trade and maquiladora activity), from continuing opportunities in telecommunications and biotech, and from growth in professional services. Housing prices have surged since 2000, and housing costs and availability could constrain growth. Like most California regions, San Diego faces challenges for expanding airport and other infrastructure capacity.

- The Sacramento region is projected to add approximately 25,000 jobs per year and to grow by 23.2% between 2003 and 2012. The Sacramento region has grown as a competitive location for activities seeking a California alternative to the higher-cost coastal regions. The growth of professional services related to state government is critical to continuing high rates of overall job growth. The region still has a large amount of vacant land, but faces challenges in accommodating the projected growth while maintaining a high quality of life.

- The San Joaquin Valley is projected to add 28,200 jobs per year and to grow by 18.7% between 2003 and 2012. The traditional resource base (agriculture, mining, timber) will see job declines in the decade ahead. Regional growth will be driven by relocation of firms and workers from the big urban areas of California, based on cost and quality-of-life considerations. The new UC campus in Merced and the long-term potential for households to live in the Valley and work in the coastal urban centers will boost the region's growth.

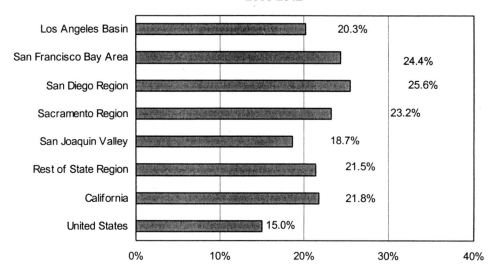

Projected Job Growth
Regions, California, and U.S.
2000-2012

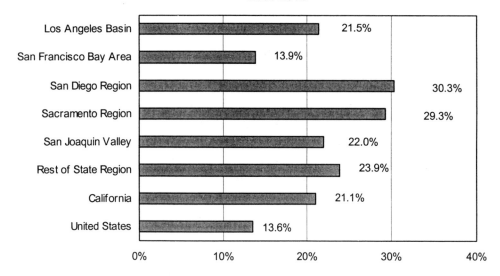

The California Economy in 2004 and 2005 (Chapter 3)

This section gives a picture of the California economy in 2004 and 2005. **The state jobs data tells a tale of two Californias.** The rate of total job losses for the state since March 2001 (1.1%) slightly exceeds the rate of national job loss (0.8%). However, California's numbers reflect two very different regional pictures.

The San Francisco Bay Area has lost nearly 400,000 jobs, while the other regions in California have added more than 200,000 jobs. The Bay Area lost more than 10% of its pre-recession job base while other regions in California posted a 2% job increase.

The state's economic regions outside the Bay Area outpaced the nation in job growth since March 2001. The state total nearly matched the national performance—despite including the large Bay Area job losses.

Non-Farm Wage and Salary Jobs (Thousands)				
	March 2001	**August 2004**	**Numerical Change**	**Percent Change**
California	14,728.0	14,561.4	-166.6	-1.1%
Bay Area	3,571.0	3,183.0	-388.0	-10.9%
California (excl. Bay Area)	11,157.0	11,378.4	221.4	2.0%
United States	132,507.0	131,575.0	-1,032.0	-0.8%

Source: EDD (Interim Series), CCSCE and U.S. Bureau of Labor Statistics

California's recent job performance is in the middle of the range for all states, as shown on the next page. The state's job losses are far smaller on a percentage basis than those in other high tech states like Massachusetts and Colorado. California also did better than most Midwestern states. California regions outside of the Bay Area were among the few areas in the nation that showed positive job growth during this period.

Manufacturing job levels have declined sharply in both the state and the nation. There were 125,000 fewer manufacturing jobs in California in August 2004 than there were at the bottom of the 1990–1994 recession. **In the current downturn, California has lost more than 300,000 manufacturing jobs.** In comparison, the nation lost more than 2.5 million manufacturing jobs during the same period.

Non-Farm Wage and Salary Jobs

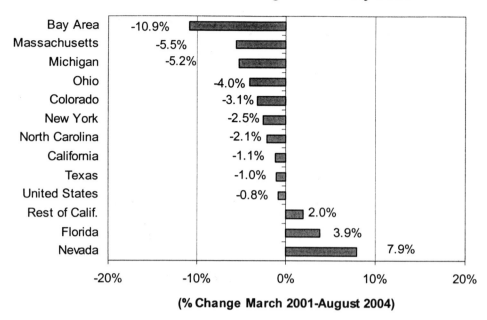

(% Change March 2001-August 2004)

Regional and Metro Area Job Trends—Definitely a Bay Area Recession

California's job losses were concentrated in the San Francisco and San Jose metropolitan areas, as shown in the table below.

Non-Farm Wage and Salary Jobs (Thousands)			
Region	July 2000	July 2003	July 2004
Los Angeles Basin	6,681	6,738	6,794
L.A. County	4,038	3,949	3,973
Orange County	1,388	1,428	1,431
Riv-San Bern Metro Area	980	1,078	1,105
San Francisco Bay Area	3,529	3,175	3,170
Oakland Metro Area	1,043	1,014	1,020
San Fran Metro Area	1,086	946	949
San Jose (Silicon Valley)	1,042	853	840
San Diego	1,186	1,237	1,257
Sacramento	833	880	881
San Joaquin Valley	1,006	1,058	1,072
California	**14,516**	**14,379**	**14,558**
United States	**132,043**	**129,814**	**131,331**

Source: California Employment Development Department; U.S. Bureau of Labor Statistics

The San Jose (Silicon Valley) metropolitan area accounted for approximately 200,000 of the state's job losses. Job levels in the San Francisco metro area fell by more than 100,000 during this period.

Strong job gains in the Riverside-San Bernardino metro area and modest gains in Orange County outweighed job losses in Los Angeles County and kept the Los Angeles Basin slightly on the plus side for job growth. The San Diego and Sacramento regions had job gains throughout most of the recession period. However, job gains in both regions have slowed in recent months.

Some Good News Emerges in 2004

Two major California sectors are reporting strong results so far in 2004: exports and foreign trade. Levels in both sectors are surging.

Exports of goods manufactured in California are up 22% for the first half of 2004. **Exports to China are up 50%.** This is a very good sign for California and the nation. China will soon be the world's largest market, aside from the United States. Historically, exports to China have lagged far behind imports from China. The recent data is a sign that export markets in China may finally be opening up.

Exports of high-value goods in computers, transportation equipment and machinery are rebounding from the post-2000 slowdown. Computer products represent California's largest export sector, and sales are up 20.8% so far in 2004. Even larger gains have been posted for transportation equipment and machinery.

Total trade volumes through California ports and airports are up nearly 15% so far in 2004. Trade volume gains in the Bay Area are leading the way, after severe declines in 2001 and 2002.

Data from EDD's "interim" series (using more up-to-date and complete payroll data) show that motion picture job levels are much higher than shown in the monthly survey. This good news is consistent with production data released by the Entertainment Industry Development Corporation.

California Economic Outlook – 2004 and 2005

There is broad agreement among economists about California's short-term economic outlook, but there is also broad agreement that these forecasts have significant uncertainty. Short-term forecasts are often wrong because external events change. **The short-term economic forecasts for California discussed below depend on achieving moderate economic growth in the nation in 2005—and there are many uncertainties about the national economic forecast.**

California's economic outlook for 2004 and 2005 includes

- Job growth of 1% (160,000) in 2004 and 2% (320,000) in 2005,

- Personal income growth of between 5% and 5.5% in each year,

- Residential building of near 200,000 units in each year,

- Substantial gains in exports and total foreign trade through California ports,

- An upturn in high tech production without substantial job gains,

- Inflation at between 2% and 2.5% in each year,

- Population growth averaging 550,000 per year, and

- Taxable sales growth keeping pace with income growth through 2005.

Issues and Challenges (Chapter 6)

Beginning with the 2003 edition of *California Economic Growth*, CCSCE addresses issues and challenges on an ongoing basis during the year and posts essays and memos on CCSCE's website, www.ccsce.com. This year's issues and challenges are related to three questions: 1) What makes a good business climate, 2) What is going on with the state budget, and 3) What role do state budget decisions play in creating a good business climate.

The debate over making California "attractive for business" has become ideological and partisan. The debate over California's budget choices remains stuck because residents continue to ask for more services without being willing to pay for the services they already have.

The "business climate" debate has three parts: 1) A bipartisan desire to see improvements in workers' compensation, energy and housing costs, 2) a continuing effort by some groups to portray the state's actual job performance as worse than it is, and 3) a lack of willingness to actively support and find ways to pay for the investments in education, infrastructure and quality of life that business and civic groups all agree are necessary to enhance the state's competitive position.

Firms often change the location of individual plants and make decisions about where to locate new facilities. The forces of globalization and the pressures to find cheaper ways to produce goods and services are part of the nation's and the state's "business environment."

Silicon Valley was "written off" in the 1970s when the first plants moved to Malaysia, and again in 1985 when chip supply ran far ahead of demand. But in the mid-1990s new innovations and the Internet created an enormous boom in the Valley, in California and in the nation. Each year, some firms go out of business and a few firms move operations to other states and countries. Each year, some new firms are created and some other firms move operations to California. The impact of these shifts can be seen by examining the state's comparative overall job growth.

The graph on page 1-12 shows the recent California "jobs performance." The graph on page 1-5 shows California's longer-term comparison to national job growth trends. Neither graph is consistent with anecdotal claims that massive numbers of firms and jobs are fleeing California.

In the early '90s, California's "jobs performance" **was demonstrably worse** than the trends in most other states, as shown on page 1-5. Even then, the explanation lay in national industry shifts (the dramatic reduction in defense spending) and had little to do with state government policies.

Different firms have different priorities. While energy costs may be critical for some firms, other factors (such as transportation infrastructure, educational opportunity, and having great communities in which to live and work) are critical for other firms. State leaders need to examine where California's economic opportunities lie and develop an economic strategy that will focus our limited resources on the most effective approaches to fostering prosperity for the broadest number of residents.

Housing is the largest spending component for most families, and it is one of the most severe "competitive hurdles" for businesses attempting to attract workers. **Housing is also the one cost area where the state's "competitive disadvantage" is very large and rising.**

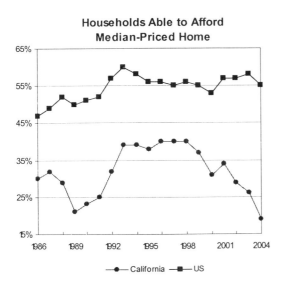

Households Able to Afford Median-Priced Home

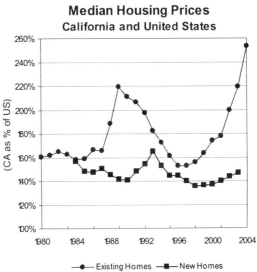

Median Housing Prices
California and United States

Although it will be challenging to develop approaches that maximize housing availability and affordability in California, there is no doubt that housing represents the largest expense for most residents—and a strong obstacle to convincing talented people to come to California.

The state is again having debates over the "costs" of a clean environment. There certainly are cases where environmental regulations do not follow the economic rule of promoting cost-effective approaches first. **On the other hand, imagine the Los Angeles Basin trying to "compete for business" if smog levels were as they were in the 1950s or 1960s.**

There is actually strong consensus that the "investment component" of creating a good business climate is important. The obstacle is not agreement, but rather the willingness to pay for the investments—and a continuing distrust of government's ability to spend money honestly and efficiently.

California remains paralyzed about the two basic budget-balancing choices: 1) cutting or reducing the rate of spending growth, and 2) increasing the rate of revenue growth. The recently adopted state budget follows the practice of recent budgets in that it relies on some spending cuts, some revenue increases and lots of borrowing and deferrals of spending to later years. The Legislative Analyst's Office projects ongoing state budget deficits of more than $8 billion per year.

There is hope that some savings can be found through eliminating "waste, fraud and abuse." In early 2004, the Governor requested a "performance review" of some state programs. The resulting report has been published and is being discussed throughout the state. While the early comment is that there are some sensible ideas in the review, the same early comments also warn that potential savings are significantly overstated.

In a real sense, the old saying is true. **We have met the enemy, and the enemy is us.** The question for someone objectively assessing California's economic prospects is whether residents and leaders can move beyond ideological gridlock to create a consensus that includes

- Business cost reductions,

- Investments in education, infrastructure and quality of life, and

- A balanced budget that reflects the collective vision of Californians for the kind of state they wish to live in and pass on to their children.

KEY CONCEPTS IN
UNDERSTANDING THE
CALIFORNIA ECONOMY

KEY CONCEPTS IN UNDERSTANDING
THE CALIFORNIA ECONOMY

There are four important concepts that are helpful in understanding how the California economy operates. These concepts are helpful both in explaining recent trends and in discussing the long-term outlook for the California economy.

The four concepts are:

- The distinction between growth in **numbers** and growth in **prosperity**.

- The importance of the state's **economic base** in determining future growth.

- How the **pool** of new opportunities in the nation and the state's **share** of U.S. job and output growth combine to determine how fast California will grow in the number of added jobs, population and households.

- The distinction between the determinants of **long-term** versus **short-term** economic growth in a state like California.

Growth in Numbers versus Growth in Prosperity

This report addresses two major questions about the California economy:

How California is Related to the U.S. Economy

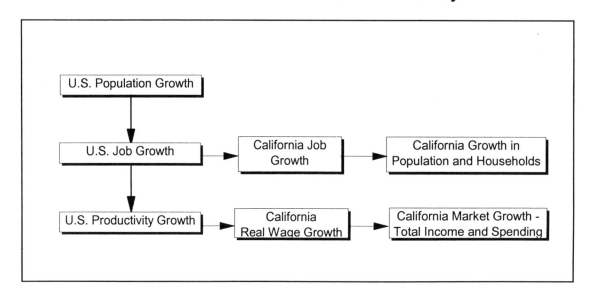

- How will California grow in **numbers**? How many more jobs, people and households will be added in California in the years ahead?

- How much will the state improve in terms of the **prosperity** of California's residents? What will the trends be for real income and spending?

The questions about numerical growth are answered by examining the **prospects for job growth** in California. The growth rate of a region like California is dependent on the decisions of individual firms to locate new facilities or expand existing ones. The growth in California's **economic base** (export industries) will determine the rate of overall job growth.

Population and household growth in California are related to job growth. California will gain new residents and require new housing units roughly in proportion to the state's job growth.

The growth in numbers in California is largely determined by the growth in numbers in the nation. Given the substantial projected growth in population and jobs in the nation, there is no doubt about the findings that California will grow significantly in terms of total jobs, population, and households.

The nation will add between 25 and 30 million residents in the next ten years and another 100 million people after that by 2050. If CCSCE's numerical growth projections are not met in 2012, they will be met and surpassed shortly thereafter. California will remain the nation's largest market by a significant degree (and with the largest projected growth in numbers) for any conceivable future planning period.

Despite the challenges facing California, **public and private decision makers in California should continue to anticipate large numerical growth**.

Growth in **prosperity** – real income and spending – has quite different determinants. The principal factor driving gains in real income and spending is **productivity growth** – increases in the productive capability of the workforce.

Productivity growth accelerated during the 1995-2000 period and has continued during the recent period of slow economic growth. The principal reasons are 1) the impact of investments in technology, 2) corporate restructuring to reduce costs and 3) the impact of the Internet on cost reduction.

As a result, real wages and incomes have risen since 1995. Living standards are at record levels for many families. For other families the 1995-2000 period reversed some, but not all, of the income losses from the previous two decades.

The outlook for future productivity gains is the brightest in many years. Nevertheless, some labor force challenges persist even in a strong economy:

- Low unemployment rates brought many workers into the labor force but their families are still in poverty because the jobs pay very low wages.

- Job skills and requirements for many middle class jobs are constantly changing which poses challenges to all workers and the economy as to how the majority of workers can have access to opportunities to upgrade their skills over their lifetime.

California's Economic Base is the Key Factor in Relative Job Growth

How fast or slowly California adds jobs compared to other areas is determined by growth in the state's **economic base**. Basic industries – the industries included in California's economic base – make a substantial share of their sales to customers outside the state. Basic industries export goods and services to areas elsewhere in the nation or world.

Basic industries produce both goods and services. Major goods-producing basic industries in California include computer equipment, electronic components, apparel, aircraft, and instruments.

Services are also an important component of California's economic base. Major service-producing basic industries include motion pictures, computer services, tourism and engineering and design services.

Basic industries are an important focus for public policy:

- *Exportable goods and services are subject to intense competition. A state competitiveness strategy means being competitive in basic industries.* Growth in jobs and sales in the state depends on how well the state's firms and workers compete – often with locations throughout the world. People involved in basic industries – whether in manufacturing apparel, filming a motion picture, or deciding where to vacation – have a choice of location.

- *Growth in the economic base will determine the opportunities for job growth and increases in income in the rest of the economy.* Prospects for employment growth in supporting activities like retail trade, medical services, construction and local education depend on employment expansion in basic industries. States with the fastest growing economic bases have the highest rates of overall employment growth.

The Pool of New Opportunities and California's Share

California's future job growth will be determined by:

- How many and what kind of jobs are created in the nation – the **pool** of new jobs?

- What **share** of new jobs will locate in the state?

The **pool** of new jobs has two important characteristics – size and composition. The size of the pool is discussed in Section 4 – the U.S. will gain substantial numbers of new residents and new jobs in the years ahead.

The composition of those jobs is also important in analyzing California's growth. Where new jobs will be (in what industries) makes a difference to the state's future economic prospects.

The finding of CCSCE's analysis is that the composition of U.S. job growth is favorable to California's economic base. The fastest sales and job growth in basic industries is occurring in industries where California has a large base of activity and a strong competitive position.

Recently, the question of California's future share of national jobs and production has received a great deal of attention. CCSCE devotes a major part of this report to reviewing recent share trends and analyzing two related issues:

- What are the likely future trends in California's share of key basic industries?

- What are the factors most likely to affect California's competitive position (i.e., share) in the future?

There is agreement that California will have the opportunity to participate in emerging growth markets.

There is agreement that California faces challenges in converting these opportunities into job and income gains. There is little agreement yet, however, on what are the most important areas of challenge or on which public policies are critical for success.

CCSCE hopes that the analysis in **California Economic Growth, 2004 Edition** will help focus these questions and provide some answers.

The Relationship of Total Job Growth to Changes in California's Economic Base – Economists look at three kinds of impacts when assessing the impact of an addition (or reduction) to the state's economic base. These are:

- Direct impacts

- Indirect (or supplier) impacts

- Induced (or consumption) impacts

The **direct** impacts are the sales and income (wages and profits) created directly by the activity. For example, an increase in medical instruments or apparel sales creates additional income and jobs.

The directly affected industry buys inputs (supplies) from many other industries. For example, medical instrument and apparel manufacturers buy additional supplies when they receive new orders. Their purchases create additional sales, income and jobs. These activities are called the **indirect** impacts of changes in basic industry sales. A portion (often large) of the purchases occurs outside California. Therefore, the indirect impacts in California of changes in basic industry sales are usually modest.

Direct, Indirect, and Total Economic Impacts

Direct Impacts		Indirect Impacts
A new order	───────────────▶	Purchase of Additional Supplies and Services
│	**Induced Impacts**	│
▼		▼
Income and Job Increases	▶ Rise in Consumer Spending ▶	Income and Job Increases
	│	
	▼	
	Total Impacts	
	Income and Job Increases	

The direct and indirect (supplier) sales create **a pool of income and profits** for residents in the state. Residents spend the income on consumer purchases and create additional sales and jobs. These jobs are **"induced"** by the impacts of the income and jobs from the direct and indirect activities. The **consumption multiplier** is another name for induced spending and jobs.

The distinctions between direct, indirect and induced spending explain how changes in basic industry activity can cause much larger changes in total jobs. The linkage explains why basic industries are critical in determining regional growth rates even though most new jobs are not in the economic base.

Long-Term Versus Short-Term Outlook and Issues

For the most part the explanation of short-term trends in the California economy depends on different factors than the key determinants of the state's long-term economic prospects. Similarly, the policy choices, especially the policy choices facing state government, vary between the short and long-term context.

Here are some examples of the difference between short-term and long-term economic determinants. In the long term, residential building is determined by population growth and affordability factors. Yet between 1989 and 1993 California experienced a 64% drop in residential building while the state added more than 2 million residents and both mortgage rates and home prices declined. As the cyclical factors diminish (as they are doing now) the construction market will again be determined by long-term job and population growth.

Long-Term Versus Short-Term Economic Growth in California		
Determinants and Issues	Short Term	Long Term
Job Growth	National and world economic cycles, cyclical fluctuations in key industries	Long-term growth trends for key industries in economic base
Housing Construction	Fluctuations in prices and buyer confidence	Household growth
Spending	Fluctuations in income **and** variations in consumer confidence	Growth in personal income
Principal Public Policy Tools	National fiscal and monetary policy; policies that affect consumer confidence	National policies in support of productivity and key industry growth. State policies to attract and retain key basic industries.

In the long run, spending and consumption related jobs are related to the growth in total jobs and income. In the short term, however, fluctuations in income and in consumer confidence can distort the spending/income ratio. For example, a sharp (and temporary) drop in spending relative to income restrained job growth in California in the early 1990s and occurred again in 2001-2003.

In the long term, job growth depends on the pool of new jobs created in the U.S. and the share that will locate in California. In the short term, however, job levels fluctuate in response to world events (e.g., economic turmoil in Asia), national economic cycles (e.g., the high levels of recent U.S. job growth), and region specific factors (e.g., the importance of technology manufacturing in California's economy and state specific cycles in construction and consumer confidence).

As a result of the difference between short and long-term growth determinants, California can face significant long-run growth prospects even though the state has entered a period of slowing growth. In the short term, many of the continuing areas of strength – foreign trade, high tech, tourism and entertainment, will be outweighed by the negative impacts of slowing economic growth inside and outside the United States.

As a result, both cyclical and permanent factors can contribute to job losses during a recession. The important points for policy analysis are 1) to keep **separate** the **analyses** of short and long-term factors and 2) to develop **separate policy responses** to short and long-term job and income growth determinants.

The distinction between long-term and short-term economic growth is especially important in the policy arena. State governments have no significant short-term economic tools. They cannot influence the world economy or the national business cycle. They cannot significantly change the confidence of homebuyers or consumers. States cannot influence cycles in key markets like aerospace.

State government policies are rarely the principal cause of cyclical fluctuations in state economies nor can state government policies do much to reverse short-term cycles.

However, state governments need not be simply passive spectators as recession impacts affect residents and business. States can advocate for federal counter-cyclical financial assistance (a very good idea in 2003) and can use state infrastructure investments as an anti-recession tool. Both ideas are examined in the *Key Issues* section.

State governments, however, have a much more significant role in long-term economic growth. State governments have a key role in **some** areas – like education, infrastructure, quality of life, and rules and regulations – which do affect the state's attractiveness for business investment.

THE CALIFORNIA ECONOMY
TO 2005

THE CALIFORNIA ECONOMY TO 2005

The Bottom Line

United States — Strong national economic growth is essential for achieving job and income growth in California. **There are no sustained periods in the past 60 years where the California economy has grown while the national economy lagged.**

Measured by jobs and income, the national economy is expanding. GDP and corporate profits are at record levels; interest rates and inflation remain low by historical standards. Yet, measured by job growth, the current "recovery" is the weakest expansion after recession since the Great Depression.

Moderate economic growth is forecast for 2005, with GDP growth expected to be between 2.8% and 3.5%. Several factors are pushing growth rates lower: Interest rates are rising, oil prices are surging and some tax incentives for corporate investment expire at the end of 2004.

Job growth will continue to be a challenge. If productivity gains remain in the 2-to-2.5% range, then GDP growth will need to be at least 3.5% per year to keep pace with labor force growth.

California — Since 2000 there have been two California economies: 1) the Bay Area, and 2) the rest of the state.

Bay Area job losses exceed the state's total job losses. Outside the Bay Area, all major economic regions of California have 1) added jobs since 2000, and 2) outpaced the nation in job growth during this period.

There are many positive indicators for the California economy in 2004. Exports of goods made in California are growing, led by high tech exports. Total trade volumes will reach record levels in 2004, led by trade with China. Motion picture production job levels are rising, according to recent EDD estimates. Technology manufacturing sales and wages are rising. Income and spending are growing.

As in the nation, California is experiencing a moderate economic recovery **except when measured by jobs.** As yet, neither economy is growing rapidly enough to create many added jobs, due to the continuing high rates of productivity growth. In high tech, for example, production levels are rising significantly—but not by enough to require companies to hire many additional workers.

Despite the headlines, California's job performance during the current recession is average among all states. This is in stark contrast to the early '90s, when California's job growth trailed the nation's by a wide margin.

The U.S. Economy

The U.S. economy experienced a mild recession in 2001. Aggressive interest rate cuts by the Federal Reserve Bank, along with tax cuts, provided stimulus to push the economy out of recession by the end of 2001.

Since the end of 2001, the national economy has experienced steady quarterly GDP growth in the range of 2% to 4% per year, as shown on page 3-5. Corporate profits have surged above $1 trillion and are forecast to be more than 50% higher in 2004 than in 2001.

In spite of these gains, job growth has lagged. National job levels remain nearly 1 million below the level in March 2001, at the beginning of the national recession. The nation has lost more than 2.5 million manufacturing jobs. Unemployment rates fell to 5.4% in August 2004 but remain above the 4% levels of late 2000 and early 2001.

In addition, some workers have dropped out of the labor force. Labor force participation rates have fallen from 67.1% in March 2001 to 66.0% in August 2004.

United States Job and Labor Force Trends March 2001 – August 2004 (Thousands)			
	March 2001	**August 2003**	**August 2004**
Non Farm Jobs	132,507.0	129,789.0	131,475.0
Manufacturing Jobs	16,931.0	14,404.0	14,421.0
Unemployment Rate	4.3%	6.1%	5.4%
Labor Force Participation Rate	67.1%	66.2%	66.0%

Source: Bureau of Labor Statistics

Sustained and above-average productivity gains have boosted GDP and corporate profits while making additional hiring less necessary. **Simply put, companies are able to produce more with fewer workers.**

Productivity growth has ranged from 2.0% to 4.5% in recent quarters. Such gains are well above the average since 1973 and should eventually translate into higher wages and benefits.

CCSCE wrote in *California Economic Growth — 2003 Edition*: "**Even though the outlook for the next six months is less robust than hoped for, eventually the U.S. economy will begin to recover sufficiently for job growth to resume, probably by the end of 2003.**"

Despite the fact that the nation has added nearly 1.7 million jobs since mid-2003, and despite the fact that manufacturing job levels have stopped falling, the current performance is the weakest jobs recovery since the Great Depression.

Job Gains
41 Months After Recession Starts

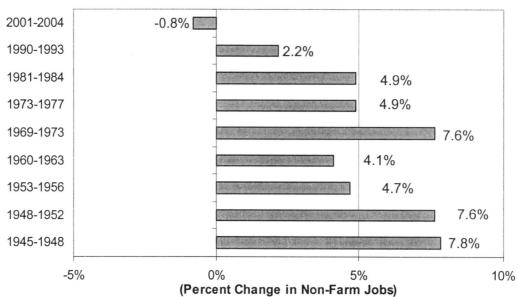

(Percent Change in Non-Farm Jobs)

The average job gain 41 months after the beginning of a recession is 4.7%, counting only the past six recovery periods. **If national job levels in August 2004 had been 4.7% above the levels of March 2001, the nation would have had an additional 7 million jobs, and California likely would have had more than 800,000 additional jobs.**

Steady and substantial cuts in interest rates were one of the nation's primary stimulus programs. During 2001 the federal funds rate was cut from 5% to below 2% in a series of bimonthly decreases. The federal funds rate was subsequently cut to 1.00%, well below the rate of inflation. This made real short-term interest rates negative.

Some stimulus is now being removed from the economy. The federal funds rate is moving back upwards, with the latest increase to 1.75% in September 2004. Tax credits for depreciation expire at the end of 2004. Higher oil prices act like a tax on spending and will lower the rate of economic growth.

Record budget deficits and projections of continuing budget deficits restrain the ability of any President or any Congress to provide additional short-term economic stimulus. The federal budget deficits also threaten long-term growth by putting upward pressure on interest rates and creating the possibility that the United States could be vulnerable if foreign nations decide to finance less of our long-term deficits.

U.S. Productivity Growth

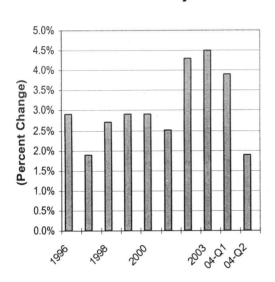

United States Corporate Profits

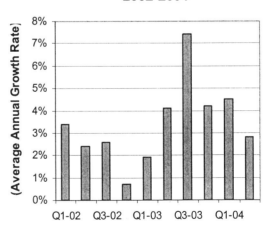

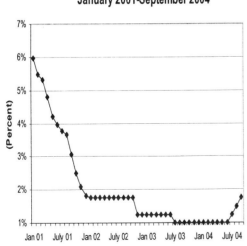

Federal Funds Rates
January 2001-September 2004

United States GDP Growth
2002-2004

The two most likely outcomes for 2005 are either 1) GDP growth in the 3.5% range and modest job gains, or 2) lower GDP growth, with job gains that may lag behind labor force growth. The nation appears to be in a period where GDP growth needs to be higher than "normal" in order to get substantial job growth.

California and U.S. Comparisons

The state jobs data tells a tale of two Californias. For the total state, job losses since March 2001 (1.1%) slightly exceed the rate of national job loss (0.8%). However, California's numbers reflect two very different regional pictures.

The San Francisco Bay Area has lost nearly 400,000 jobs while the other regions in California have added more than 200,000 jobs. The Bay Area lost more than 10% of its pre-recession job base while other regions in California posted a 2% job increase.

The state economic regions outside of the Bay Area outpaced the nation in job growth since March 2001, and the state total nearly matched the national performance—despite including the large Bay Area job losses.

Non-Farm Wage and Salary Jobs (Thousands)				
	March 2001	August 2004	Numerical Change	Percent Change
California	14,728.0	14,561.4	-166.6	-1.1%
Bay Area	3,571.0	3,183.0	-388.0	-10.9%
California (excl. Bay Area)	11,157.0	11,378.4	221.4	2.0%
United States	132,507.0	131,575.0	-1,032.0	-0.8%

Source: EDD (Interim Series), CCSCE and U.S. Bureau of Labor Statistics

California's recent job performance is in the middle of the range for all states, as shown on the next page. The state's job losses are far smaller on a percentage basis than those in other high tech states like Massachusetts and Colorado. California also did better than most Midwest states. California regions outside of the Bay Area were among the few areas that showed positive job growth during this period.

Non-Farm Wage and Salary Jobs

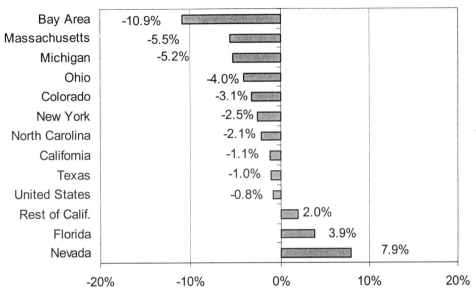

	%
Bay Area	-10.9%
Massachusetts	-5.5%
Michigan	-5.2%
Ohio	-4.0%
Colorado	-3.1%
New York	-2.5%
North Carolina	-2.1%
California	-1.1%
Texas	-1.0%
United States	-0.8%
Rest of Calif.	2.0%
Florida	3.9%
Nevada	7.9%

(% Change March 2001-August 2004)

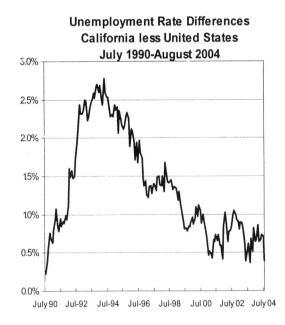

**Unemployment Rate Differences
California less United States
July 1990-August 2004**

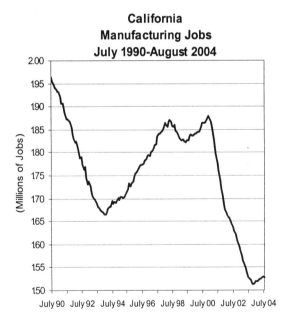

**California
Manufacturing Jobs
July 1990-August 2004**

In the 1990-94 recession, California's unemployment rate was as much as 2.7% higher than the national rate. This signifies that the downturn was much more severe in the state. Currently, the state's unemployment rate has ranged between .5% and 1.0% above the national rate, and the unemployment rate "gap" is smaller than it was three years ago.

In August 2004 California's unemployment rate was 5.8% compared to the nation's 5.4%. At the low in 2000, California's unemployment rate was 4.9% compared to the nation's low of 3.9%.

Manufacturing job levels have declined sharply in both the state and the nation. A comparison, using the new NAICS data, shows that the number of manufacturing jobs in California in August 2004 was more than 125,000 below the level at the bottom of the 1990-94 recession, and that **California has lost more than 300,000 manufacturing jobs in the current downturn.**

The nation lost more than 2.5 million manufacturing jobs during this period. Again, there are "two Californias" with regard to manufacturing job losses. The Bay Area's manufacturing job losses have been severe and far above the national manufacturing job loss rate. Manufacturing job levels in the other regions of California have been in line with the national performance.

The prospects for 2005 are discussed at the end of this chapter.

Regional and Metro Area Job Trends—Definitely a Bay Area Recession

California's job losses were concentrated in the San Francisco and San Jose metropolitan areas, as shown in the table below.

Non-Farm Wage and Salary Jobs (Thousands)			
Region	July 2000	July 2003	July 2004
Los Angeles Basin	6,681	6,738	6,794
L.A. County	4,038	3,949	3,973
Orange County	1,388	1,428	1,431
Riv-San Bern Metro Area	980	1,078	1,105
San Francisco Bay Area	3,529	3,175	3,170
Oakland Metro Area	1,043	1,014	1,020
San Fran Metro Area	1,086	946	949
San Jose (Silicon Valley)	1,042	853	840
San Diego	1,186	1,237	1,257
Sacramento	833	880	881
San Joaquin Valley	1,006	1,058	1,072
California	**14,516**	**14,379**	**14,558**
United States	**132,043**	**129,814**	**131,331**

Source: California Employment Development Department; U.S. Bureau of Labor Statistics

The San Jose (Silicon Valley) metropolitan areas accounted for approximately 200,000 of the region's and state's job losses. Job levels in the San Francisco metro area fell by more than 100,000 during this period.

Strong job gains in the Riverside-San Bernardino metro area and modest gains in Orange County outweighed job losses in Los Angles County and kept the Los Angeles Basin slightly on the plus side for job growth. The San Diego and Sacramento regions had job gains throughout most of the recession period. Job gains in both regions have slowed in recent months.

The San Joaquin Valley posted strong gains in non-farm jobs, but farm job losses restricted overall job growth. The Valley job growth was largely in population-serving sectors as the region experienced more rapid population gains in recent years.

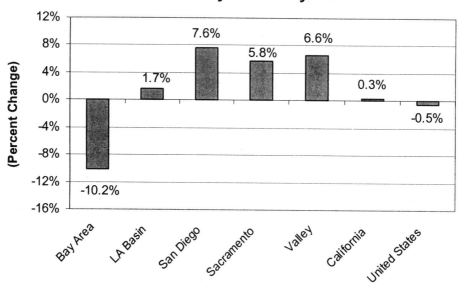

Non-Farm Job Growth
July 2000 - July 2004

Since 1994, the Los Angeles Basin has seen job growth slightly exceed the national average. The Basin has also avoided large job losses in this downturn, although job growth has been minimal since 2000.

The San Joaquin Valley trailed both the state and the nation in job growth throughout most of the mid and late 1990s. After that time, however, the Valley's job growth continued while the state and nation experienced job losses. As a result, by August 2004 the Valley had pulled ahead of both the state and the nation in job growth rates since 1994.

Jobs in the San Diego and Sacramento regions have outpaced the state and nation since 1994, **including during the period since 2000.**

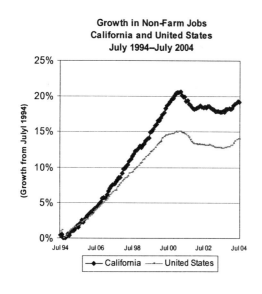

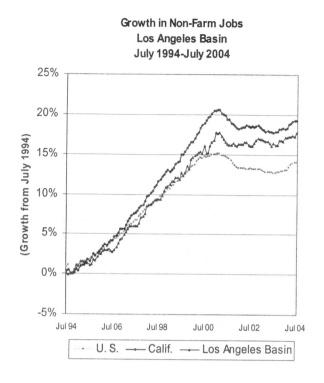

**Growth in Non-Farm Jobs
Los Angeles Basin
July 1994-July 2004**

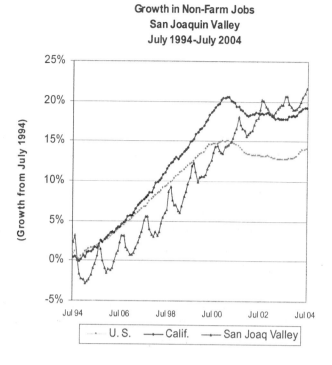

**Growth in Non-Farm Jobs
San Joaquin Valley
July 1994-July 2004**

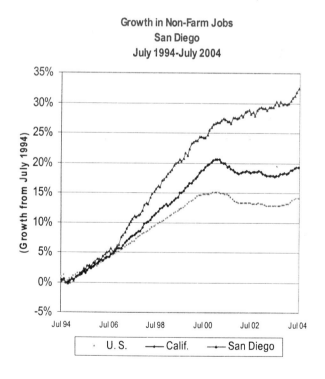

**Growth in Non-Farm Jobs
San Diego
July 1994-July 2004**

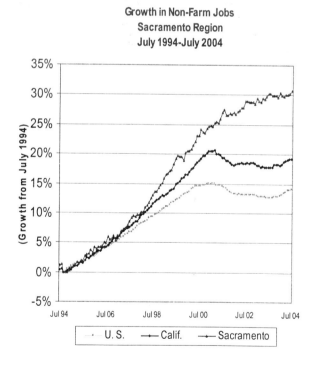

**Growth in Non-Farm Jobs
Sacramento Region
July 1994-July 2004**

Some Good News Emerges in 2004

Two major California sectors are reporting strong results so far in 2004: Export and foreign trade levels are surging.

Exports of goods manufactured in California are up 22% for the first half of 2004. **Exports to China are up 50%.** This is a very good sign for California and the nation. China will soon be the world's largest market, aside from the United States. Historically, exports to China have lagged far behind imports from China. The recent data is a sign that export markets in China may finally be opening up.

Exports of high-value goods in computers, transportation equipment and machinery are rebounding from the post-2000 slowdown. Computer products represent California's largest export sector, and sales are up 20.8% so far in 2004. Even larger gains have been posted for transportation equipment and machinery.

Total trade volumes through California ports and airports are up nearly 15% so far in 2004. Trade volume gains in the Bay Area are leading the way after severe declines in 2001 and 2002.

Data from EDD's "interim" series (using more up-to-date and complete payroll data) show that motion picture job levels are much higher than shown in the monthly survey. This good news is consistent with production data released by the Entertainment Industry Development Corporation.

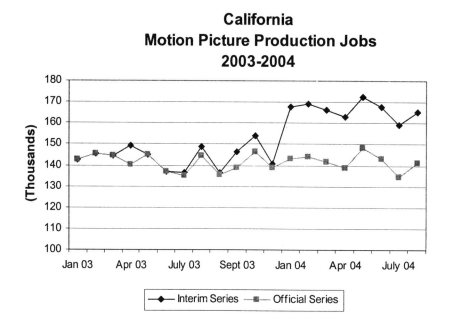

**California
Motion Picture Production Jobs
2003-2004**

California Export Growth

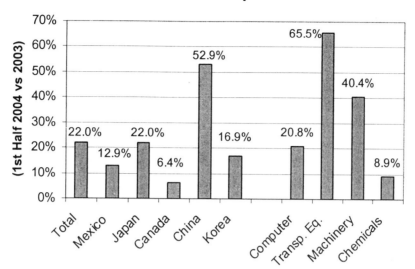

California Customs Districts
Growth in Foreign Trade

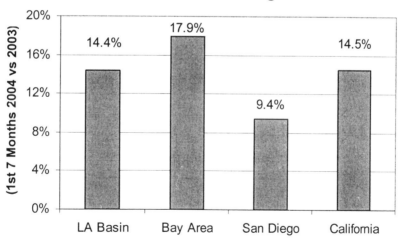

Personal Income is Growing in California

Total personal income in California rose 3.9% in 2003. Based on 1st quarter 2004 data, it is currently growing at 4.8%.

This is a sharp decline from the 10.5% growth posted in 2000, but it is far better than the weak gains experienced in 2001 and 2002.

Wage and salary income rose 5.1% in the 1st quarter of 2004. Average wage levels turned up (even including in the Bay Area), and there was a small increase in stock option income. Wage and salary income accounts for more than half of total personal income, and changes in wage and salary income are the major determinant of changes in total personal income.

Benefits rose at the same rate as wages and salaries. This is the first time in many quarters that benefits did not increase faster than wage income.

The dramatic drop in personal income growth after 2000, led by the sharp fall in stock option income, caused a decline in state income tax collections. This in turn created a budget gap between revenues and expenditures at the state level. Personal income is now growing at more normal rates, but not fast enough to close the budget deficits projected for future years.

Property income (dividends, interest and rents) grew very slowly between 2000 and 2003 but increased to a 4.0% growth rate in the 1st quarter of 2004. Property income should grow at higher rates in the near term as interest rates rise and companies increase dividends to keep pace with corporate profit growth.

The largest gain in personal income came from transfer payments as 1) unemployment insurance payments surged, 2) public medical payments (Medicare and MediCal) increased, and 3) Social Security income rose modestly.

	California Personal Income (Percent Change)		
	1999-2000	**2002-2003**	**2003-2004 Q1**
Total Personal Income	10.5%	3.9%	4.8%
Wages and Salaries	12.8%	3.3%	5.1%
Other Labor Income (Benefits)	11.6%	6.7%	5.1%
Proprietors Income	6.9%	6.0%	5.1%
Property Income	9.1%	0.6%	4.0%
Transfer Payments	4.4%	6.8%	5.5%

Source: California Department of Finance

Taxable Sales Decline in 2003 and 2004

Taxable sales were up 6.0% in the first quarter of 2004—the best performance since the fourth quarter of 2000. Taxable sales estimates for the last half of 2003 were also revised upward.

Revenue estimates from the California Department of Finance through August 2004 indicate that the long period of slow sales growth is finally over, and that the period of higher gains that began in the first quarter of 2004 should continue when data for the rest of the year is released.

The decline in taxable sales growth hit city, county and transit district budgets throughout California. It has created substantial problems for completing all of the projects that voters were promised when the taxes were approved. The rebound in taxable sales growth will help, but it will not recover the revenue losses from 2001 and 2002.

	California Taxable Sales ($Billions)				
	1st Quarter	2nd Quarter	3rd Quarter	4th Quarter	Year
2002	$101.0	$111.0	$112.2	$116.8	$440.9
2003	104.5	114.5	115.7	119.7	454.3
2004	110.8				
% Change - 2002-3	3.5%	3.1%	3.1%	2.5%	3.0%
% Change - 2003-4	6.0%				

Source: California Board of Equalization – percentages calculated from unrounded data

Construction — A Pretty Good Year Considering the Economy

In 2003, residential permit levels rose by 16.6% to their highest level since 1989. In the first seven months of 2004, permit levels are up 4.7%. Housing price levels surged in 2003, and are continuing to rise rapidly in 2004.

Nonresidential and public works construction results were more mixed. Nonresidential construction was down 4.2% in 2003, but it is up 9.9% for the first seven months of 2004.

California Nonresidential and Public Works Construction ($Billions)			
	Jan.-July 2003	Jan.-July 2004	Percent Change
Industrial	$.8	$.8	2.0%
Office	.7	.9	32.8%
Alterations & Additions	3.3	3.5	5.2%
Other	1.7	1.8	6.4%
Total Nonresidential	**$8.1**	**$8.9**	**9.7%**
Heavy (Civil Works)	$4.3	$5.0	16.6%
Public Buildings	5.7	5.4	-4.4%
Total Public Works	**$10.0**	**$10.5**	**4.6%**
Public Works & Nonresidential	**$18.1**	**$19.4**	**7.2%**

Source: Construction Industry Research Board

Public works construction reached $16.5 billion in 2003, exceeding the $13.9 billion in new nonresidential building. Public works construction is up another 4.6% in the first seven months of 2004.

Nonresidential construction appears to have turned up in most regional markets, signaling the end to the downturn since 2000. Recent state and local bond measures, along with increases in federal transportation spending, should translate into significant continuing gains in public works spending.

New residential construction rose in 2003 in terms of both units and valuation. Residential building is up slightly over 2003 levels in the first seven months of 2004.

The Los Angeles Basin is posting strong gains in construction so far in 2004. Nonresidential valuation is up 16.7%, and the number of residential permits is up 11.3% after a strong showing in 2003.

Nonresidential construction is up slightly in all regional markets in 2004 except in the San Joaquin Valley, where valuation levels are flat compared to the first seven months of 2003. Residential permit levels are up in the Sacramento and San Joaquin Valley regions but down slightly in San Diego and down by nearly 20% in the Bay Area.

California Construction Trends ($Billions) January — July						
	Nonresidential Permit Values			Residential Permits (Thousands)		
	2003	2004	% Change	2003	2004	% Change
Los Angeles Basin	$3.6	$4.2	16.7%	48,933	54,485	11.3%
San Francisco Bay Area	1.8	1.9	5.6%	16,120	13,151	-18.4%
San Diego	0.7	0.7	5.6%	11,011	10,433	-5.2%
Sacramento	0.7	0.7	4.4%	13,170	14,517	10.2%
San Joaquin Valley	0.9	0.9	-0.3%	16,973	19,261	13.5%
Other	0.4	0.5	7.3%	9,063	8,795	-3.0%
California	**$8.1**	**$8.9**	**9.9%**	**115,270**	**120,642**	**4.7%**

Source: Construction Industry Research Board

Resale Housing Market Sees Record Highs for Prices and Lows for Affordability

Median resale prices reached record levels in June or July of 2004 in every major regional market in California—including the Bay Area, where nearly 400,000 jobs have been lost since 2000.

Median resale housing prices exceeded $450,000 in California in the summer of 2004. This was a new record level. Median resale prices in Orange County are now well above $600,000 and now equal price levels in Santa Clara County and the Bay Area.

Median resale prices surged in California's lower-priced markets, including the Riverside-San Bernardino, Sacramento and Central Valley markets. Median prices are above $300,000 in the Sacramento and Inland Empire markets, and these markets are now more expensive than in nearly all Western markets outside of California.

Median price gains are far outpacing inflation in all California markets, with the largest recent gains occurring in the more moderately priced markets. While the highest prices are still found in the Bay Area and Orange County, **price growth** since 1996 is similar among regional markets. In fact, Santa Clara County has the **lowest** rate of median home price gain since 1996.

California
Median Resale Housing Prices

Counties/Regions	July 1996	July 2000	July 2004	Percent Change 1996-2000	Percent Change 2000-2004	Percent Change 1996-2004
California	$182,416	$243,240	$463,540	33.3%	90.6%	154.1%
Orange	$211,711	$315,730	$648,590	49.1%	105.4%	206.4%
Riverside-San Bernardino	$114,380	$138,560	$317,820	21.1%	129.4%	177.9%
San Diego	$180,000	$271,760	$582,490	51.0%	114.3%	223.6%
San Francisco	$278,820	$459,920	$651,150	65.0%	41.6%	133.5%
Central Valley	$108,210	$140,670	$283,650	30.0%	101.6%	162.1%
Sacramento	$118,000	$150,640	$325,060	27.7%	115.8%	175.5%
Los Angeles	$174,330	$211,150	$448,800	21.1%	112.6%	157.4%
Santa Clara	$290,930	$550,720	$640,000	89.3%	16.2%	120.0%
Calif. Consumer Price Index				11.3%	11.7%	24.3%

Source: California Association of Realtors

During the past four years, the largest increases in median resale prices were in the Inland Empire (+129.4%), followed closely by Sacramento, Los Angeles and San Diego. The highest median prices are in the Bay Area ($651,150), Orange County ($648,590) and Santa Clara County ($640,000).

Median Resale Home Prices
California
July 1990-July 2004

Median Resale Prices
Los Angeles County

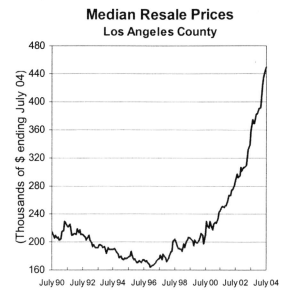

Median Resale Prices
Orange County

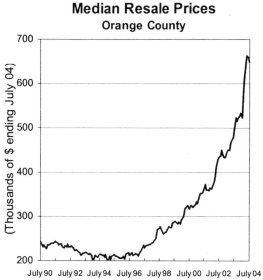

Median Resale Prices
San Diego County

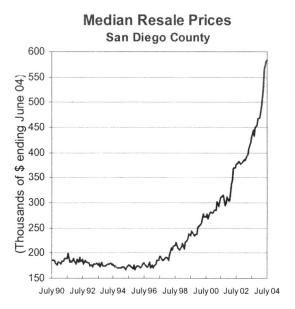

Median Resale Prices
Santa Clara County

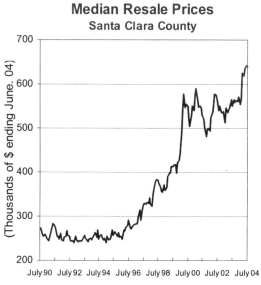

3-19

California Economic Outlook – 2004 and 2005

There is broad agreement among economists about California's short-term economic outlook, but there is also broad agreement that these forecasts have significant uncertainty. Short-term forecasts are often wrong because external events change. **The short-term economic forecasts discussed below for California depend on achieving moderate economic growth in the nation in 2005—and there are many uncertainties about the national economic forecast.**

California's economic outlook for 2004 and 2005 includes:

- Job growth of 1% (160,000) in 2004 and 2% (320,000) in 2005

- Personal income growth of between 5% and 5.5% in each year

- Residential building of near 200,000 units in each year

- Substantial gains in exports and total foreign trade through California ports

- An upturn in high tech production without substantial job gains

- Inflation at between 2% and 2.5% in each year

- Population growth averaging 550,000 per year

- Taxable sales growth keeping pace with income growth through 2005

These forecasts are generally in line with those recently released by the highly respected UCLA Anderson forecast.

Major threats include 1) a downturn in housing prices if job growth does not accelerate, 2) continuing large budget deficits at the state and federal level, and 3) the possibility that national economic growth will lag as interest rates rise and oil prices remain high.

THE U.S. ECONOMY IN
THE DECADE AHEAD

THE U.S. ECONOMY IN THE DECADE AHEAD

Summary

- U.S. population is projected to grow by 2.7 million each year, or approximately 1% per year to 2012. Foreign immigration is projected to remain near 1 million each year, with both legal and undocumented immigration continuing near current levels for the next ten years.

- The largest population growth will occur in the 55-64 age group (+11.5 million) and the 65+ age group (+ 7 million). Hispanic residents will account for approximately half of projected population growth and will account for 15.5% of U. S. population in 2012.

- Productivity growth has remained very high since 2000, allowing the economy to expand even while job levels remain below those when the 2001 recession began. CCSCE projects that productivity will grow by 2.4% per year to 2012, lower than during the past eight years but well above the average since 1973. The projected productivity growth will support GDP growth of 3.5% per year and strong growth in wages and income.

- The nation is projected to add approximately 2 million jobs per year between 2002 and 2012. Half of the gains are in two sectors—Professional and Business Services and Educational and Health Services. **Manufacturing job levels are projected to remain near 2002 levels as productivity gains offset rising sales levels.**

- The largest amount of job growth is projected for professional and technical occupations and for service occupations. Net job creation will account for less than half of job openings in the next ten years. For every five openings created by job growth, nearly 10 openings will occur from the need to replace workers who retire or change occupations. As a result, job openings will occur in occupations and industries where there is no job growth.

The Importance of Long-Term U.S. Trends to California

National trends in job and income growth create the opportunities and context for job and income gains in California. The number and kind of jobs that are added in the nation will shape the amount and pattern of job growth in California.

Productivity growth (i.e., how fast real output per worker is changing) is the principal determinant of income growth in both the nation and California. The prospects for real income gains (i.e., sustained improvement in average living standards) will be determined by how fast worker productivity can be increased.

Population Growth

Population growth remained high in the nation between 2000 and 2003. The U.S. added 8.6 million residents in the three years ending July 1, 2003, for an average of just below 2.9 million people per year. The nation is on pace to add another 2.8 million residents by July 1, 2004.

Foreign immigration has continued at high levels even in a post–9/11 world. Net immigration, including undocumented immigration, is estimated at near 1.2 million per year since 2000.

In 2004 the Census Bureau published new national population projections to 2050. The new projections show an increase of 26.8 million residents between 2000 and 2010 and also between 2002 and 2012.

Population growth in the next ten years will be lower, both in absolute numbers and in average annual growth rate, than population growth in the 1990s. The nation is projected to add 26.8 million residents between 2002 and 2012, down from 29.4 million in the 1990s. Population growth will slow from 1.1% per year in the 1990s to 0.9% per year between 2002 and 2012.

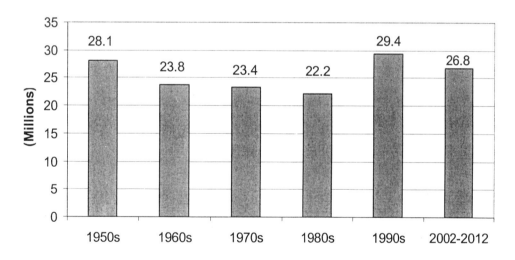

**Population Growth by Decade
United States**

The recent estimates and new projections assume that undocumented immigration will continue near current levels of approximately 300,000 per year.

Growth in Working Age Population

America's workforce is aging rapidly as shown in the next graph. Most of the growth in the nation's working-age population will occur among older workers.

- The largest growth (11.5 million) is in the pre-retirement (55-64) cohort. Their decisions about work and retirement will profoundly affect the nation's economy in this decade and the next.

- There will be little growth in the 35-54 age cohort. An increase in the 45-54 age cohort (4.4 million) will be nearly offset by a decrease in the 35-44 age cohort (-3.9 million).

- The youngest working-age cohorts (18-24 and 25-34) will grow (+5.6 million) in the coming decade, raising college enrollment and creating a slowly growing pool of new workers. Their skills and training will begin to impact the economy in the coming years.

Population Growth by Age Group
United States
2002-2012

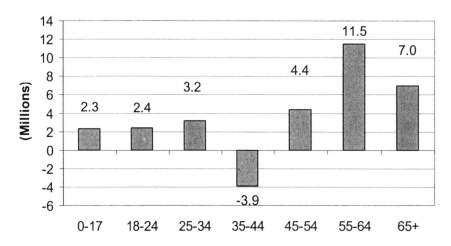

Labor Force Growth

U.S. labor force growth in the 2002-2012 decade will be determined by two conflicting trends:

1) More workers are moving into the older age groups, where labor force participation begins to decline. As shown in the next table, the labor force participation rate for men aged 25-54 was 91.0% in 2002. The participation rate for men aged 55-64, the fastest-growing age group in the decade ahead, was 69.2% for the same time period.

2) Labor force participation rates are now rising for older workers. As shown in the next table, the Bureau of Labor Statistics projects that participation rates will rise for both men and women over 55 in the decade ahead.

For women in the 55-64 age cohort, BLS projects a sharp increase in participation rates—from 55.2% in 2002 to 60.6% in 2012. While BLS projects no significant change in participation rates for men aged 55-64, CCSCE expects that these rates will rise as baby boomers fill this cohort between now and 2010. **Labor force participation rates are expected to rise substantially for both men and women over 65.**

Total labor force participation rates fell in the United States after 2000, going from 67.1% for 1997–2000 to a low of 65.9% in early 2004. The projections in this report assume a reversal of the recent decline, resulting in a small increase in the nation's total labor force participation rate—from 66.6% in 2002 to 67.2% in 2012. The increase will result primarily from continuing gains in labor force participation rates for women and older workers.

United States Labor Force Participation Rates 1982 – 2012				
	1982	**1992**	**2002**	**2012**
Total	64.0%	66.4%	66.6%	67.2%
Men	**76.6%**	**75.8%**	**74.1%**	**73.1%**
25-54	94.0%	93.0%	91.0%	91.0%
55-64	70.2%	67.0%	69.2%	69.9%
65 +	17.8%	16.1%	17.9%	20.8%
Women	**52.6%**	**57.8%**	**59.6%**	**61.6%**
25-54	66.3%	74.6%	75.9%	79.3%
55-64	41.8%	46.5%	55.2%	60.6%
65 +	7.9%	8.3%	9.8%	12.1%

Source: Bureau of Labor Statistics

The nation's labor force will grow in numbers an average of 1.7 million per year between 2002 and 2012, similar to the 1.7 million-per-year pace of the 1990s.

The growth in percentage will be 1.11% per year, slightly faster than 0.90% annual growth expected for population.

United States Total Labor Force 1992 – 2012 (Millions)				
			Annual Percent Change	
1992	**2002**	**2012**	**1992-2002**	**2002-2012**
128.1	144.9	162.3	1.26%	1.11%

Source: Bureau of Labor Statistics

After 2012, labor force growth will slow dramatically and fall **below** the rate of population increase.

- The period to 2012 is expected to be the last decade of rapid growth in female labor force participation rates. By 2012, the female rate for ages 25-54 will reach 79.3%, the closest ever to the participation rate for men. In 1980, the male participation rate for ages 25-54 was 30% above the female rate; by 2010, the gap is projected to be less than 12%.

- After 2012, rising retirement levels will restrain labor force growth. The first baby boomers reach 65 in 2012. Even if they keep working longer than previous generations, retirement levels will rise rapidly.

U.S. Productivity Growth

Productivity growth is the principal determinant of growth in real income. Growth in productivity—the ability to produce more goods and services per hour of work—is the key to rising real wages and a rising standard of living.

The 1947–1973 period was the "Golden Era" of United States productivity growth. Annual productivity gains during these twenty-six years averaged 3.0%, enough to double living standards in 23 years.

During the following twenty years, productivity growth fell substantially. Recently revised data, including the impact of software growth on the economy, shows that productivity grew by 1.6% per year between 1973 and 1995. At that rate, living standards double in 44 years.

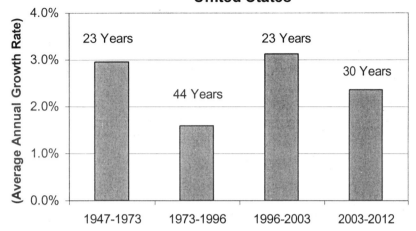

Growth in Output per Hour
Time for Doubling of Living Standards
United States

There is strong evidence that the nation has reversed the decline in productivity growth that started in 1973. Three major events have turned the tide:

1) The nation's firms have made significant capital investments in technology and new equipment in the 1980s and 1990s.

2) Corporate restructuring and the explosion of Internet access and activities have lowered costs in many sectors of the economy.

3) The purchase of more inputs—goods and services—from abroad has lowered the costs of production and gets counted as an increase in productivity growth.

As a result, productivity growth has averaged 3.1% per year since 1996. At this pace, living standards double in 23 years.

Moreover, productivity growth continued during the recent economic slowdown. Preliminary estimates show that productivity grew by 4.8% in 2002 and by 4.3% in 2003. The evidence is stronger today than at any point in the 1990s that the upturn in productivity growth is for real and can be factored into projections of future economic growth.

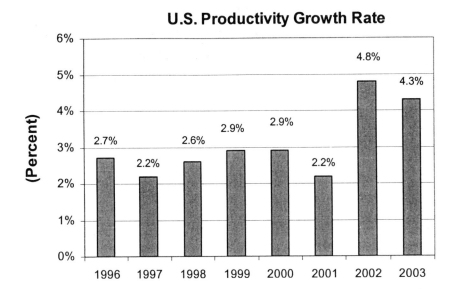

U.S. Productivity Growth Rate

A Range of Productivity and GDP Projections

CCSCE uses a range of productivity projections in developing the income and spending projections reported in *California Economic Growth*. These projections reflect the wide range of possible futures for U.S. productivity growth. Moreover, the projections reveal the substantial payoff to living standards from even modest sustained increases in productivity growth.

U.S. Productivity Growth Rate 2003-2012	
Low	1.6% per year
Middle	2.4% per year
High	3.1% per year

The low projection (1.6% per year) represents the 1973–1995 experience. The middle projection represents our estimate of a reasonable and conservative rate of long-term productivity gains, given the favorable trends cited above. The high projection represents a continuation of the average productivity gains of the 1996–2003 period.

The middle projection of 2.4% productivity growth per year is used in developing the baseline income and spending projections in later chapters of this report.

Implications for GDP Growth

Productivity growth will be the principal determinant of how well the U.S. economy does in the decade from 2002 to 2012.

- Under the low-growth scenario, gross domestic product (GDP) would grow by 2.7% annually. This represents a sharp decline from the 3.2% annual gains of the 1980s and the 3.3% average GDP increase in the 1990s.

- In the middle-growth scenario, GDP grows at 3.5% per year.

- With high productivity gains, GDP grows by 4.2% a year, higher than the growth experienced in the 1970s and 1980s.

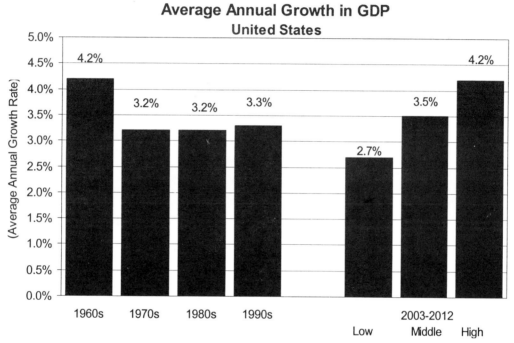

Average Annual Growth in GDP
United States

Different rates of productivity growth have a substantial impact on levels of individual income.

Gross Domestic Product (Trillions of 2003$)	
2000	$10.1
2003	$11.0
2012	
Low	$14.0
Middle	$15.0
High	$15.9

With 2.4% annual productivity gains (the middle-growth projection), the U.S. economy would be **$1 trillion larger** in 2012 than it would be with the low-growth projection—**a difference of $3,000 for every person in the nation**. If productivity growth increased to 3.1% annually (the high-growth projection), each resident would have yet an additional $2,860 in 2012.

The amount of revenues available to meet federal, state and local government budget priorities will depend critically on the future role of productivity growth.

Job Growth

Total U.S. job growth between 2002 and 2012 is projected to be 21.3 million (2.1 million per year). This is comparable to the 20.7 million jobs added between 1992 and 2002. The **rate** of job growth is expected to slow somewhat, dropping from 1.56% per year between 1992 and 2002 to 1.39% per year between 2002 and 2012.

The 2002–2012 growth rate is affected by the fact that 2002 was a recession year with total job levels approximately 2 million below their 2000 total.

			Annual Percent Change	
United States Total Jobs 1992 – 2012 (Millions)				
1992	**2002**	**2012**	**1992-2002**	**2002-2012**
123.3	144.0	165.3	1.56%	1.39%

Source: Bureau of Labor Statistics, CCSCE

The new BLS job national projections are based on industry data organized by NAICS (North American Industry Classification System) categories. The NAICS–based historical data and projections replace the previous data, which were organized by SIC codes.

Job growth by major industry category is shown in the next table. Nearly half of all U.S. job growth to 2012 is in two sectors: Professional and Business Services, and Educational and Health Services. The Educational and Health Services sector, which includes social assistance sectors such as childcare, is projected to increase by 31.8% (5.1 million jobs), with most of the growth occurring in health services.

Professional and Business Services are projected to increase by 30.4% (4.9 million jobs). These two sectors also had the largest job growth between 1992 and 2002.

The number of manufacturing jobs is projected to decline slightly between 2002 and 2012, after falling by 1.5 million in the previous decade. Construction job levels will increase by 1 million and keep pace with the overall job growth rate. Other major sectors with substantial projected job growth include Government (with 2.5 million jobs in state and local government), Leisure and Hospitality and Retail Trade (each with 2.1 million jobs) and Other Services (1 million added jobs).

United States **Jobs By Major Industry Group** **1992-2012** **(Thousands)**					
	1992	**2002**	**2012**	**Change** **1992-2002**	**Change** **2002-2012**
Farm	2,639	2,245	1,905	-394	-340
Natural Resources & Mining	610	512	451	-98	-61
Construction	4,608	6,732	7,745	2,124	1,013
Manufacturing	16,799	15,307	15,149	-1,492	-158
Wholesale Trade	5,110	5,641	6,279	531	638
Retail Trade	12,828	15,047	17,129	2,219	2,082
Transp, Warehousing & Utilities	4,188	4,805	5,685	617	880
Information	2,641	3,420	4,052	779	632
Financial Activities	6,540	7,843	8,806	1,303	963
Professional & Business Services	10,969	16,010	20,876	5,041	4,866
Educational & Health Services	11,891	16,184	21,329	4,293	5,145
Leisure & Hospitality	9,437	11,969	14,104	2,532	2,135
Other Services	4,240	5,348	6,362	1,108	1,014
Government	18,786	21,489	24,019	2,703	2,530
Self Employed	9,889	9,775	9,865	-114	90
Total Jobs, CCSCE Definition	**121,174**	**142,326**	**163,757**	**21,152**	**21,431**
Secondary Jobs	2,051	1,688	1,562	-363	-126
Total Jobs, BLS Definition	**123,325**	**144,014**	**165,319**	**20,689**	**21,305**

Source: Bureau of Labor Statistics

Other major industry sectors with above-average growth prospects include Other Services (+19.0%), Information (+18.5%), Transportation and Warehousing (+18.3%) and Leisure and Hospitality (+17.8%).

The U.S. Bureau of Labor Statistics uses two measures of total jobs. The first measure, which CCSCE uses throughout this report, includes all wage and salary jobs plus the number of people who say that self-employment is their principal job. The U.S. total for this measure is 163,757,000 jobs in 2012.

The U.S. Bureau of Labor Statistics also uses a second measure of total jobs. It includes approximately 1.6 million self-employed jobs for people who say that self-employment is their secondary job. The U.S. total for this second measure that includes secondary jobs is 165,319,000 for 2012. These secondary jobs are included in the occupational tables shown in the following sections of this chapter.

Occupations

The 2000 Standard Occupational Classification system contains a major revision in occupational categories. The ten major occupational categories now in use are shown in the table below. As a result of the revision, direct comparisons of projected and historical patterns of occupational change before 2000 are not possible.

United States Occupational Change 2002 – 2012 (Thousands of Jobs)				
	2002	2012	Growth 2002 – 2012	Percent Growth 2002 – 2012
Management, Business and Financial	15,501	17,883	2,382	15.4%
Professional and Related	27,687	34,147	6,459	23.3%
Service	26,569	31,905	5,336	20.1%
Sales and Related	15,260	17,231	1,971	12.9%
Office and Administrative Support	23,851	25,464	1,613	6.8%
Farming, Fishing and Forestry	1,072	1,107	35	3.3%
Construction and Extraction	7,292	8,388	1,096	15.0%
Installation, Maintenance and Repair	5,696	6,472	776	13.6%
Production	11,258	11,612	354	3.1%
Transportation and Material Moving	9,828	11,111	1,282	13.0%
Total - All Occupations	**144,014**	**165,319**	**21,305**	**14.8%**

Source: Bureau of Labor Statistics

The fastest growth is projected for professional occupations, including doctors, lawyers, teachers, scientists and engineers. Professional occupations will add 6.5 million jobs to 2012 and will increase by 23.3%. This is far higher than the overall rate of job growth (14.8%).

Service occupations will add 5.3 million jobs and increase by 20.1%. Major service occupations include food preparation, waiters and waitresses, security occupations, janitorial and health care assistance jobs. Professional (34.1 million) and service occupations (31.9 million) will be the two largest occupational groups in 2010.

Sales, office and administrative support jobs will increase by 3.6 million to total 42.7 million in 2012. However, both categories will experience below-average job growth: 12.9% for sales occupations and 6.8% for office support occupations.

Construction, repair, production and transportation occupations will all grow, adding a combined 3.5 million jobs by 2012. **It is important to remember that the number of openings in all occupations exceeds the amount of net job growth because retirements and occupational shifts create "replacement" job openings.**

There will be 21.3 million net new jobs created between 2002 and 2012, but this will make up less than half of the total new job openings—56.3 million new job openings, according to the BLS projections. The difference is accounted for by people leaving the labor force and by people permanently changing occupations. So, job openings will occur in each occupation to replace existing workers—even if there is no net job growth.

Examples of the comparative magnitude of new job growth and replacement job openings are as follows:

- Managerial occupations (2.4 million net new jobs + 2.9 million replacement jobs)

- Professional occupations (6.5 million net new jobs + 5.3 million replacement jobs)

- Sales occupations (2.0 million net new jobs + 4.9 million replacement jobs)

- Office support occupations (1.6 million net new jobs + 5.9 million replacement jobs)

- Construction, Production and other manual occupations (3.5 million net new jobs + 7.9 million replacement jobs)

Six of the seven fastest-growing occupations are related to health care and social services. Medical assistants are the fastest-growing occupational group (+59%), followed by network analysts (+57%) and physician assistants (+49%).

The fastest-growing occupations are spread among the four wage quartiles. In the Wage Quartile column of the table below, 1 represents the highest-paying 25% (quartile) of all occupations and 4 represents the bottom 25% of occupations in terms of average pay. Six of the fifteen fastest-growing occupations are in the top wage quartile, two are in the second quartile, six are in the third quartile and one is in the bottom quartile.

United States Occupations with Fastest Growth 2002 – 2012 (Thousands of Jobs)					
	2002	2012	Numerical Growth 2002 - 2012	Percent Growth 2002 - 2012	Wage Quartile ---------
Medical Assistants	365	579	215	59%	3
Network Syst. & Data Comm. Analysts	186	292	106	57%	1
Physician Assistants	63	94	31	49%	1
Social & Human Service Assistants	305	454	149	49%	3
Home Health Aides	580	859	279	48%	4
Medical Records & Health Info. Techs.	147	216	69	47%	3
Physical Therapist Aides	37	54	17	46%	3
Comput. Softw. Engrs. (Applications)	394	573	179	46%	1
Comput. Softw. Engrs. (Syst. Software)	281	409	128	45%	1
Physical Therapist Assistants	50	73	22	45%	2
Fitness Trainers & Aerobics Instructors	183	264	81	44%	3
Database Administrators	110	159	49	44%	1
Veterinary Technologists & Technicians	53	76	23	44%	3
Hazardous Mats. Removal Workers	38	54	16	43%	2
Dental Hygienists	148	212	64	43%	1

Source: Bureau of Labor Statistics

The fastest-growing occupations (shown in the table above) are substantially different from the occupations that will have the largest number of new jobs (shown in the following table).

Registered nurses will add the most jobs for a single occupational group (623,000), for a 27% increase to 2012. The U.S. will also need 603,000 more postsecondary teachers (+38%) and 595,000 more retail salespersons (+15%).

Three of the fast-growing occupations are in the highest pay quartile—registered nurses, postsecondary teachers and managers. However, seven of the fifteen occupations with the largest projected number of new jobs are in the bottom pay quartile—including retail salespersons, food preparation workers and cashiers (each with +454,000 jobs), janitors (+414,000), waiters and waitresses (+367,000) security guards (+317,000) and teacher assistants (+294,000).

United States
Occupations with Largest Growth
2002 – 2012
(Thousands of Jobs)

	2002	2012	Numerical Growth 2002 - 2012	Percent Growth 2002 - 2012	Wage Quartile ---------
Registered Nurses	2,284	2,908	623	27%	1
Postsecondary Teachers	1,581	2,184	603	38%	1
Retail Salespersons	4,076	4,672	596	15%	4
Customer Service Representatives	1,894	2,354	460	24%	3
Food Prep/Serving Wrkrs., incl. Fast Fd	1,990	2,444	454	23%	4
Cashiers, except Gaming	3,432	3,886	454	13%	4
Janitors & Cleaners, exclu. Maids/hskp.	2,267	2,681	414	18%	4
General & Operations Managers	2,049	2,425	376	18%	1
Waiters and Waitresses	2,097	2,464	367	18%	4
Nursing Aides, Orderlies, Attendants	1,375	1,718	343	25%	3
Truck Drivers, Heavy & Tractor-Trailer	1,767	2,104	337	19%	2
Receptionists & Information Clerks	1,100	1,425	325	29%	3
Security Guards	995	1,313	317	32%	4
Office Clerks, General	2,991	3,301	310	10%	3
Teacher Assistants	1,277	1,571	294	23%	4

Source: Bureau of Labor Statistics

United States Population Growth by Ethnic Group

The population share of each major ethnic group (except white non-Hispanics) is projected to increase between 2002 and 2012. For example, Hispanic residents will account for 15.5% of U.S. population in 2012, up from 13.3% in 2002. The White non-Hispanic share of U.S. population is projected to decline to 64.3% in 2012, down from 68.5% in 2002.

Nearly half (12.0 million) of the projected 26.9 million population gain will be accounted for by Hispanic residents. Black and White non-Hispanic population groups will each account for approximately 5 million additional residents.

United States Population Trends 2002 – 2012 (Millions)

	Population 2002	Population 2012	Growth Of Population 2002 – 2012	Percent Of Population 2002	Percent Of Population 2012
Hispanic	38.1	50.1	12.0	13.3%	15.9%
White (non-Hispanic)	196.8	202.1	5.3	68.5%	64.3%
Black	36.7	41.4	4.7	12.8%	13.2%
Asian	11.4	15.0	3.6	4.0%	4.8%
All Other	7.5	9.7	2.2	2.6%	3.1%
Total Population	**287.5**	**314.3**	**26.8**	**100.0%**	**100.0%**

Source: U.S. Census Bureau
Note: Groups do not add up to Total Population because Black, Asian and All Other groups also include Black Hispanics, Asian Hispanics and All Other Hispanics.

THE CALIFORNIA
ECONOMY TO 2012

THE CALIFORNIA ECONOMY TO 2012

The Bottom Line

Jobs

California will outpace the nation in job growth to 2012. The state will add approximately 391,000 jobs per year between 2003 and 2012. This represents a 21.8% gain, compared to the nation's projected 15.0% gain.

California has maintained a strong competitive position in major basic industries through the recent economic downturn. **Shares** of manufacturing and venture capital activity remain near record highs. Foreign trade volumes are rising and California's **share** foreign trade has increased in 2004.

- California has an above-average share of fast-growing basic industries.

- California is projected to achieve modest **share increases** in key basic industry sectors including, professional and business services, diversified manufacturing and wholesale trade and transportation.

- As a result, California is projected to account for 13.1% of the nation's basic industry jobs in 2012—up from 12.4% on 2003.

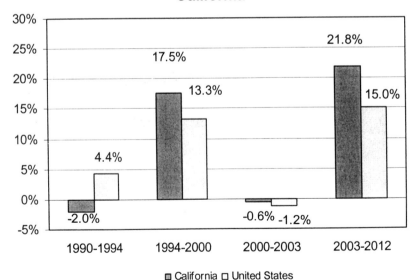

Past and Future Job Growth
California

□ California □ United States

- California faces substantial opportunities and equally substantial challenges relative to future job growth. The opportunities are explored later in this chapter. The challenges are summarized at the end of Chapter 1 and are analyzed in more detail in essays posted on CCSCE's website, www.ccsce.com.

Income

Productivity growth should push incomes and living standards higher for most Californians. CCSCE's projection of productivity growth for the next ten years (2.4% per year) is the highest since *California Economic Growth* was first published in 1977.

- Real (i.e., inflation-adjusted) per capita income is projected to increase by 2.8% per year between 2003 and 2012 to reach $42,796, measured in 2003 dollars. Per capita income was 5.3% above the national average in 2003. It is projected to be 4.6% higher than the national average in 2012.

- Total real personal income is projected to increase by 4.3% annually between 2003 and 2012 — outpacing the nation's projected 3.8% annual gains. California's share of U.S. personal income is projected to increase from 13.0% in 2003 to 13.6% in 2012.

Construction

Construction levels are projected to increase based on 1) continuing growth in jobs, population and households and 2) rising levels of public construction.

California is projected to add 4.9 million residents and 1.7 million households between 2003 and 2012. New housing production has reached 200,000 units per year, which is close to the 235,000 units per year needed to keep pace with the projected growth in households. The good news is that more communities are recognizing the benefits of allowing more housing, and they are rezoning excess industrial and commercial land for housing. The challenge is that affordability levels have fallen to record lows in most California housing markets.

Californians continue to approve infrastructure bonds in record levels, and public construction will be a strong positive for the California economy. In addition, measures to allow local communities to pass local taxes and bonds for infrastructure with less than a 2/3 voting majority are gaining support. Nonresidential construction levels have fallen since 2000. No significant upturn in nonresidential building is expected to occur before 2006.

The California Economy According to NAICS

Beginning in 2003, all jobs data for the nation, state and metropolitan areas will be compiled using the 2002 North American Industry Classification System (NAICS). Historical data for 1990 through 2003 is available through a cooperative effort of the California Employment Development Department (EDD) and the United States Bureau of Labor Statistics (BLS). State and regional jobs estimates for years before 1990 are not available for NAICS industry sectors.

A description of the differences between NAICS and SIC industry classifications is presented in Appendix A.

A Short Summary of the Difference Between NAICS and SIC Industry Descriptions

There are two major changes between the NAICS criteria for classifying industries and the previous Standard Industrial Classification (SIC) structure of industries:

- NAICS groups industries according to similar production processes.

- NAICS includes many new industries (primarily those dealing with information and technology) and a much more detailed description of the broad services sectors.

A complete description of the NAICS structure and changes can be found at the Bureau of Labor Statistics website, www.bls.gov/bls/naics.htm, and at the Census Bureau website, www.census.gov/epcd/www/naics.html.

Publishing was switched from Manufacturing to Information, a new major industry. Contract manufacturing activities were switched from Services (they had been in SIC 87, Management Services) into Manufacturing. Other major switches include moving Eating and Drinking Establishments from Retail Trade to the new Leisure and Hospitality sector, and major switches between Retail and Wholesale Trade. These reflect the NAICS emphasis on what an establishment does, rather than who it sells to. Telecommunication activities were switched from Transportation, Communications and Utilities to the new Information sector.

With the introduction of NAICS, many new industries were added in order to reflect the growth of new economic activities **and** the increasing importance of services. There are now four major service sectors—Professional and Business Services, Educational and Health Services, Leisure and Hospitality and Other Services that are formed primarily from industries which used to be in the SIC Services sector.

California's Economic Base

Economists assess job growth prospects for states and regions by examining the growth prospects for what economists call *basic industries*.

Basic industries sell primarily to markets outside the state—markets in other states and other countries. Because basic industries do not depend on local markets, firms have a choice of where to locate production facilities. As a result, regions and states "compete" for the location of firms in basic industries. The location decisions of these firms determine how fast a state like California will grow relative to other states in the nation.

Most jobs are what economists call *population serving*. Jobs in major sectors such as retail trade, health care, local government and finance primarily serve local markets within the region and do not sell much to outside areas. These jobs increase as a result of overall growth in population—part of which is determined by the growth rate in basic industry jobs.

CCSCE examines trends in 90 basic industries, as shown on Appendix Table A-1. In 2003, these industries in California's economic base accounted for almost 5.2 million (32%) of California's 16.2 million total jobs.

To explain trends in California's economic base, CCSCE combines the 90 basic industries into eight major sectors. These eight sectors and their 2003 job totals are shown in the tables on pages 5-9 and 5-11.

Non-basic jobs (i.e., those serving the local population) account for two out of every three jobs in the state. **Growth in the number of non-basic jobs is determined by how successful the state is in attracting basic industry production and jobs.**

Eight Major Sectors in California's Economic Base

California's economic base has been changing and adjusting to world market forces for more than 30 years. In the 1950s and 1960s, and again briefly in the 1980s, defense spending was a growth force in California's economic base. In the 1970s and again in the 1990s, growth in high technology manufacturing and diversified manufacturing industries offset declines in the defense-related sectors.

The new NAICS industry data allows CCSCE and readers to analyze California's economic base with an updated set of industries. These new industries reflect changes in the structure of the state's economic base and in the relative importance of individual basic economic activities.

CCSCE has developed eight major sectors for grouping industries in California's economic base. The composition of these eight sectors is slightly different for analyzing trends in economic regions. It is explained on pages 7-4 and 7-18.

The eight major sectors are as follows:

- High Tech Manufacturing
- Diversified Manufacturing
- Professional and Business Services
- Basic Information Services
- Wholesale Trade and Transportation
- Tourism and Entertainment
- Government
- Resource Based

Total Basic Jobs

Job and production levels for basic industries are significantly more volatile than those for population-serving industries. Job levels in basic industries rise and fall with the economic cycle and with cycles in foreign trade and tourism. Population-serving industries show a relatively steady upward trend as population grows.

The number of basic industry jobs fell sharply in each of the last two California recessions, as shown on page 5-9. California lost nearly 600,000 basic industry jobs between 2000 and 2003, while total job levels fell by less than 100,000 during the same period.

California's share of the nation's basic industry jobs is a key measure of how well the state is doing compared to the nation. As shown on the bottom of page 5-11, California's **share** of U.S. basic industry jobs remains near record levels.

In the early 1990s recession, California's share of the nation's basic industry jobs fell sharply, from 12.1% in 1990 to 11.3% in 1994. However, in the 2000–2003 period, California's share fell by only 0.1%, from 12.5% to 12.4%. So, by this measure the high tech downturn did not affect the state nearly as much as the aerospace downturn of a decade ago.

California is projected to add 1.1 million basic industry jobs (+22.0%) between 2003 and 2012. Because the state's economic base is expected to grow more rapidly than the nation's, California's share of U.S. basic industry jobs is projected to reach a record high level of 13.1% in 2012.

Total Basic Jobs

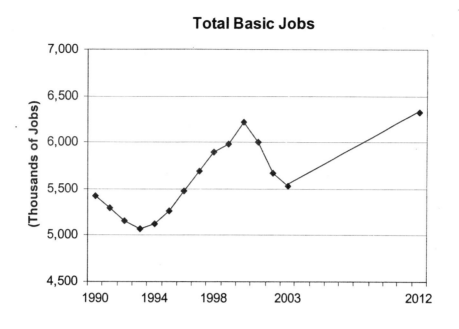

Total Basic Jobs

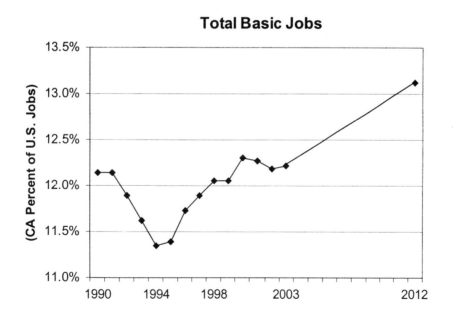

Basic Jobs by Major Basic Industry Category

Historical data and projections for CCSCE's eight basic industry categories for California and the United States are shown on page 5-9.

The structure of the state's and the nation's economic base is compared below.

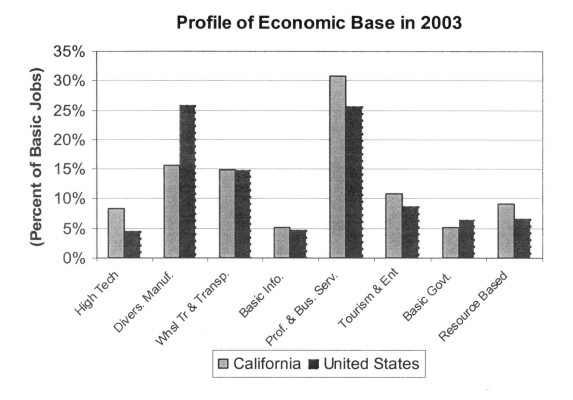

Profile of Economic Base in 2003

California's economic base is more heavily concentrated in High Tech Manufacturing and Professional and Business Services. This is true even after the large job losses in these sectors since 2000. Thus California has a larger share of basic jobs in high-wage sectors than does the nation.

The biggest difference in economic structure relates to Diversified Manufacturing, where the nation has a higher concentration. This is true even though California has been gaining share of total Diversified Manufacturing jobs in the nation.

As a result of Hollywood film production, California has a slightly above-average share in Tourism and Entertainment. It has a slightly below-average share of basic jobs related to federal government activities, including defense.

The share of basic jobs in Information and Wholesale Trade and Transportation is similar between the state and nation.

California **Jobs by Major Basic Industry Sector** **1994-2012** **(Thousands)**					**Numerical Change**		
	1994	**2000**	**2003**	**2012**	**1994-2000**	**2000-2003**	**2003-2012**
High Tech Manufacturing	519.8	558.2	438.4	439.3	38.4	-119.8	0.9
Diversified Manufacturing	855.4	987.8	819.0	882.5	132.4	-168.8	63.5
Wholesale Trade & Transp.	658.8	772.9	766.3	942.0	114.1	-6.6	175.7
Basic Information Services	201.5	336.1	268.6	390.2	134.6	-67.5	121.6
Prof. & Business Services	1,170.4	1,744.7	1,596.6	2,269.6	574.3	-148.1	673.0
Tourism & Entertainment	481.1	582.5	560.7	712.1	101.4	-21.8	151.4
Government	333.9	282.2	267.6	261.1	-51.7	-14.6	-6.5
Resource Based	518.5	516.2	472.2	424.8	-2.3	-44.0	-47.4
Total Basic Jobs	**4,730.4**	**5,771.3**	**5,180.5**	**6,321.6**	**1,040.9**	**-590.8**	**1,141.1**

Source: EDD

United States **Jobs by Major Basic Industry Sector** **1994-2012** **(Thousands)**					**Numerical Change**		
	1994	**2000**	**2003**	**2012**	**1994-2000**	**2000-2003**	**2003-2012**
High Tech Manufacturing	2,433.7	2,611.1	2,094.4	2,079.6	177.4	-516.7	-14.8
Diversified Manufacturing	11,456.9	11,480.6	9,506.6	9,946.7	23.7	-1,974.0	440.1
Wholesale Trade & Transp.	6,353.3	7,202.8	6,748.9	7,539.1	849.5	-453.9	790.2
Basic Information Services	1,705.7	2,473.5	2,137.4	2,846.0	767.8	-336.1	708.6
Prof. & Business Services	8,736.2	12,346.8	11,635.1	15,497.3	3,610.6	-711.7	3,862.2
Tourism & Entertainment	3,269.3	4,054.9	3,942.3	4,858.5	785.6	-112.6	916.2
Government	3,018.0	2,865.0	2,756.0	2,778.7	-153.0	-109.0	22.7
Resource Based	3,785.6	3,200.9	3,011.2	2,628.0	-584.7	-189.7	-383.2
Total Basic Jobs	40,758.7	46,235.6	41,831.9	48,173.9	5,476.9	-4,403.7	6,342.0

The number of jobs in the largest industries for each of the eight major basic industry groups is shown on page 5-11. More detailed information about each basic industry sector is analyzed below.

The first sector to be examined is Wholesale Trade and Transportation. A discussion of foreign trade is included, as that is an area of significant competitive advantage for California.

Wholesale Trade and Transportation

The new NAICS sector is similar to the SIC-based Transportation and Wholesale Trade sector. Most of the transportation industries (air, rail, and water) have been split into two components: direct services and support services. As an example, the airlines are included in air transportation, while airport activities are included in support activities.

The table below shows the components of Wholesale Trade and Transportation used by CCSCE in analyzing California's economic base.

The largest number of jobs is in wholesale trade, which is now split into three subcategories—durable goods, non-durable goods and electronic markets (wholesale business over the Internet) and brokers.

California Wholesale Trade and Transportation Jobs 1994-2012 (Thousands)						
	1994	2000	2003	2012	1994-2000	2000-2003	2003-2012
Merchant Wholesalers, Durable Gds	296.9	365.0	346.0	406.8	68.1	-19.0	60.8
Merchant Wholesalers, NonDurable Gds	187.6	223.6	233.2	288.9	36.0	9.6	55.7
Whlsl Electronic Mkts. & Agents & Brkrs.	60.6	56.4	72.2	106.8	-4.2	15.8	34.6
Air Transportation	63.8	68.4	54.2	75.1	4.6	-14.2	20.9
Rail Transportation	15.5	14.0	12.9	12.9	-1.5	-1.1	0.0
Water Transportation	5.0	4.2	4.2	4.1	-0.8	0.0	-0.1
Pipeline, Scenic & Sightseeing Transp.	6.5	6.3	6.1	5.5	-0.2	-0.2	-0.6
Support Activities for Water Transp.	9.2	15.5	18.2	18.6	6.3	2.7	0.4
Other Support Activities for Transp.	13.7	19.5	19.3	23.3	5.8	-0.2	4.0
Transportation and Wholesale Trade	**658.8**	**772.9**	**766.3**	**942.0**	**114.1**	**-6.6**	**175.7**

Source: EDD

California
Major Sectors in Economic Base
2003
(Thousands of Jobs)

High Tech Manufacturing	**438.4**	
Computer & Peripheral Equip. Mfg.		65.5
Communications Equip. Mfg.		28.4
Semiconductor & Electronic Comp. Mfg.		108.1
Electronic Instrument Manufacturing		107.0
Aerospace Product & Parts Mfg.		73.4
Pharmaceutical & Medicine Mfg.		38.8
Diversified Manufacturing	**810.1**	
Wood Product Manufacturing		39.6
Fabricated Metal Product Mfg.		138.8
Machinery Manufacturing		86.7
Furniture & Related Product Mfg.		62.9
Medical Equipment & Supplies Mfg.		49.1
Apparel Manufacturing		89.0
Chemicals except Pharmaceuticals		39.6
Plastics & Rubber Products Mfg.		59.8
Wholesale Trade & Transportation	**766.3**	
Merchant Wholesalers, Durable Goods		346.0
Merchant Wholesalers, Nondurable Gds		233.2
Wholesale Elec. Mkts & Agents & Brokers		72.2
Air Transportation		54.2
Basic Information Services	**268.6**	
Software Publishers		44.7
Telecommunications		121.4
ISPs, Web Search Portals & Data Proc.		48.6
Professional & Business Services	**1,596.6**	
Legal Services		138.7
Acntg., Tax Prep. & Bookkeeping Svcs.		103.5
Architectural, Engnrg & Related Svcs.		149.3
Computer Syst. Design & Related Svcs.		166.2
Mgmt., Scientific & Tech. Consltg. Svcs.		111.1
Scientific Research & Developmt Svcs.		95.1
Mgmt. of Companies & Enterprises		255.6
Employment Services		441.6
Tourism and Entertainment	**560.7**	
Motion Picture & Sound Recording		135.2
Arts, Entertainment & Recreation		233.9
Accommodation		191.6
Government	**267.6**	
Department of Defense		58.2
Other Federal Government		200.5
Resource Based	**472.2**	
Farm		375.0
Total Basic Jobs	**5,180.5**	

Source: EDD. See Appendix A, Table A-1, for a complete list.

Jobs in the direct transportation services (air, rail and water) have fallen since 1994. The events of 9/11 have transformed the market for air travel and most airlines are currently operating with reduced schedules and employment levels. Support activities for transportation have grown along with activity at ports and airports. The growth related to water transportation should continue as trade expands, but support services for air travel will need time to recover.

Job levels in wholesale trade have risen and are projected to continue rising in the decade ahead. The main drivers are continued growth in the California economy and the state's strong position as a center for international trade and as a distribution center for goods coming to and from other parts of the country.

California is projected to add more than 150,000 jobs in wholesale trade between 2003 and 2012. As shown on page 5-13, job levels in the Wholesale Trade and Transportation sector have risen since 1990, with small declines in each of the recession periods. By 2012 there should be nearly 1 million jobs in the sector.

California's share of national jobs has risen since 1990, overcoming a drop in the early '90s to reach a record 11.4% in 2003. The state's share of U.S. Wholesale Trade and Transportation jobs is projected to increase to 12.5% in 2012.

Foreign Trade

The volume of foreign trade is a major driver of the growth in wholesale trade jobs. Foreign trade has grown faster than the national economy during the past decade. It is projected to grow faster again in the decade ahead. The real value of exports is projected to increase by 74.0% between 2002 and 2012—more than twice as fast as GDP (+33.9%). Imports are projected to rise by 66.5% during the same period. Between 1992 and 2002, imports rose faster than exports.

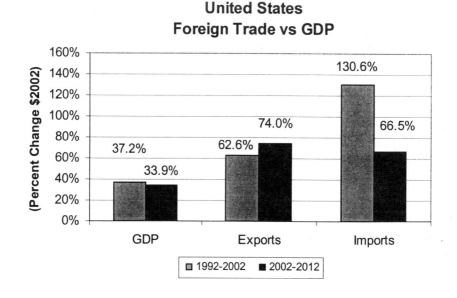

United States
Foreign Trade vs GDP

Wholesale Trade and Transportation

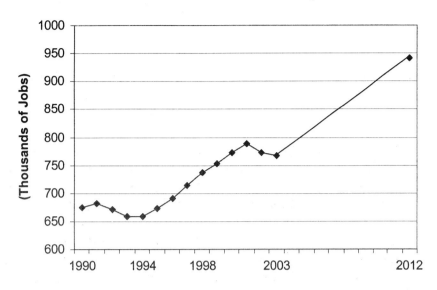

Wholesale Trade and Transportation

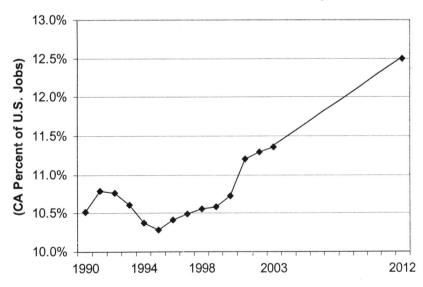

Foreign trade activity is surging in 2004, as reported in Chapter 3. Trade volumes could recover all of the losses since 2000 and reach record levels late in 2004 or early in 2005. The remainder of this chapter looks at California's long-term trade trends.

Exports of goods and services produced in California, trade activities at California's ports and airports and related activities in wholesale trade and finance all represent ways in which foreign trade helps the California economy expand.

Foreign Trade in the California Economy — Two sets of data are regularly collected about foreign trade in California. Data are collected on the volume of foreign trade (imports and exports combined) that passes through the three California customs districts—Los Angeles, San Francisco, and San Diego.

The customs district data have two distinct uses. First, they are the only source of data on imports—amount, type and country of origin. Second, the customs district data provide a measure of total trade volume—not just exports produced in California. Some jobs in wholesale trade, finance, and the goods movement industries are related to total trade volume regardless of whether the goods and services are produced or consumed in the state.

Data are also available from the U.S. Department of Commerce on exports produced in California. These data allow analysis of the amount and kinds of goods made in California for export.

Customs District Data — The customs district data for California confirms two findings. Even with the recent downturn,

- Foreign trade has been a fast-growing sector in California.

- California maintains a high share of national trade activity (although the state's share has fallen in recent years).

Between 1990 and 2000, the volume of trade (excluding services) handled by California customs districts grew by an annual average gain of 9.0% in dollar volume. The volume of U.S. trade grew by 8.6% per year during the same period. Both growth rates exceeded the growth of the overall economy.

Trade volumes fell after 2000. By 2003, California's average foreign trade growth rate had fallen to 5.9% per year for the 1990-2003 period. The state's foreign trade growth rate was lower than the nation's for the same 1990-2003 period.

California Foreign Trade Value of Exports and Imports 1990 - 2003 ($Billions)			
	Exports	**Imports**	**Total**
1990	$68.6	$97.1	$165.7
2000	$148.6	$243.6	$392.2
2003	$113.6	$236.7	$350.3
Average Annual Growth Rate 1990 – 2003			
California	4.0%	7.1%	5.9%
United States	5.1%	7.8%	6.7%

Source: U.S. Department of Commerce

California's share of total U.S. foreign trade increased steadily between 1979 and 1995. California's ports and airports handled 11.6% of U.S. volume in 1979. By 1995, the state's customs districts had increased the state's share to 21.3%.

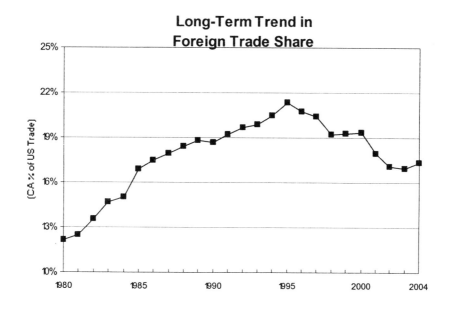

By 2003, however, California's share had fallen to 16.9%—the lowest level since 1986. The decline in share has two principal components: (1) the sharp slide in exports of high tech manufacturing goods and (2) the recent slowdown in growth rates in parts of Asia, particularly in Japan. Even after this substantial decline in share, however, California still accounts for 17% of national trade activity—far higher that the state's 12% share of total income.

As described in Chapter 3, California's trade volumes **and** trade share are rebounding in 2004:

- High tech exports and Asian trade are growing again.

- California's ports and airports are investing billions of dollars in facilities expansion and related transportation improvements. This is one infrastructure area where the public and private sectors are investing heavily.

The Los Angeles Customs District handled a record $235.0 billion in trade volume in 2003. The Los Angeles District had a gain of 120% between 1990 and 2003, slightly below the national average. Los Angeles passed New York again in 2002 as the nation's largest customs district in terms of dollar volume. The Los Angeles Customs District is up 14.4% in dollar volume through July 2004.

Foreign Trade by Customs District ($Billions)			
	1990	2000	2003	% Change 1990 vs. 2003
Los Angeles	$106.7	$230.0	235.0	120.3%
San Francisco	51.2	127.2	79.6	55.3%
San Diego	7.8	35.0	35.7	360.0%
California	165.7	392.2	350.3	111.4%
United States	$888.2	$2,028.8	$2,069.0	132.9%

Source: U.S. Department of Commerce; excludes services

The San Francisco Customs District had nearly a 150% gain in trade volume between 1990 and 2000—driven by rapidly rising tech exports. During the 1990s, Bay Area trade growth far outpaced Southern California gains.

Between 2000 and 2003, the picture changed dramatically. Bay Area trade volume fell by 37.5%, from $127.2 billion in 2000 to $79.6 billion in 2003. The decline in tech trade accounted for most of the state's trade drop and pushed the Bay Area well behind Southern California in trade growth since 1990.

Trade volumes in San Diego, driven by long-term gains in trade with Mexico, have increased by nearly 400% since 1990 and are up again so far in 2004.

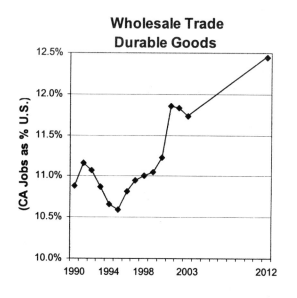

Wholesale Trade Durable Goods

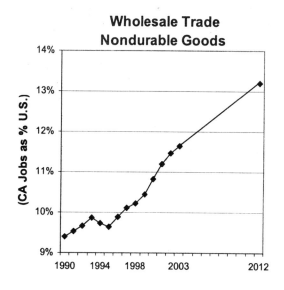

Wholesale Trade Nondurable Goods

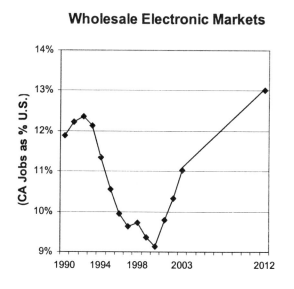

Wholesale Electronic Markets

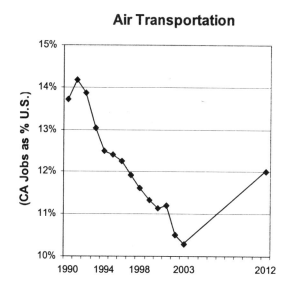

Air Transportation

Exports Produced in California

Exports produced in California rose from $58.4 billion in 1990 to $119.6 billion in 2000. They then fell to $94.0 billion in 2003.

Despite the recent downturn, exports of goods produced in California are up sharply over 1990 levels. Markets with the largest growth include Mexico (which is now California's largest export market, at $14.9 billion in 2003—up from $4.7 billion in 1990), Canada (just behind Japan, at $11.2 billion—up from $5.8 billion in 1990), and Mainland China (up from $.7 billion in 1990 to $5.5 billion in 2003).

All export markets except Mainland China and Hong Kong had declining export volumes between 2000 and 2003. The largest decline was with Japan, where export levels fell from $16.4 billion in 2000 to $11.8 billion in 2003.

California Top Export Markets 1990-2003 ($Billions)			
	1990	**2000**	**2003**
Mexico	$4.7	$17.5	$14.9
Japan	10.3	16.4	11.8
Canada	5.8	14.1	11.2
China	.7	3.5	5.5
South Korea	3.8	6.9	4.8
Taiwan	3.2	7.4	4.4
U.K.	3.4	6.0	4.4
Hong Kong	1.7	4.1	4.2
Germany	3.7	5.3	3.6
Netherlands	1.8	5.0	3.4
Total Exports	**$58.4**	**$119.6**	**$94.0**

Source: U.S. Department of Commerce

Approximately half of the exports produced by California firms are in one category—computers and electronic products. These exports went from $49.5 billion in 1999 to $61.4 billion in 2000, and then back down to $36.7 billion during the worldwide slowdown in high tech purchases. **High tech exports are rising at double-digit rates in 2004.**

In 2003 the second-largest category of exports was non-electrical machinery ($9.4 billion), followed by transportation equipment (with exports near $8.6 billion).

Chemical exports was one of the categories to increase between 2000 and 2003. It rose to $6.0 billion.

California Top Export Industries 1999-2003 ($Billions)			
	1999	2000	2003
Computers, Elec. Products	$49.5	$61.4	$36.7
Machinery, except Elec.	8.7	13.8	9.4
Transportation Equipment	8.8	8.2	8.6
Chemicals	4.0	4.8	6.0
Misc. Manufacturing	3.8	4.1	4.9
Crops	2.9	3.6	4.8
Food Products	3.2	3.4	4.2
Electrical Equipment	2.9	4.0	2.9
Total Exports	**$97.9**	**$119.6**	**$94.0**

Source: U.S. Department of Commerce

Exports of Services

Services are an important and often overlooked category of foreign trade. Service exports from the United States totaled $279.5 billion in 2002—roughly one-third the size of goods exports.

The largest component of service exports is travel and transportation—$112.7 billion in 2002 after two straight years of decline. The fastest-growing category is royalties and licenses, which increased by 10.7% per year since 1997.

Business and professional services, financial services, education and film and TV have all grown by between 8% and 10% since 1997. California firms will eventually benefit from access to Asian and world markets in financial, retail, engineering and consulting services.

CCSCE estimates that California accounts for approximately 20% of U.S. services exports. On this basis, California services exports would have been $55.9 billion in 2002.

United States
Exports of Goods and Services
($Billions)

	1997	2000	2002	Average Annual Growth Rate 1997-2002
Goods Exports	$728.5	$812.8	$736.3	0.2%
Private Services Exports	237.9	283.5	279.5	3.3%
Transportation & Travel	121.3	132.9	112.7	-1.5%
Royalties, Licenses	33.2	43.2	44.1	10.7%
Film & TV	5.9	8.6	9.8	9.3%
Education	8.3	10.3	12.8	9.1%
Financial Services	12.5	19.3	19.9	9.7%
Bus. & Prof. Services	44.0	55.2	65.4	8.2%
Other	7.3	7.6	7.8	1.3%
Gross Domestic Product	$8,304.3	$9,817.0	$10,480.8	4.8%

Source: U.S. Department of Commerce

Total Exports — Total exports produced in California were just under $150 billion in 2003. Agricultural exports in 2003 are estimated at $9.0 billion, including processed food products.

California
Total Value of Exports
2003
($Billions)

Manufacturing and Mining	$85.0
Services (2002)	55.9
Agricultural Products	9.0
Total Exports	**$149.9**

Sources: U.S. Dept. of Commerce; CCSCE

Professional and Business Services

The new NAICS sector combines elements of the SIC-based professional and business services, legal, computer and management services categories. The NAICS sector has much more detail—ten individual industries—and it and includes the new and separate category for management of companies (headquarters and district office operations). Because most employment service jobs "serve" other basic industry sectors, CCSCE also includes employment services in this basic industry category.

The Professional and Business Services sector is projected to be the nation's largest and fastest-growing basic industry group, adding nearly 4 million jobs between 2003 and 2012. The projected job growth rate for Professional and Business Services (33.9%) is more than double the projected growth rate for total jobs. In addition, wage levels in Professional and Business Services are among the highest of all basic industry groups.

United States
Comparison of Job Growth Rates
2003-2012

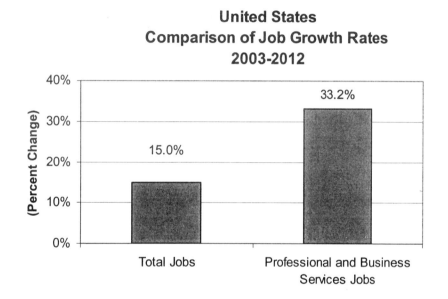

Professional and Business Services is the largest basic industry sector in California, and it has added the most jobs since 1994. As shown on page 5-23, job levels rose steadily throughout the 1990s before falling during the recent recession. Sector job levels reached a high of over 1.7 million in 2000 and remained near 1.6 million in 2003.

California's share of Professional and Business Services jobs has fluctuated between 13.5% and 14.5% since 1990.

California's job levels and share are projected to increase in the decade ahead.

The Professional and Business Services sector is projected to add 673,000 jobs between 2003 and 2012. California's share of national sector jobs is projected to increase from 13.7% in 2003 to a record 14.6% in 2012. As a result, California is projected to show above-average growth in this fastest-growing basic industry sector.

California has an above-average share of the nation's jobs in each subsector of Professional and Business Services. Substantial job growth is projected for two reasons: 1) the nation will experience large job growth in most of the individual Professional and Business Services industries and 2) California is projected to increase the state's share of the nation's jobs modestly in most industries. Even so, the state's share of the nation's jobs will remain below the highest share levels of the 1990s.

California Professional and Business Services Jobs 1994-2012 (Thousands)						
	1994	2000	2003	2012	1994-2000	2000-2003	2003-2012
Legal Services	124.8	127.4	138.7	172.9	2.6	11.3	34.2
Accounting, Tax Preparation & Bookkeeping Services	101.4	99.0	103.5	158.8	-2.4	4.5	55.3
Architectural, Engineering & Related Services	114.1	155.0	149.3	169.7	40.9	-5.7	20.4
Specialized Design Services	16.0	23.3	23.0	29.2	7.3	-0.3	6.2
Computer Systems Design & Related Services	87.5	204.8	166.2	292.9	117.3	-38.6	126.7
Management, Scientific & Technical Consulting Services	58.3	94.9	111.0	162.0	36.6	16.1	51.0
Advertising & Related Services	56.0	71.6	60.5	76.1	15.6	-11.1	15.6
Scientific R & D Services & Other Prof. Services	120.1	144.7	147.2	179.6	24.6	2.5	32.4
Mgmt. of Companies & Enterprises	237.0	330.7	255.6	326.7	93.7	-75.1	71.1
Employment Services	255.2	493.3	441.6	701.7	238.1	-51.7	260.1
Professional & Business Services	**1,170.4**	**1,744.7**	**1,596.6**	**2,269.6**	**574.3**	**-148.1**	**673.0**

Source: EDD

Three industries—Computer System Design (which includes programming services), Employment Services (which includes temporary help agencies) and Management of Companies—accounted for the most job growth in the 1990s. They are now the largest of the ten industry groups within Professional and Business Services.

Professional and Business Services

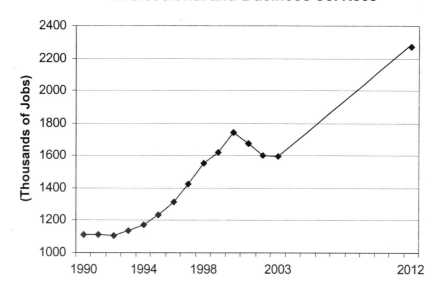

Professional and Business Services

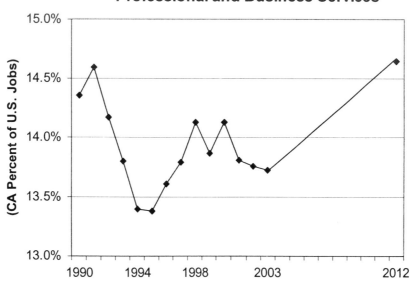

The number of computer system design jobs more than doubled, from 87,500 in 1994 to 204,800 at the peak in 2000. The number of employment services jobs nearly doubled, from 255,200 in 1994 to 493,300 in 2000. The number of management jobs increased from 237,000 in 1994 to 330,700 at the peak in 2000.

These same three sectors lost approximately 175,000 jobs between 2000 and 2003. Recent losses in computer design and management were heavily concentrated in the Bay Area.

The sector-by-sector graphs on pages 5-25 and 5-27 show a clear picture of the trends in each component of Professional and Business Services.

The number of computer services jobs in California is projected to increase by more than 125,000 between 2003 and 2012. The state's share of the nation's jobs is projected to reach 16.3% in 2012, up from 15.0% in 2003 but below the peak level of 18.1% in 1992.

Legal service jobs increased between 2000 and 2003, finally surpassing the early '90s peak level. There were 138,700 legal service jobs in 2003. That number is expected to grow to 172,900 in 2012. California's share of legal services jobs dropped in the early 1990s and has recovered only slightly since 2000. The state's share of national jobs is projected to increase to 13.0% in 2012, up from 12.2% in 2003 but below the high of 14.2% in 1991.

Job levels in accounting services remained relatively stable between 1994 and 2003. The state's share of the nation's jobs fell sharply during the 1990s and has recovered modestly after 1999.

The number of accounting services jobs is projected to increase by nearly 50% between 2003 and 2012, based on substantial national job growth in this sector plus projected share gains for California. The state's share of accounting services jobs is projected to increase to 14.7% in 2012, up from 12.7 in 2003 but still well below the high of 17.7% in 1991.

Architectural and Engineering Services is the fourth-largest component of Professional and Business Services in 2003, with 149,300 jobs. Job levels have grown substantially since 1994, and further job increases are expected by 2012. California's share of national jobs has fluctuated between 11.5% and 13.5%, ending at 12.2% in 2003. Share gains to 13.0% are projected for 2012.

The majority of jobs in architectural and engineering services are oriented to new construction and renovation in California **and** worldwide. **California is the site of 7 of the top 10 design firms in the United States, as well as 6 of the top 10 global design firms.**

Legal Services

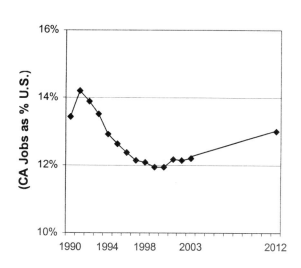

Accounting Services

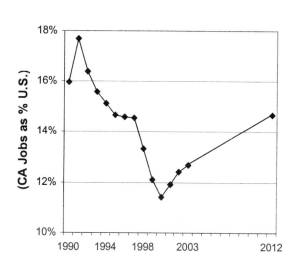

Architectural and Engineering Services

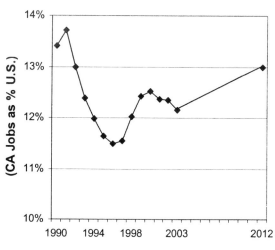

Computer Services

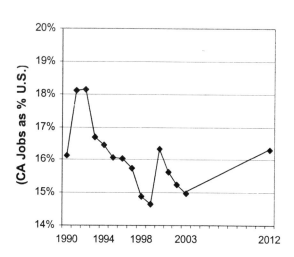

Job levels in scientific R & D and other professional services began rising steadily in 1996, reaching a record level of 147,200 jobs in 2003. These firms conduct original research and testing in a variety of scientific fields, including biotechnology. Further job growth is projected, with California accounting for 14.5% of national jobs in 2012.

Management, scientific and technical consulting posted a 90% increase in job levels between 1994 and 2003, reaching a record 111,000 jobs. As with most of the professional and business services industries, California firms serve state, national and worldwide markets. The sector is projected to add more than 50,000 jobs by 2012 and to account for 14.2% of national sector jobs.

Employment services job levels nearly doubled between 1994 and 2000, before sliding back to 441,600 jobs in 2003. Job levels are rising again and are projected to reach over 700,000 by 2012, when California is projected to account for 14.0% of national jobs in this sector—the highest share since 1990.

California had an increase of 93,700 jobs in management of companies between 1994 and 2000. This new category includes headquarters and district office jobs. At the peak in 1999, California had 18.6% of all U.S. jobs in this sector. The state's job levels and share fell substantially after 2000, as many dot-com companies disappeared. Job and share levels are projected to increase, but these gains will mostly only recover the losses since 2000.

High Tech Manufacturing

The high tech manufacturing sector has three major components: (1) the new NAICS version of the old SIC-based non-defense high tech sector, including computer, communications equipment, electronic components and instruments; (2) the new NAICS version of the old aircraft, missile and defense electronics sector (aerospace) and (3) pharmaceuticals.

Non-defense high tech manufacturing was one of the driving forces behind California's economic growth in the 1980s and 1990s. The state experienced rising levels of sales, profits and new venture capital **and** increased its share of national high tech activity on nearly every indicator.

Then came the stock market collapse in technology shares, a decline in business capital investment, falling exports and a major drop in new venture capital funding. Two questions arise from the 2000–2003 experience:

- Is high tech manufacturing still a growth sector?

- Has California lost competitive position, as it did in aerospace a decade ago?

The answers are **yes** to high growth and **no** to loss of share.

Management, Scientific and Technical Consulting

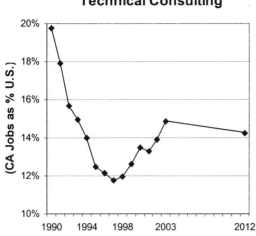

Scientific, R&D and Other Professional Services

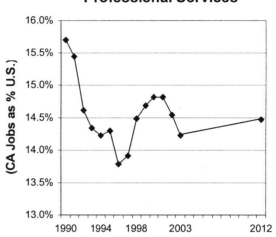

Management of Companies

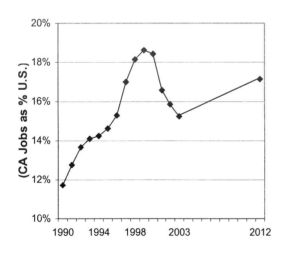

Employment Services

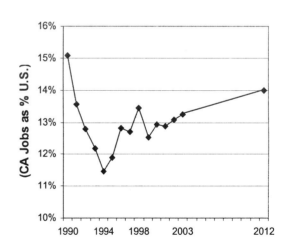

High tech is a major growth area (measured by projected output growth), yet job levels are projected to remain near current levels. Productivity growth in high tech manufacturing is allowing companies to keep pace with higher and higher sales levels without requiring much, if any, additional hiring.

On the other hand, higher levels of tech production do create jobs in associated industries, including professional and business services and wholesale trade.

The United States Bureau of Labor Statistics projects that real high tech production will increase by more than 150% between 2002 and 2012—more than four times as fast as GDP growth. Yet national high tech job levels are projected to remain near current levels.

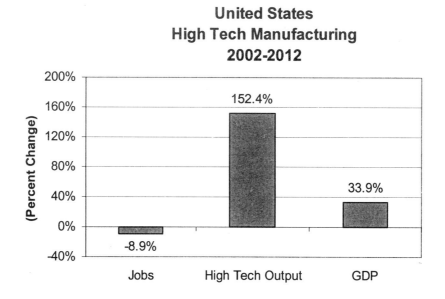

**United States
High Tech Manufacturing
2002-2012**

California continues to account for approximately 21% of U.S. high tech manufacturing jobs. The state's share remained between 20.9% and 21.7% after 1994. So there has been no significant gain or loss in share for the past decade. California's share of high tech manufacturing jobs is approximately twice as large as the state's share of total jobs.

CCSCE's high tech manufacturing sector combines our previous high tech and aerospace sectors and adds pharmaceuticals. As a result, the new job trends must be interpreted with the understanding that aerospace job losses were large and continuing throughout the 1990s, as shown on the table on page 5-30.

High Tech Manufacturing

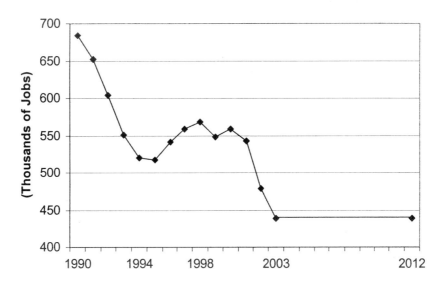

High Tech Manufacturing

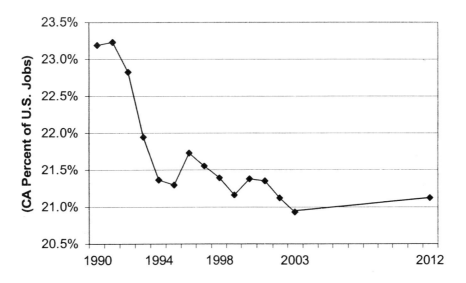

The aerospace and electronic instrument industries are now added to the high tech sector in recognition that **future** growth in these industries will depend significantly on the application of commercial technologies and innovations to defense production.

California High Technology Manufacturing Jobs 1994-2012 (Thousands)							
	1994	2000	2003	2012	1994-2000	2000-2003	2003-2012
Computer & Peripheral Equip. Mfg.	68.0	83.7	65.5	52.8	15.7	-18.2	-12.7
Communications Equipment Mfg.	33.0	43.8	28.4	38.9	10.8	-15.4	10.5
Audio & Video Equipment Mfg.	12.2	13.5	8.3	9.2	1.3	-5.2	0.9
Semiconductor & Elec. Component Mfg.	117.4	154.3	108.1	109.4	36.9	-46.2	1.3
Electronic Instrument Manufacturing	127.6	118.5	107.0	98.9	-9.1	-11.5	-8.1
Magnetic Media Mfg. & Reproducing	16.0	16.0	8.9	11.6	0.0	-7.1	2.7
Aerospace Product & Parts Mfg.	117.6	90.5	73.4	64.4	-27.1	-17.1	-9.0
Pharmaceutical & Medicine Mfg.	28.0	37.9	38.8	54.1	9.9	0.9	15.3
High Technology Manufacturing	**519.8**	**558.2**	**438.4**	**439.3**	**38.4**	**-119.8**	**0.9**

Source: EDD

The high tech manufacturing sector lost a substantial number of jobs in the 1990–1994 period, as aerospace job levels plummeted, and again during the past three years as non-defense high tech job levels fell. During the 1994–2000 period, non-defense high tech job levels rose and more than offset continuing losses in aerospace (which now includes aircraft and missiles) and electronic instrument manufacturing.

Job trends for individual high tech sectors are shown above. Trends in California's share of U.S. jobs are shown on pages 5-31 and 5-33.

NAICS industry code 334 is Computer and Electronic Products. It includes five primarily non-defense sectors and electronic instrument manufacturing, where most of the former defense electronics firms are located.

Computers and Peripheral Equipment

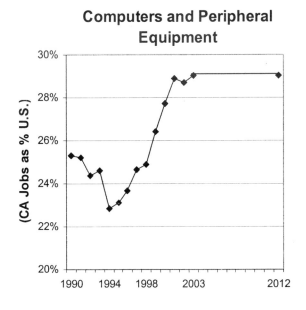

Communications Equipment

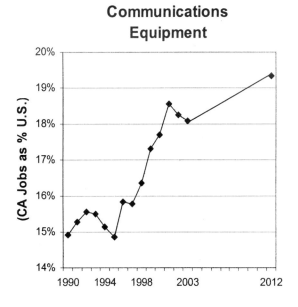

Semiconductor Manufacturing

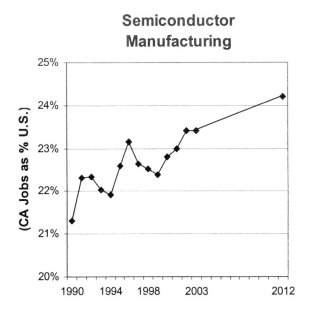

Electronic Instruments

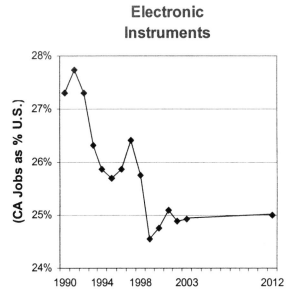

Job levels in computer and electronic products fell during the early 1990s, based primarily on declines in electronic instrument manufacturing. They rose in the late 1990s during the high tech boom and then fell sharply after 2000 as rising productivity and falling sales reduced employment levels.

California's share of national high tech jobs remains near record levels, despite the large loss of high tech manufacturing jobs in the Bay Area. California accounted for 24% of national high tech jobs in 2003, and that share is projected to continue to 2012. **Moreover, the state's share of high tech production is even higher (in the 28%–30% range) because the state's high tech workers have above-average productivity.**

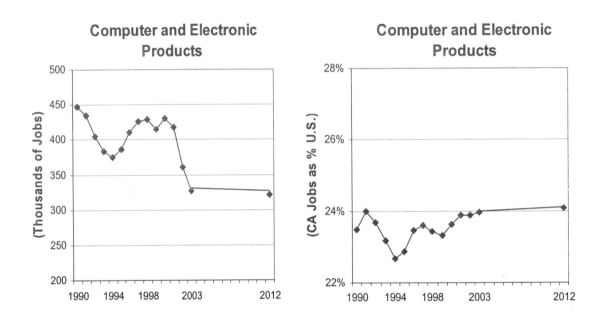

For the three major non-defense high tech manufacturing sectors—computers, communications equipment and semiconductors—California has posted fairly steady share gains since 1990, as shown on the graphs above. Small additional share gains are projected for communications equipment and semiconductors, while California's share of computer and peripheral equipment jobs is projected to remain near 29%.

Job levels are projected to decline slightly in computers and peripheral equipment, rise slightly in communications equipment and remain near current levels in semiconductors.

Job and share levels for electronic instrument manufacturing in California fell after 1990. The sector lost approximately 20,000 jobs between 1994 and 2003 and is projected to lose another 8,100 jobs by 2012.

Audio and Video Equipment

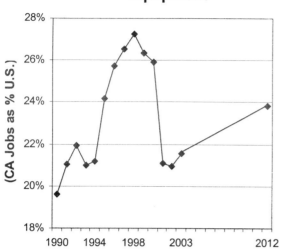

Magnetic Media

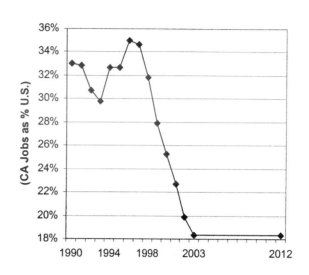

Aerospace

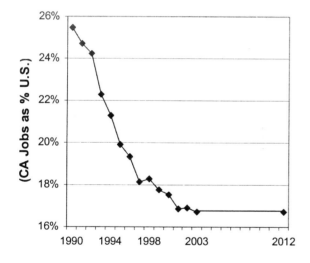

Pharmaceuticals

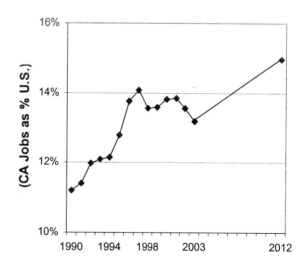

Aerospace job levels fell substantially between 1990 and 1994 in California, and the state's share of national aerospace jobs fell as well. Some firms transferred operations to other areas or closed their California operations. The drop in share was dramatic, as shown on page 5-33.

Aerospace job levels in California continued to decline after 1994, and the state's share of national aerospace jobs continued to decline as well. By 2003 California's share of aerospace jobs had fallen from near 25% to near 17%. By 2012 California's aerospace job levels are projected to have declined to 64,400, from 214,000 in 1990. **In most high tech manufacturing sectors, job levels are projected to decline or remain constant despite substantial increases in production levels.**

Part of the high tech boom (in both manufacturing and services) was fueled by a surge in venture capital funding. Studies show that much of the job growth in Silicon Valley came from newly formed and relatively small firms.

Venture capital funding in California increased from $2 billion per quarter in early 1997 to $5 billion per quarter in early 1999. For the next two years, funding averaged between a low of $7 billion per quarter to a high of over $20 billion per quarter in the Internet boom period.

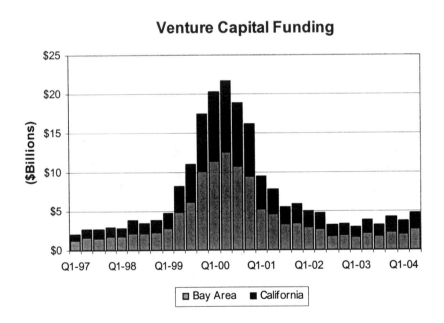

Venture Capital Funding

On an annual basis, venture capital funding increased from $6.1 billion in 1997 to $44.2 billion in 2000. **After 2000, venture capital funding in California fell to a low of $8.0 billion in 2003 before it began to recover in 2004.**

California Venture Capital Funding 1995-2003 ($Billions)							
	1995	**1997**	**1998**	**1999**	**2000**	**2001**	**2003**
Los Angeles/Orange	$.5	$.8	$1.4	$3.7	$6.5	$2.2	$1.0
Sacramento/N. Calif.	.0	.0	.1	.1	.3	.2	.1
San Diego	.3	.5	.6	1.3	2.3	1.6	.8
San Francisco Bay Area	1.9	4.8	6.3	18.9	35.1	12.9	6.1
California	**$2.7**	**$6.1**	**$8.4**	**$24.0**	**$44.2**	**$16.9**	**$8.0**
Calif. Share of U.S.	**34.2%**	**39.6%**	**38.4%**	**42.7%**	**41.0%**	**39.4%**	**42.6%**

Source: Price Waterhouse Coopers/Venture Economics/NVCA

Venture capital funding followed the same pattern of activity as high tech manufacturing jobs between 2000 and 2003–**large declines in activity levels, but no declines in share.** California accounted for 43.7% of national venture capital funding at the peak in 1999. The share remained above 40% and reached a record high of 44.7% in 2003.

Pharmaceuticals have been the steady growth component of California's high tech manufacturing sector. Job levels increased from 28,000 in 1994 to 38,800 in 2003. California is projected to gain another 15,000 pharmaceutical jobs by 2012.

In addition, California firms have posted steady gains in the share of national jobs. The state is projected to outpace the nation in pharmaceutical job growth to 2012.

Pharmaceuticals is not the only component of California's biotech and bioscience sector.

California has a leadership position in biotech R&D. As shown in the tables on page 5-36, California firms account for between 1/3 and 1/2 of biotech sales, jobs, profits and R&D spending among public biotech firms.

It remains difficult to assess how fast the industry will grow. Exciting opportunities in agriculture, health care, and environmental cleanup have produced continuing growth in R&D, sales, and employment. As yet, however, there has been no explosion of growth as in the early days of the computer and semiconductor industries.

Public Biotechnology Industry in 2002 Number of Firms	
San Francisco Bay Area	62
New England	52
San Diego	28
New Jersey	24
Mid-Atlantic	20
Los Angeles/Orange County (11th)	13

Source: Ernst & Young

California's niche is in R&D from existing companies and university-based research efforts. Major regional public-private partnership initiatives are underway in the Bay Area and San Diego to strengthen California's competitive position as an R&D leader.

Public Biotech Companies ($Billions)	Employees		Product Sales		R & D	
	2001	2002	2001	2002	2001	2002
Bay Area	34,983	31,844	$7.4	$9.0	$3.3	$3.6
Los Angeles-Orange	25,976	27,091	5.5	7.2	1.1	4.2
New England	24,452	24,447	3.9	4.8	2.7	2.8
San Diego	7,534	8,569	1.4	1.6	.8	.8
Total U.S.	141,238	142,878	$25.3	$30.3	$11.5	$16.3

Source: Ernst & Young

There are a number of excellent sources on state and national biotech trends: 1) the Biotechnology Industry Organization at www.bio.org, 2) the California Healthcare Institute at www.chi.org and 3) Ernst and Young. In addition the California Employment Development Department (www.edd.ca.gov) has a recent report on California's biomedical sector.

Diversified Manufacturing

The new NAICS Diversified Manufacturing sector is similar to CCSCE's SIC-based sector in previous editions of this report. Two changes are that (1) CCSCE moved pharmaceuticals to the high tech sector and (2) publishing is now in the NIACS Information sector.

Diversified manufacturing is projected to show below-average growth in the nation to 2012, measured both by job **and** output growth. National job levels in diversified manufacturing are projected to show no increase between 2002 and 2012. Output growth is projected to trail GDP growth during this period.

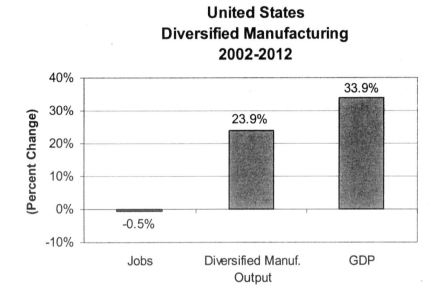

Diversified manufacturing played an important role in California's economic growth during the late 1990s. These industries added more than 130,000 jobs between 1994 and 2000. Reaching a total of nearly 1 million jobs in 2000, this became California's second-largest basic industry sector.

California firms posted job gains in the 1990s while their national counterparts had relatively constant job levels. As a result, California's share of national diversified manufacturing production slowly increased in the 1990s—a trend that is projected to continue in the decade ahead.

Despite the widespread publicity about manufacturing jobs "leaving" California, the overall numbers for diversified manufacturing tell a different story. First, California's share of national diversified manufacturing jobs rose during the late 1990s, from 7.5% in 1994 to 8.6% in 2000.

After 2000, both the state and the nation did lose a substantial number of diversified manufacturing jobs. The nation lost nearly 2 million diversified manufacturing jobs while California lost nearly 200,000 sector jobs. These losses were the result of 1) the recession, 2) productivity growth outpacing sales growth and 3) some loss of competitive share to other countries.

However, California's share of U.S. diversified manufacturing jobs in 2003 was 8.6%, the same as in 2000.

California has two advantages in competing for diversified manufacturing jobs: 1) California is closer to fast-growing domestic and foreign markets than other regions and 2) many California facilities are newer than facilities in other regions. As a result, a higher share of plant closures is occurring in other states, particularly in the Midwest.

California also has a competitive advantage in some diversified manufacturing sectors such as apparel, furniture and toys where design is an important component of overall competitive advantage. California is an acknowledged leader in many design areas.

California also has a number of cost and other disadvantages, including higher costs for housing, workers' compensation insurance and energy. Moreover, the state is struggling to provide enough infrastructure and maintain a high quality of life.

California's share of diversified manufacturing jobs is projected to increase slightly, from 8.6% in 2003 to 8.9% in 2012. Job levels are projected to rise by 63,500. However, job levels in California and the nation are expected to remain below the levels achieved in 2000, as output growth is not projected to be high enough to regain many of the lost jobs.

Diversified Manufacturing

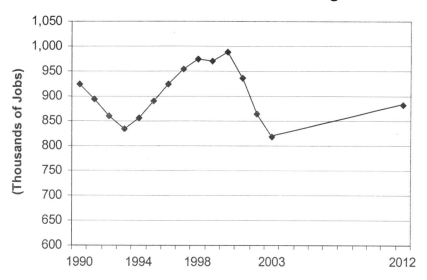

Diversified Manufacturing

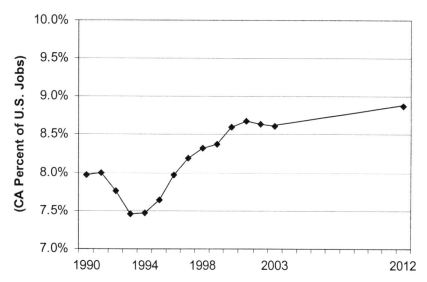

Historical job levels and projected growth for major diversified manufacturing sectors are shown below. Many sectors follow the following pattern:

- Job levels rose between 1994 and 2000.

- Job levels fell between 2000 and 2003.

- Job levels are projected to increase between 2003 and 2012.

- The projected job levels in 2012 are below the levels in 2000.

- California's share of national jobs is constant or rising slowly.

California Diversified Manufacturing Jobs 1994-2012 (Thousands)							
	1994	2000	2003	2012	1994-2000	2000-2003	2003-2012
Wood Products	29.1	37.6	31.8	43.3	8.5	-5.8	11.5
Primary Metal Products	27.7	30.9	25.2	29.3	3.2	-5.7	4.1
Fabricated Metal Products	139.3	173.3	138.8	161.2	34.0	-34.5	22.4
Machinery	90.7	108.5	86.7	106.6	17.8	-21.8	19.9
Electrical Equipment & Appliance	37.3	44.1	36.6	38.4	6.8	-7.5	1.8
Transportation Equip. (exc. Aerospace)	54.9	62.7	55.9	60.8	7.8	-6.8	4.9
Furniture & Related Products	58.4	76.7	62.9	75.2	18.3	-13.8	12.3
Medical Equipment & Supplies	41.6	51.8	49.1	55.4	10.2	-2.7	6.3
Other Miscellaneous Manufacturing	40.9	51.5	42.6	46.4	10.6	-8.9	3.8
Beverage Products	27.9	33.0	35.7	34.6	5.1	2.7	-1.1
Textiles	31.7	37.6	30.0	27.6	5.9	-7.6	-2.4
Apparel	123.9	122.6	89.0	64.4	-1.3	-33.6	-24.6
Paper Products	35.9	35.4	30.1	29.1	-0.5	-5.3	-1.0
Chemicals (except Pharmaceuticals)	42.3	43.7	39.6	37.0	1.4	-4.1	-2.6
Plastics & Rubber Products	65.3	73.1	59.8	69.2	7.8	-13.3	9.4
Leather Products	8.7	7.0	4.9	4.2	-1.7	-2.1	-0.7
Diversified Manufacturing	**856.4**	**987.8**	**819.0**	**882.5**	**131.4**	**-168.8**	**63.5**

Additional industry detail is shown for 2003 on Table A-1 in Appendix A.

Apparel

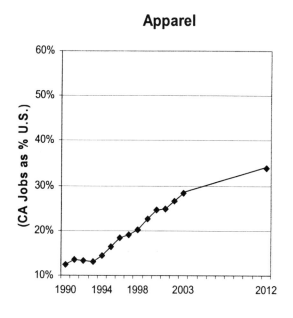

Chemicals
Excluding Pharmaceutical

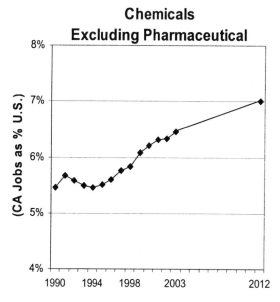

Fabricated Metal Products

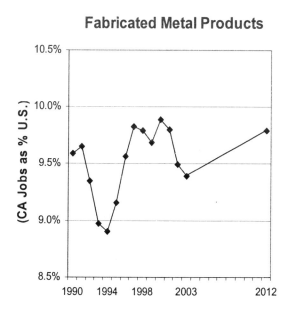

Machinery Manufacturing

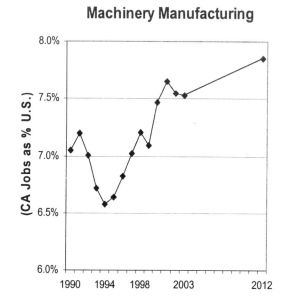

Between 1985 and 2000, apparel jobs increased substantially, reaching a high of 137,500 in 1996. During this period, national apparel job levels fell steadily. Apparel job levels reached a low of 89,000 in 2003.

The California apparel industry is based on the state's talent in fashion and design. Apparel and textiles have made steady gains in share of national production and jobs. California had 28.5% of national apparel jobs in 2003—up from 12.5% in 1990. State apparel sales were $16.7 billion in 2001 (this is the latest sales data available).

The apparel industry is under increasing pressure from imports. Job levels in the nation and state are falling and are projected to decline further by 2012. CCSCE projects that job levels in California will fall by a smaller percentage than in the nation, based on competitive advantage in design for markets that are harder to serve with overseas production.

By 2012 the number of apparel jobs in California is projected to decline to 64,400, even as the state's share of national jobs increases to 33.9%. Programs to increase the use of technology in apparel design and manufacture, such as those run at L.A. Trade Tech Community College, are one approach to maximizing the opportunities for apparel jobs in the state.

Fabricated metal products is the largest diversified manufacturing sector in California, based on number of jobs. Job levels rose to a peak of 173,300 in 2000 after falling between 1990 and 1994. Job levels fell to 138,800 in 2003 but are projected to rebound to 161,200 in 2012. Industry sales in California were $26.0 billion in 2001.

California's fabricated metal product industry now has 9.4% of U.S. sector jobs. The state's share is projected to increase to 9.8% in 2012, slightly below the high share of 9.9% in 2000.

Machinery manufacturing is the next-largest diversified manufacturing industry in California after fabricated metal products and apparel. The state had 86,700 machinery manufacturing jobs in 2003, down from 108,500 in 2000. Industry sales in California were $19.1 billion in 2001.

Machinery job levels are projected to increase by nearly 20,000 between 2003 and 2012, based on rising national job levels and a small increase in the state's share of national jobs. California accounted for between 6.5% and 7.5% of U.S. machinery manufacturing jobs between 1990 and 2003. The state's share is projected to increase from 7.5% in 2003 to 7.9% in 2012.

Wood Products

Furniture

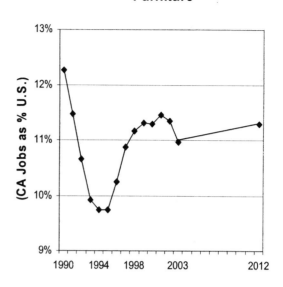

Paper Products

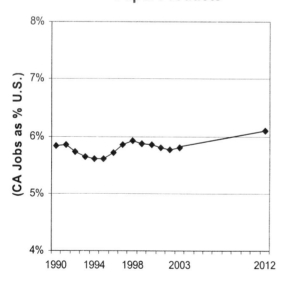

Plastic & Rubber Products

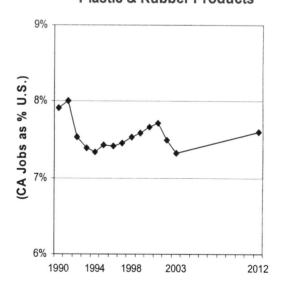

The chemical sector (excluding pharmaceuticals) has accounted for approximately 40,000 jobs since 1990. Job levels have declined slowly since 2000. They are projected to fall to 37,000 by 2012 as national industry job levels fall. The chemical sector (excluding pharmaceuticals) had sales of $11.5 billion in 2001.

The state's share of national sector jobs increased from 5.5% in 1990 to 6.5% by 2003. It is projected to reach 7.0% in 2012. This means that the industry is shrinking more in the rest of the country than in California, as measured by job levels.

Construction markets have been expanding since 1994. Job levels in furniture and wood products (excluding sawmills) rose between 1994 and 2000. In 2000, industry job levels reached to 114,300, up from 87,500 in 1994. The NAICS data show sales of $6.2 billion for wood products in 2001 and $8.0 billion for furniture—down from a high of $14.9 billion in 2000.

The furniture and wood products industry will certainly benefit from the projected rebound in construction activity in the decade ahead. CCSCE projects a continued increase in job levels and modest gains in the state's share of national jobs. Furniture design and manufacture also is one of Southern California's craft industries where a concerted region-wide effort could bring this California industry to a new level of international competitiveness.

California plastic and rubber products firms accounted for $13.7 billion in sales in 2001. Job levels rose between 1994 and 2000, fell between 2000 and 2003, and are projected to increase upwards toward the 2000 level in 2012. California accounts for approximately 7.5% of the national industry as measured by jobs.

California had 101,700 jobs in miscellaneous manufacturing in 2003. These were split evenly between two components—medical equipment and supplies and other miscellaneous manufacturing. In 2001, medical equipment and supplies had California-based sales of $12.1 billion; other miscellaneous manufacturing had sales of $7.3 billion.

California's share of jobs in each miscellaneous manufacturing segment has increased since 1990 and is projected to remain near record levels. The number of jobs is projected to increase to 111,800 in 2012.

Transportation equipment (excluding aerospace) accounted for 55,900 jobs in California in 2003, with 41,300 of these jobs in motor vehicles. California has major design centers for most leading auto firms in the nation and world. Job and share levels are projected to remain relatively constant to 2012.

Electrical Equipment

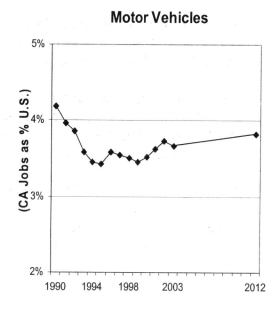

Motor Vehicles

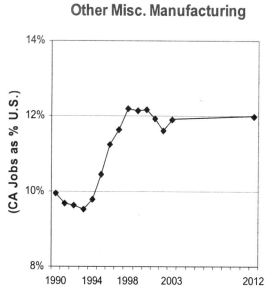

Medical Equipment

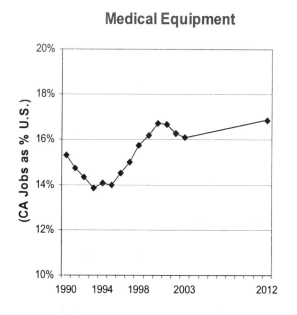

Other Misc. Manufacturing

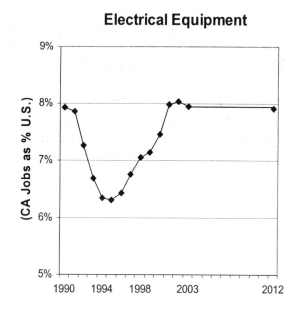

Future Prospects

The data shows clearly that California has not lost competitive advantage in this large sector. After rebounding from the early '90s recession, California firms captured 8.6% of the national sector in 2003—**just below the highest share ever**.

The diversified manufacturing sector remains important for California's economic base. Even though the national industry will not have job growth in the years ahead, production will increase. The Bureau of Labor Statistics projects that output in the sector will increase by 24% between 2002 and 2012.

The growth in output will be enough to slow the job losses in diversified manufacturing. Nevertheless, diversified manufacturing faces the same paradox that high tech faces—rising sales with few new jobs. Productivity growth will lead to gains in real wages, as well as job gains in industries that supply goods and services to diversified manufacturing firms.

CCSCE's projections assume that the era of large share gains for most diversified manufacturing industries in California has ended. The projections assume that in most industries the state's share of U.S. jobs and output recovers to near 1990 levels but does not increase thereafter.

However, share gains are expected to continue in a few industries, which will push the state's share of the sector higher. CCSCE projects that California will account for 8.9% of national diversified manufacturing jobs in 2012.

The future of diversified manufacturing in the state and nation is tied to

- The ability of the U.S. industry to adopt "high tech" production approaches.

- The ability of small and medium-sized firms to expand.

- The development of regional industry clusters where:

  — Private firms collaborate in supplier-producer-customer partnerships.

  — The public and private sector collaborate on public investment and rules and regulation uses.

Many regions within California have exciting initiatives underway (public-private partnerships) that could result in California firms capturing a higher-than-projected share of U.S. diversified manufacturing jobs and output.

This page intentionally left blank.

Basic Information Services

Basic Information Services is a new basic industry sector. It includes software, publishing, telecommunications, ISPs, web search portals and other basic information services.

Information Services is a new major industry sector under the NAICS definitions, and basic information services is a new CCSCE major basic industry sector. Note that CCSCE has moved motion picture production from the Information sector to CCSCE's Tourism and Entertainment basic industry group in the tables, graphs and discussion below.

California Basic Information Services Jobs 1994-2012 (Thousands)							
	1994	2000	2003	2012	1994-2000	2000-2003	2003-2012
Software Publishers	25.2	48.1	44.7	78.6	22.9	-3.4	33.9
Radio & Television Broadcasting	24.8	29.2	27.9	30.0	4.4	-1.3	2.1
Cable & Subscription Broadcasting	15.2	26.1	25.1	39.0	10.9	-1.0	13.9
Telecommunications except Cable	106.7	134.8	113.1	144.0	28.1	-21.7	30.9
Internet & Other Telecom.	29.6	97.9	57.8	98.6	68.3	-40.1	40.8
Basic Information Services	**201.5**	**336.1**	**268.6**	**390.2**	**134.6**	**-67.5**	**121.6**

Source: EDD

The basic information services sector increased by nearly 70% between 1994 and 2000. It reached a peak job level of 336,100 jobs in 2000. Substantial job losses after 2000 still left the sector with substantial job growth since 1994.

California's share of national basic information jobs fell after 1990, rose sharply during the Internet boom and fell back after 2000. In 2003 California accounted for 12.6% of national sector jobs—a share that is projected to increase to 13.7% in 2012.

All segments of basic information services grew rapidly between 1994 and 2000. The largest job growth was in Internet-related activity—the ISP, Web Search Portals and Data Processing Services sector. Job levels rose from 29,600 in 1994 to 97,900 in 2000—more than a threefold increase.

Software publishing job levels rose from 25,200 in 1994 to 48,100 in 2000. Job levels in the radio and TV and cable broadcasting sectors also increased during this period.

Basic Information Services

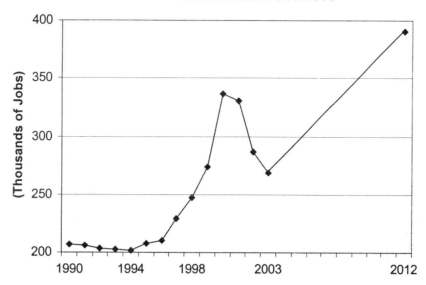

Basic Information Services

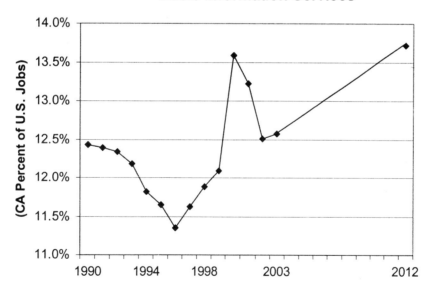

Substantial job losses occurred in the Internet sector as many firms went out of business between 2000 and 2003. However, job levels remained relatively constant in the other subsectors during this period.

Telecommunications is the largest single industry in basic information services. It is a mixture of faster-growing sectors, such as wireless communications resellers, where job levels fell substantially during the past ten years. Overall sector job levels increased from 106,700 in 1994 to 134,800 in 2000, and then fell to 113,100 in 2003.

Job levels in the California basic information sector are projected to grow by nearly 50% between 2003 and 2012, for a gain of 121,600 jobs. The largest job gains are projected for software publishing and Internet-related activities.

Projected national industry growth is the basic cause of California's projected job growth in this sector. Most subsectors had a sharp increase in the state's share of national jobs during the Internet boom, followed by a drop in share.

Output is projected to grow rapidly in this sector, far outpacing GDP growth. Job growth would be larger were it not for the high rates of productivity growth anticipated in information services.

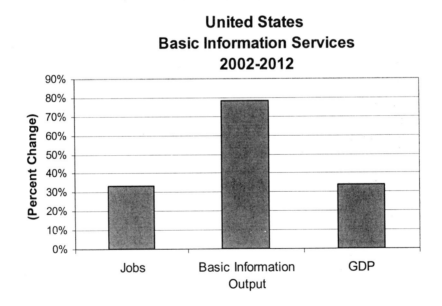

United States
Basic Information Services
2002-2012

Software Publishing

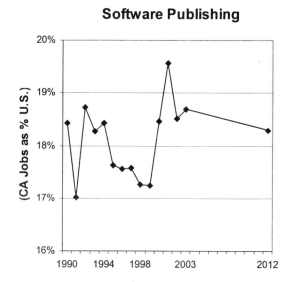

Cable & Subscription Broadcasting

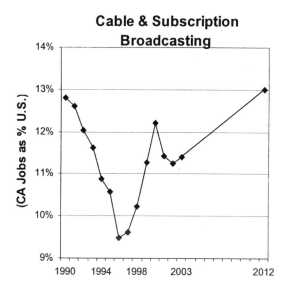

Telecommunications Excluding Cable

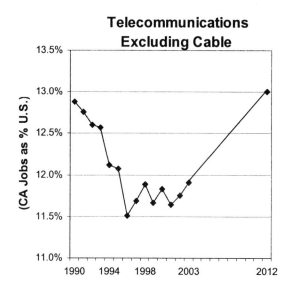

Internet & Other Telecommunications

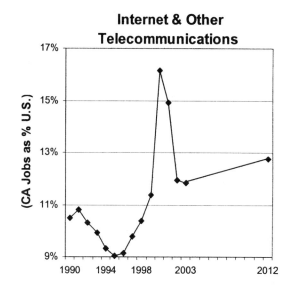

Tourism and Entertainment

The NAICS Tourism and Entertainment sector is an updated and expanded version of the previous SIC-based sector that included hotels, motion picture production and amusements.

CCSCE now includes accommodation (hotels), motion picture production, and the arts, entertainment and recreation industry in the tourism and entertainment industry of California's economic base. Tourism and entertainment serve California, U.S., and international consumers. California is a major destination for worldwide vacation travel and possesses some of the world's finest recreational attractions.

The sector has strong long-term growth prospects based on rising disposable income in the United States and abroad. As incomes rise, families can and do increase spending on travel and entertainment. Job levels nationally in the tourism and entertainment sector are projected to increase more than 50% faster than the projected overall job growth rate.

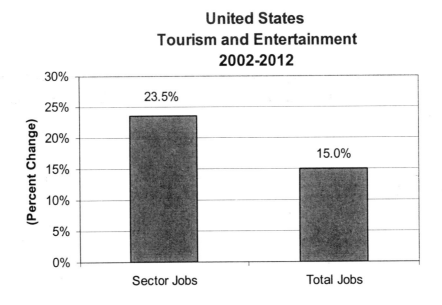

Tourism and entertainment job levels fell temporarily after 2000, as international travel was hard hit by the 9/11 events. Motion picture job levels also fell. Substantial job growth is projected between 2003 and 2012, and more than 150,000 additional jobs are expected in the sector.

California has an above-average share of national tourism and entertainment jobs, but the share has declined from near 16% to near 14% during the past ten years. California's share is projected to increase slightly, from 14.2% in 2003 to 14.7% in 2012.

Tourism and Entertainment

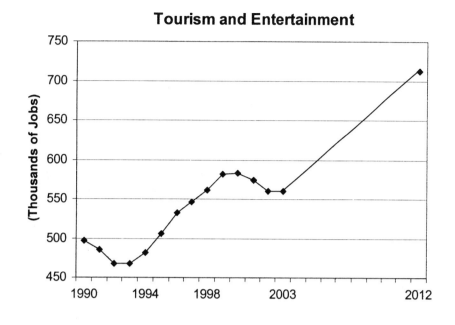

Tourism and Entertainment

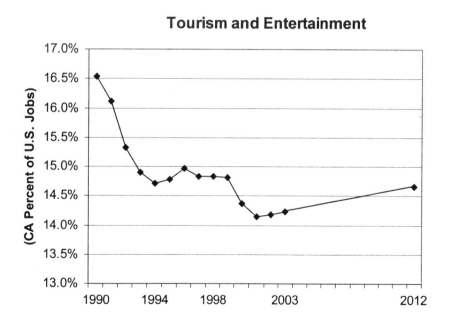

Travel and Tourism

Travel growth stopped after 2000, with 9/11 and the recession causing a decline in international travel and a reduction in business travel. Domestic leisure travel markets have shown continued growth. CCSCE expects that both international and business travel will grow again as the economy recovers, assuming that international tensions return to more normal levels.

World travel is, over the long-term, a strong growth industry. It is driven by rising incomes throughout the world, especially, in Pacific Rim nations. While Asian tourism has declined recently, the long-term growth potential remains very strong—especially with the prospects of rising income and more travel freedom in China.

California also provides tourism and entertainment services to domestic consumers. The state is a major market for domestic business and vacation travel for the same reasons that attract foreign visitors. Californians also travel within the state and use California's world-class amusement and recreational facilities.

The California Travel and Tourism Commission publishes data related to California's tourism industry (http://gocalif.ca.gov). The following section is drawn from their data. Travel volumes have been flat to down since 2000. The data do, however, illustrate the **size** of the tourism sector in California.

In 2003, travel spending in California totaled an estimated $78.2 billion—virtually the same as in 2000. This includes spending by Californians and out of state travelers.

California received 316 million person trips (a trip of more than 50 miles that is not for work or school) to and through the state in 2003. This was up from 243 million in 1996 and 289 million in 2000. Approximately 265 million trips were made by California residents, 44 million were made by travelers from other states and 7 million were made by international travelers.

California Tourism and Entertainment 1994-2012 (Thousands)							
	1994	2000	2003	2012	1994-2000	2000-2003	2003-2012
Motion Picture & Sound Recording	124.2	170.0	135.2	176.1	45.8	-34.8	40.9
Arts, Entertainment & Recreation	181.5	216.1	233.9	307.4	34.6	17.8	73.5
Accommodation	175.4	196.4	191.6	228.7	21.0	-4.8	37.1
Tourism and Entertainment	**481.1**	**582.5**	**560.7**	**712.1**	**101.4**	**-21.8**	**151.4**

Sources: EDD

Air travel is important for business and leisure travel, even though most travel in California is done by residents. Air travel is the mode for nearly 20% of business trips and 49% of leisure trips by nonresidents.

Air travel was down in 2001 and again in 2002 and 2003. Finally, in the early part of 2004, air travel into and out of California was rising again. From 2000 through 2003, the largest drops were at San Jose and San Francisco airports. Oakland airport added flights, and San Diego reported small losses.

Air Arrivals 2003 (Millions)				
	Domestic	Vs 02	International	Vs. 02
Los Angeles	20.1	-2.5%	7.3	-1.3%
San Francisco	11.0	-5.6%	3.3	-7.9%
San Diego	7.5	2.5%	.1	-11.9%

Source: California Department of Tourism, 2004 Fast Facts (http:gocalif.ca.gov)

California receives 21% of all overseas tourism to the United States. Domestically, California captured 11.5% of the tourism market in 2002—up from 9.8% in 1997, despite the sharp Bay Area losses after 9/11.

California Share of U.S Travel Market

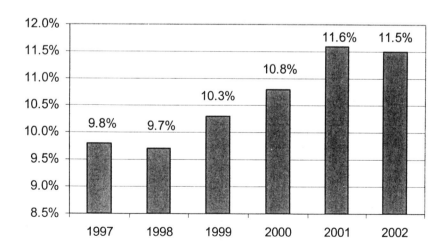

California has some of the nation's major tourist attractions. The opening of California Adventure at Disneyland in 2001 is one of many expansions planned throughout the state.

California Top Ten Amusement/Theme Parks (Millions of Visitors)	2000	2003
Disneyland, Anaheim	13.9	12.7
Disney's California Adventure		5.3
Universal Studios Hollywood	5.2	4.6
Sea World, San Diego	3.6	4.0
Knott's Berry Farm, Buena Park	3.5	3.5
San Diego Zoo	3.0	3.0
Six Flags, Magic Mountain, Valencia	3.3	3.0
Santa Cruz Beach Boardwalk	3.0	3.0
Paramount's Great America, Santa Clara	1.8	1.9
Monterey Bay Aquarium, Monterey	1.8	1.7

Source: California Department of Tourism, 2003 Fast Facts

Because more than 80% of tourist travel is from California residents, the income growth projected for state residents should provide a firm base for expansion in tourist spending in the decade ahead.

Motion Picture Production

Motion picture production is one of the largest high-wage sectors in the California economy. Between 1994 and 2000 the industry added 45,800 jobs and maintained a relatively steady 45% share of national motion picture production job levels. Moreover, it is estimated by the industry that, for every 100 wage and salary jobs counted in the official statistics, there are another 50 jobs held by self-employed individuals, and California's share of these jobs may be even higher.

Job levels dropped sharply after 2000, according to the published EDD estimates. The threat of "runaway production" captured the industry headlines after 2000. Still, production levels remained high—although there has been a shift from motion picture production to TV production in recent years.

In September 2004, EDD released motion picture production job estimates based on more recent data. It found that job levels were 20,000–25,000 jobs higher than in the official estimates. These new estimates are shown on page 5-57.

California
Motion Picture Production Jobs
1990--2003

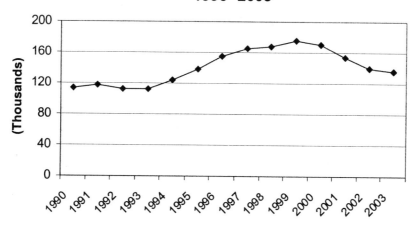

California
Motion Picture Production Jobs
2003-2004

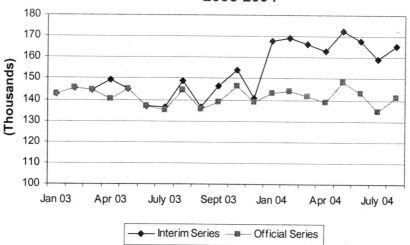

Data on production days are published by the Entertainment Industry Development Corporation and are shown on their website, www.eidc.org. CCSCE made estimates for 2004 based on actual data for the first six months of the year.

Southrn California
Production Days by Major Type
1995-2004

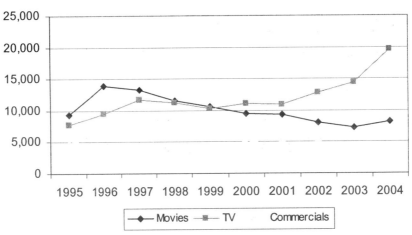

The data show a decline in motion picture production days and an offsetting increase in production days for TV and commercials.

The explosive growth of motion picture and television exports continues, despite recent international financial turmoil. Film and tape rental exports rose from $1.9 billion in 1991 to $9.9 billion in 2002. These figures demonstrate the strong international demand for U.S. entertainment products.

U.S. Film Exports

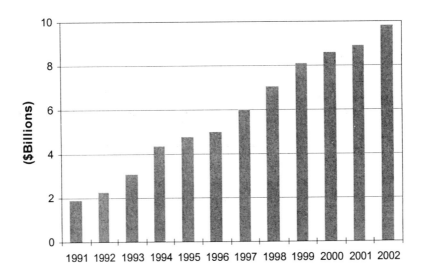

Motion Picture Production

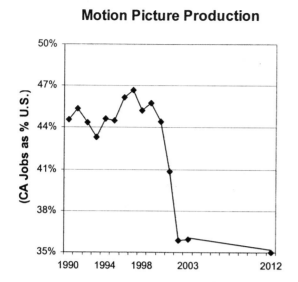

Arts, Entertainment & Recreation

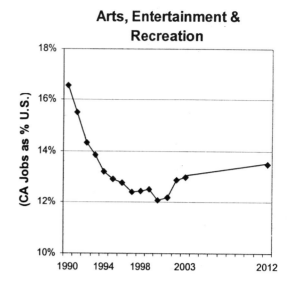

Accommodations

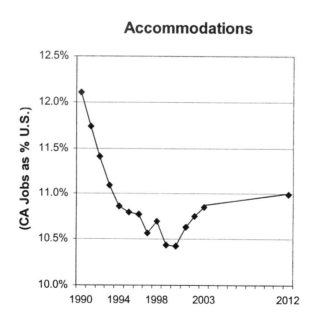

Future Prospects

Travel and tourism markets should grow over the next ten years. Incomes are projected to increase, Pacific Rim economic growth should continue and California continues to be the site of world-class tourist attractions.

One new factor, casino gambling, has not been factored into CCSCE's projections. California is in the midst of passing agreements that should lead to a substantial increase in casino gambling under laws that allow Native American tribes to operate casino facilities. It is reasonable to assume that associated activities—hotels and restaurants—will grow along with casino gambling.

In addition, the recent upward revision of California's motion picture production job estimates was not received in time to incorporate into the *California Economic Growth — 2004 Edition* projections. If these data had been available, it is likely that CCSCE's motion picture production job projections would be 20,000 to 40,000 higher.

The market for entertainment media is exploding with the new ability to receive and play movies on computers and with the surge in new home entertainment technologies.

Government

The basic industry government section involves federal defense and non-defense activities. Federal government jobs are split between Department of Defense (including civilian jobs at military bases) and other federal government activity, including the Postal Service.

Department of Defense job levels fell in the early '90s with the first rounds of base closures. They continued falling through 2003, when there were just 54,000 California jobs remaining in this subsector of the state economy. California has had approximately 200,000 non-defense federal government jobs since 1990.

Federal government job levels are projected to remain relatively constant to 2012.

	Government 1994-2012 (Thousands)						
	1994	2000	2003	2012	1994-2000	2000-2003	2003-2012
Department of Defense	104.1	60.7	58.2	54.0	-43.4	-2.5	-4.2
Other Federal Government	220.8	212.2	200.5	207.1	-8.6	-11.7	6.6
Government	**324.9**	**272.9**	**258.7**	**261.1**	**-52.0**	**-14.2**	**2.4**

Source: EDD

Resource Based

The resource-based economic basic sector has five industries: farm, logging, mining, sawmills and fruit and vegetable preserving. CCSCE includes self-employed farm workers within the farm category.

California Resource Based 1994-2012 (Thousands)							
	1994	2000	2003	2012	1994-2000	2000-2003	2003-2012
Farm (including self-employed)	426.9	441.1	407.6	370.5	14.2	-33.5	-37.1
Logging	4.1	3.5	2.6	2.0	-0.6	-0.9	-0.6
Mining	23.0	23.0	19.4	15.3	-0.0	-3.6	-4.1
Sawmills	8.5	8.8	7.8	7.3	0.3	-1.0	-0.5
Fruit and Vegetable Preserving	46.0	39.8	34.8	29.6	-6.2	-5.0	-5.2
Resource Based	518.5	516.2	472.2	424.8	-2.3	-44.0	-47.4

Source: EDD

Farm

California's agricultural industry employed 407,600 workers in 2003 to produce an output valued at $27.5 billion in 2002. Agricultural exports in 2002 were $9.0 billion, including processed foods. Agricultural sales and exports have stayed in a narrow range for the past five years.

California Agriculture in 2002 ($Millions)					
Crops		**Exports**		**Counties**	
Milk and Cream	$3,812	Almonds	$829	Fresno	$3,416
Grapes	2,579	Cotton	514	Tulare	$3,200
Nursery Products	2,347	Wine	486	Monterey	2,812
Lettuce	1,278	Grapes	367	Kern	2,586
Cattle	1,229	Dairy	301	Merced	1,730
Almonds	1,190	Oranges	303	San Joaquin	1,368
Strawberries	991	Tomatoes	215	Stanislaus	1,344
Flowers	948	Walnuts	184	San Diego	1,297
Tomatoes	926	Rice	183	Riverside	1,224
Hay	914	Beef	168	Ventura	1,161
Total	**$27,478**	**Total**	**$6,468**	**Total**	**$27,478**

Source: California Department of Agriculture

The leading farm products in 2002 were milk and cream products ($3.8 billion), grapes ($2.6 billion) and nursery products ($2.3 billion). Leading export products were almonds ($829 million), cotton ($514 million) and wine ($486 million). Leading agricultural counties were Fresno ($3.4 billion), Tulare ($3.2 billion) and Monterey ($2.8 billion).

California's share of national agricultural production, measured by dollar value, has remained relatively stable in the 1990s. However, California's share of farm wage and salary jobs has risen because California farms use a large amount of paid labor relative to farms in other states.

CCSCE expects that farm and food product sales will continue to grow along with the overall economy. Because expected sales growth is modest relative to productivity increases, industry employment should fall in the decade ahead.

The largest industries in terms of jobs, sales and exports are farming and fruit and vegetable preserving. Farm sales have been stable at near $27 billion for several years, and sales for the fruit and vegetable preserving industry have been near $10 billion since 1997.

Resource Based

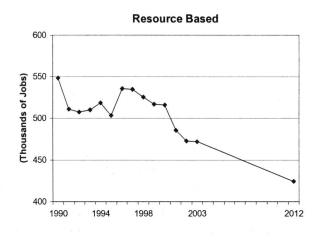

Resource Based

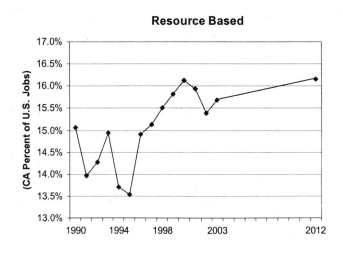

Total Jobs

Total jobs in California are projected to increase to 19.1 million in 2012 as a result of the growth in California's economic base. Job growth in California will outpace the national average because jobs in the state's economic base will grow faster than in the nation. California is projected to have 12.0% of U.S. jobs in 2012. This is up from 11.3% in 2003 and 10.9% in 1994.

California jobs are projected to grow by 2.2% per year between 2003 and 2012. This is after having grown by 2.4% per year in the 1980s and 1.7% per year between 1994 and 2003. Job levels in the nation are projected to increase by 1.6% per year during the 2003–2012 period. This is higher than the 1.3% annual rate between 1994 and 2003.

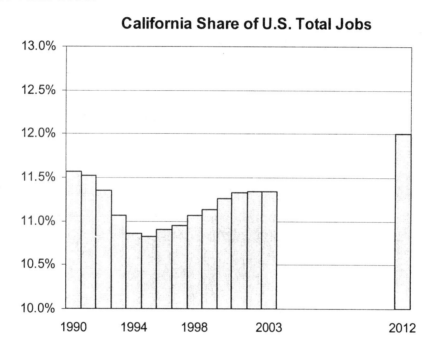

California Share of U.S. Total Jobs

California and United States Total Jobs 1979-2012 (Thousands)						Average Annual Growth Rate	
	1979	1994	2000	2003	2012	1994-2003	2003-2012
California	10,932.0	13,813.1	16,232.9	16,140.5	19,629.5	1.7%	2.2%
United States	101,401.5	127,235.7	144,132.4	142,336.9	163,756.8	1.3%	1.6%
CA % of U.S.	10.8%	10.9%	11.3%	11.3%	12.0%		

Sources: BLS; EDD; CCSCE

Jobs by Major Industry Group

Job trends for major NAICS industry sectors in California between 1994 and 2012 are shown below.

California
Jobs By Major Industry Group
1994-2012
(Thousands)

| | 1994 | 2000 | 2003 | 2012 | Numerical Change | | |
					1994-2000	2000-2003	2003-2012
Farm	379.7	408.5	375.0	347.4	28.8	-33.5	-27.6
Natural Resources and Mining	27.1	26.5	22.0	17.3	-0.6	-4.5	-4.7
Construction	475.3	731.0	788.8	949.8	255.7	57.8	161.0
Manufacturing	1,683.8	1,857.5	1,544.9	1,646.6	173.7	-312.6	101.7
Wholesale Trade	545.1	644.9	651.4	802.5	99.8	6.5	151.1
Retail Trade	1,358.8	1,559.4	1,589.9	1,985.6	200.6	30.5	395.7
Transp, Warehousing & Utilities	447.3	517.2	480.7	637.5	69.9	-36.5	156.8
Information	395.8	575.4	471.4	634.3	179.6	-104.0	162.9
Financial Activities	770.3	795.1	886.8	1,028.6	24.8	91.7	141.8
Professional & Business Serv.	1,586.4	2,246.0	2,108.1	2,950.3	659.6	-137.9	842.2
Educational and Health Serv.	1,212.0	1,398.0	1,536.3	2,141.7	186.0	138.3	605.4
Leisure and Hospitality	1,143.8	1,332.6	1,397.6	1,730.2	188.8	65.0	332.6
Other Services	420.5	486.7	505.8	642.8	66.2	19.1	137.0
Government	2,093.2	2,318.1	2,426.5	2,733.8	224.9	108.4	307.3
Self Employed	1,273.9	1,336.1	1,355.3	1,410.9	62.2	19.2	55.5
Total Jobs	**13,813.1**	**16,232.9**	**16,140.5**	**19,659.5**	**2,419.8**	**-92.4**	**3,518.9**

Sources: 1994-2003 — EDD with CCSCE estimate of self-employed based on 1990, 2000 Census data; 2012 — CCSCE

Professional and Business Services will be California's largest major industry sector in 2012. It is projected to have nearly 3 million jobs. The sector includes the basic industry components described earlier in this chapter, as well as other office and business support services.

The Professional and Business Services sector is projected to have the largest job gain between 2003 and 2012, a repeat of the sector's leading job growth between 1994 and 2003.

The number of manufacturing jobs in California in 2012 is projected to be near the 1994 level, after having grown in the late 1990s and fallen sharply between 2000 and 2003. Manufacturing sales and exports are projected to show substantial growth, but productivity gains will limit the potential for job creation in the sector.

Retail Trade and Educational and Health Services are California's two largest population-serving sectors. Each is projected to have approximately 2 million jobs in 2012. The two sectors combined are projected to contribute 1 million added jobs in California by 2012. This growth is supported by the projected gains in population and income.

The Leisure and Hospitality sector includes the basic industry components described earlier, as well as food services (including fast-food and other restaurants). Leisure and Hospitality is projected to be the state's fifth-largest major industry sector, with 1.7 million jobs in 2012. This represents a gain of 332,600 jobs over 2003 levels.

Construction and Financial Activities are each projected to have approximately 1 million jobs in 2012, and to add approximately 150,000 jobs between 2003 and 2012. This job growth is supported by rising population and income levels and the construction and financing needs of a growing state.

Total Population

Based on anticipated job growth in the state, CCSCE projects that California will add 4.9 million residents between 2003 and 2012. By 2012, California is projected to have 40.8 million residents. The state will continue to grow faster than the nation. California's population will increase by 13.5%, while the national growth rate is projected to be 8.2%.

California and United States					
Population Growth					
2000-2012					
(Resident Population in Thousands)					
	2000	**2003**	**2012**	**Growth 2003-2012**	**Percent Growth**
California	33,871.6	35,934.0	40,800.0	4,866.0	13.5%
United States	281,421.9	290,818.0	314,800.0	23,990.0	8.2%
California as % of U.S.	12.0%	12.3%	13.0%	20.3%	

Sources: 2000 — Census Bureau; 2003, July I— Census Bureau and DOF; 2012, July 1 — CCSCE

Between 2003 and 2012, growth is projected to average 540,700 per year— compared to 421,200 annual population increases in the 1990s. Nevertheless, projected growth will be far less on a percentage basis than gains in the 1970s and 1980s.

In the decade ahead, California's population is projected to increase by 1.4% per year. In the 1990s growth averaged 1.3% per year, and in the 1980s the state population grew by 2.3% annually.

California will capture a large share of the nation's population growth. The state will get 20.3% of U.S. population growth in the decade ahead, compared to 27.4% of national population growth in the 1980s and 12.8% in the 1990s. By 2012, California will account for 13.0% of the U.S. population. This is up from 12.4% in 2000 and 10.5% in 1980.

Foreign immigration is expected to continue near current levels for both legal and undocumented immigrants. Migration from other states is expected to nearly equal the number of residents who leave California to live in other states.

Population Growth by Major Age Group

The projections presented below are adapted from those published by the California Department of Finance in 2004. There are significant changes in where population growth is occurring by age group.

Between 2003 and 2012 the largest population growth is projected in the 55–64 age group—nearly 1.4 million residents. Nearly 1 million persons will be added in both the 65+ and 20–34 age groups. The number of young adults will rise in the years ahead, after having fallen slightly since 1990. Population growth will also move from the 35–54 age group to the 55+ age group between 2003 and 2012.

The number of persons under the age of 20 in California rose by 1.9 million between 1990 and 2003. Growth will continue, but at a lower level between 2003 and 2012, with the addition of 730,000 residents under 20 years of age.

California Population by Age Group 1990 – 2012 (Thousands)					
Age Group		**Age Group Population**		**Numerical Change**	
---	**1990**	**2003**	**2012**	**1990-2003**	**2003-2012**
0-19	8,701.2	10,631.2	11,361.3	1,930.0	730.0
20-34	8,021.0	7,824.1	8,801.4	-196.9	977.3
35-44	4,727.7	5,561.6	5,622.3	833.9	60.7
45-54	2,927.1	4,834.4	5,587.8	1,907.4	753.3
55-64	2,202.8	3,218.2	4,594.8	1,015.4	1,376.6
65+	3,248.7	3,864.5	4,832.5	615.8	968.1
Total Population	**29,828.5**	**35,934.0**	**40,800.0**	**6,105.5**	**4,866.0**

Source: California Department of Finance, adjusted to CCSCE 2012 projection

Population Growth by Ethnic Group

California's Hispanic population is projected to increase by 5 million, or 45.5%, between 2000 and 2012. Hispanic population growth is projected to account for nearly 80% of the state's total population increase.

Asian population is projected to increase by 1.2 million, or 32.3%, during the same time period. The Black population is projected to grow by nearly 500,000 residents, while the White Non-Hispanic population is projected to fall by nearly the same amount. The largest percentage increase is projected for the multi-race and American Indian population—a gain of 52.3% between 2000 and 2012.

Ethnic Group	Ethnic Group Population		Numerical Growth	Percent Growth
---	2000	2012	1990-2003	2003-2012
White Non-Hispanic	16.048.0	15,553.8	-494.2	-3.1%
Hispanic	11,083.0	16,123.6	5,040.6	45.5%
Asian	3,746.3	4,954.6	1,203.8	32.3%
Black	2,222.8	2,732.7	509.9	22.9%
Multi-Race, American Indian	831.9	1,275.2	443.3	53.3%
Pacific Islander	111.2	160.1	48.9	44.0%
Total Population	**34,043.2**	**40,800.0**	**6,756.8**	**19.8%**

California
Population by Ethnic Group
2000 – 2012
(Thousands)

Sources: 2000 — DOF as of July 1; 2012 — DOF adjusted to CCSCE projection of total population

Total Households

Household growth depends on 1) job and population growth, 2) the age composition of the population and 3) conditions affecting household formation rates, such as affordability, supply conditions and the ethnic composition of the population. New household projections have been prepared using 2000 Census data about household formation rates by age and ethnic group.

Job and population growth, as discussed earlier, will be far higher between 2003 and 2012 than in the 1990s.

The bottom line of CCSCE's new household projection analysis is that these factors mostly point toward a large increase in household formation in California.

Age Trends

The number of residents under the age of 20 rose as a share of California's population in the 1990s—from 29.2% in 1990 to 30.1% in 2000. As a result, the adult population, which is the household-forming group, grew more slowly than average. This was a negative factor for household formation.

Between 2003 and 2012, the 20-and-older population will grow more rapidly than the 0–19 age group. By 2012, the 0–19 age group will account for 27.8% of California's population. The above-average growth of the adult population will be a positive factor in pushing household growth higher.

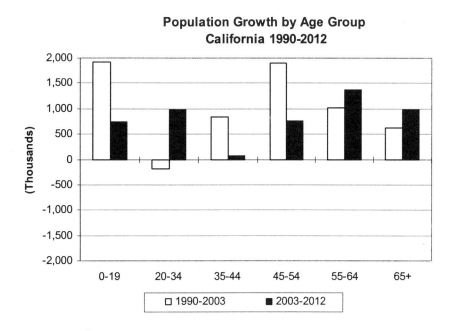

There are significant changes in the age distribution of population growth for the adult population:

- There will be a gain of nearly 1 million in the 20–34 age group. By contrast, the population in this age group—where people often get their first home or apartment—fell by nearly 200,000 between 1990 and 2000.

- There will be less growth in the 35–53 age groups compared to the 1990s.

- There will be a substantial increase in growth of California's population in two age groups, ages 55–64 and 65+. This trend is important because these groups have the highest housing demand per 1,000 people—the result of divorces, separations and deaths.

State Household Projections to 2010

CCSCE has prepared three sets of household projections based on different assumptions about household formation rates.

The **demographic trend projections** assume that the household formation rates by age and ethnic group reported in the 2000 Census will remain constant to 2012. As a result, the major forces affecting household growth are the projected changes in total population and population by age and ethnic group.

The demographic trend projections result in the highest rate of household growth— 226,800 per year between 2004 and 2012. Meeting these projections will require an increase in the level of annual housing construction from the current production of 190,000–200,000 units per year. Housing production needs to be approximately 10% above the level of household growth to account for second home purchases and the demolition of existing housing. These projections could also be considered conservative, in that they assume no increase in the propensity to form households as income rises for recent immigrants and their children.

The table below shows that the household formation rates (the number of households formed for every 100 residents aged 15 and above) for Hispanic and Asian populations are substantially below the rates for the White Non-Hispanic population. If the formation rates for Hispanics and Asians increase by 2012, overall household formation in California will be above the 216, 4000 annual growth cited above.

	California Household Formation Rates by Age and Ethnic Group 2000				
Age Group	**All Ethnic Groups**	**Black**	**Asian**	**Hispanic**	**White (Non-Hispanic)**
15-24	11.0%	13.1%	9.5%	8.8%	13.4%
25-34	40.7%	46.1%	34.9%	35.4%	46.6%
35-44	50.7%	53.2%	45.4%	46.7%	53.9%
45-54	55.1%	58.9%	49.6%	50.1%	57.7%
55-64	57.0%	65.4%	47.1%	49.0%	60.3%
65-74	59.2%	69.0%	41.9%	50.4%	63.5%
75+	62.1%	65.6%	43.7%	50.3%	65.5%
Total	**44.1%**	**47.7%**	**37.3%**	**34.4%**	**50.9%**

Source: 2000 Census

	California Alternative Household Projections 1990-2010 (Thousands)				
				Average Annual Growth	
Households	1990 Census	2004 Jan. 1	2012 July 1	1990-2004	2004-2012
Demographic Trend	10,380.9	12,015.8	13,963.8	118.9	226.8
Current Trend			13,512.6		176.1
Midway Projection			13,738.2		202.6

CCSCE has also prepared two lower sets of household growth projections. In the **current trends projections**, CCSCE assumes that the decline in household formation rates in the 1990s will be continued. This alternative is possible if 1) California's housing supply disincentives are not reduced, 2) income gains do not materialize as expected or 3) the cultural patterns of multi-family households for immigrants remain stronger for recent immigrants than for previous generations despite rapid gains in income.

The current trend assumptions result in approximately 450,000 fewer households being formed in California by 2012. Household growth will equal nearly 1.5 million, or roughly 175,000 per year between 2004 and 2012.

Finally, CCSCE has a **midway projection** household growth alternative, which is roughly midway between the demographic trends and current trends projections.

The midway projection alternative will result in just over 13.7 million households in 2012. Household growth would average 202,600 per year between 2004 and 2012.

Midway Projection Used in 2004 Edition

CCSCE will use the midway household growth projection (202,600 per year) in the 2004 edition of this report. As discussed at the end of this chapter and elsewhere in this report, recent housing price increases have caused housing affordability to fall to all-time lows throughout California. These high housing prices, along with the difficulties in getting new housing approved in some communities, could reduce housing construction below the levels suggested by demographic trends.

Even though most California regions are adopting plans to accommodate more housing, supply constraints may continue in many regions.

Income and Spending

This section describes the past and projected growth of income and spending in California. All data are expressed in 2003$.

Bottom Line

Real per capita and average household income fell between 2000 and 2003. There were two principal causes: 1) a sharp decline in stock option income as tech company profits and stock prices plummeted and 2) a slowing in wage growth resulting from the national economic downturn. The California performance in these years is affected by the very sharp income losses in the San Francisco Bay Area.

Long-term income growth is still projected for California, based on continuing gains in productivity and jobs. As discussed in Sections 3 and 4, productivity growth has been, and is projected to continue to be, much higher than previously anticipated.

Total, Per Capita and Average Household Income

In 2003, California represented 13.0% of the national market in terms of income and spending – by far the largest state economy. The state's nearly $1.2 billion in total personal income compares with $702 million for New York and $650 million for Texas.

In 2000, fueled by a surge in stock option income, California had 13.1% of the nation's personal income and ranked as the world's 5th largest economy. Currently, the state ranks 6th after three years of stagnating real income.

Comparison of California and U.S. Income Trends

In 2000, per capita income in California was 10.8% above the U.S. average. Since 2000, per capita income in the state has lagged behind national growth rates because real per capita income in the Bay Area fell sharply as stock option income plummeted. In 2003, California's per capita income was 5.4% above the national average.

Average wage levels in California ($42,576 in 2003) were approximately 13% above national levels down from 17% above in 2000. Average household income ($100,923) was 20.1% above the national level.[1]

---

[1] CCSCE uses per capita and average household income series based on estimates of **total personal income** prepared by the U.S. Department of Commerce. Census estimates (based on the **money income** definition) are lower than the ones based on total personal income because the money income definition excludes non-money income items like fringe benefits and there is underreporting in the money income surveys.

The comparisons between state and national income levels were affected in 2000 by the substantial surge in stock option income in California and since then by the sharp drop in option income. The long-term state/national income ratio probably lies between the reported 2000 and 2003 levels.

California and United States Comparison of Income Measures 2003			
	California	United States	California as % of U.S.
Total Personal Income (Billions)	$1,197.6	$9,199.0	13.0%
Per Capita Income	$33,326	$31,632	105.4%
Average HH Income	$100,923	$84,009	120.1%
Average Wage (2001)	$42,576	$37,752	112.8%

Sources: U.S. Department of Commerce and Bureau of Labor Statistics; CCSCE

Wage Trends

Average wage levels in California remained 10%-12% above the national average throughout the long California recession in the early 90's. Wage growth in California in the late 1990s – adjusted for inflation – outpaced the nationwide gains.

California had the sixth highest average wage in 2003 – $42,576. Average wages in the state were 12.8% above the national average. State average wages rose slightly faster than the national average in 2003 after two years of below average performance.

Average Annual Pay

	2000	2002	2003	Percent Change 2000-2003
District of Columbia	$52,965	$57,914	$60,435	14.1%
Connecticut	$45,486	$46,852	$48,311	6.2%
New York	$45,358	$46,328	$47,239	4.1%
New Jersey	$43,676	$45,182	$46,325	5.0%
Massachusetts	$44,168	$44,954	$46,318	6.1%
California	$41,207	$41,419	$42,576	3.3%
Delaware	$36,535	$39,684	$40,956	6.6%
Maryland	$36,395	$39,382	$40,696	6.9%
Illinois	$38,045	$39,688	$40,548	12.1%
United States	$35,320	$36,764	$37,752	11.8%

Source: U.S. Bureau of Labor Statistics

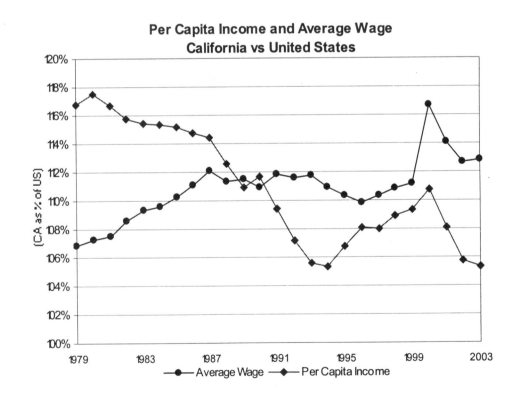

Per Capita Income and Average Wage
California vs United States

Projected Income Growth in California — Total **real** personal income (in 2003$) is projected to grow at 4.3% annually in California between 2000 and 2010. Total income will rise from $1.2 trillion in 2000 to more than $1.7 trillion in 2012.

The California market will continue to grow faster than the nation. United States income growth is projected at 3.8% per year to 2010. California's projected 4.3% real (i.e., inflation adjusted) annual gain compares with the 4.6% annual growth between 1994 and 2000. Real wage gains will be higher in the coming decade and offset a decline in the rate of population growth.

The income growth rates to 2012 projected here include some "rebound" affect from the recent period of slow growth and slightly overstate the underlying rate of productivity and real wage growth. However, the projections do not assume a return to the high levels of stock option income experienced in 2000.

Real per capita income is projected to grow by 2.8% annually between 2003 and 2012 compared to 3.3% in the 1994-2000 period. Per capita income (in 2003$) is projected to increase from $33,326 in 2003 to $42,796 in 2012.

California Income Levels and Growth 1990-2012 (2003$)			
	Per Capita Income	Average HH Income	Total Personal Income (Billions)
1990	$30,652	$88,075	$914.3
1994	$29,125	$84,890	$918.1
2000	$35,322	$104,526	$1,202.4
2003	$33,326	$100,923	$1,197.6
2012	$42,796	$126,081	$1,746.1
Low Projection	$39,192	$115,564	$1,599.0
High Projection	$44,706	$131,707	$1,824.0
Average Annual Growth Rates			
1994-2000	3.3%	3.5%	4.6%
2000-2003	-1.8%	-1.2%	-0.1%
2003-2012	2.8%	2.5%	4.3%
Low Projection	1.8%	1.5%	3.3%
High Projection	3.3%	3.0%	4.8%
U.S. Projection	2.9%	3.0%	3.8%

Sources: 1990 - 2003 — U.S. Department of Commerce (deflated by CCSCE); 2012 — CCSCE

Average household income in 2000 surpassed 1990 levels (measured in 2003$) by 19% after falling in the early 1990s. The strong rebound in real average household income between 1994 and 2000 (+3.5% per year) was created by job gains and the continuing increase in the number of workers per household.

After a temporary decline between 2000 and 2003, real average household income is projected to grow by 2.5% annually between 2003 and 2012. Average household income, adjusted for inflation, is projected to increase from $100,923 in 2003 to $126,081 in 2012.

There are several different measures of average household income. CCSCE uses a measure of total personal income per household, which is estimated as $100,923 in 2003. The Census bureau publishes measures of average household money income, which excludes fringe benefits and other non-monetary income. CCSCE's estimate of average household money income in 2003 is $69,764.

The Census Bureau also publishes an estimate of median household money income (half of all households have more than the median and half have less). CCSCE's estimate of 2003 median household income in California is $50,901. Average household income exceeds median income because a large share of total income gains are received by high-income households.

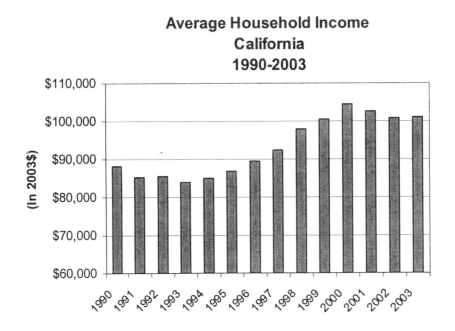

Average Household Income
California
1990-2003

California Alternative Measures of Household Income 2003	
Average Household Personal Income	$100,923
Average Household Money Income	$69,764
Median Household Money Income	$50,901

The Basis for Projecting Income Gains — CCSCE projected the growth in total personal income in California by examining two trends:

- Growth in income per job

- Growth in total jobs

CCSCE projects that productivity will grow by 2.4% per year in California and income per job in California will grow by 2.3% per year above the rate of inflation as average hours per job decline slightly. The basis for productivity projections is explained in Section 4.

CCSCE expects that average wages will grow at the same rate in California as in the nation.

California Components of Real Income Growth Average Annual Growth			Percent Growth 2003-2012		
	1980-1990	1990-2000	Low	Moderate	High
Total Personal Income	3.4%	2.6%	3.3%	4.3%	4.8%
Per Capita Income	1.1%	1.3%	1.8%	2.8%	3.3%
Population	2.3%	1.3%	1.4%	1.4%	1.4%

CCSCE Recommends Reviewing a Range of Income Projections. The answer to the question, "How much will prosperity increase in California?" depends on the rate of productivity growth and, therefore, the rate of real wage growth in the state and nation. Since there is uncertainty about whether and how much productivity growth will improve, CCSCE has prepared a range of income and spending projections.

Low income projections were based on the assumption of 1.4% annual growth in income per job. High income alternatives were developed assuming growth in income per job of 2.8% per year.

Total personal income in 2012 is projected to range between $1,599 billion and $1,824 billion. The projected real growth rates range from 3.3% per year (low) to 4.8% (high) compared with the 4.3% baseline projection.

Growth in per capita income is projected to range from 1.8% per year (low) to 3.3% per year (high) compared with the 2.8% annual growth projected in the "most likely" alternative.

The difference between the low and high annual income growth rates for California is equal to $225 billion in 2012. Depending on how the nation meets the productivity challenge, average inflation-adjusted household incomes in California will increase by approximately $15,000 (15%), $25,000 (25%), or $31,000 (31%) between 2003 and 2012.

Taxable Sales

Taxable sales have fallen sharply since 2000 as a result of two main factors: 1) the national and state economic slowdown and 2) the substantial decline in business to business sales, particularly in high tech and in the Bay Area.

Real sales fell from $483.1 billion in 2000 (in 2003$) to $454.0 billion in 2003 or by 2.0% per year. Taxable sales fell faster than income with the result that the percent of personal income spent on taxable sales fell to 37.9% — the lowest level ever recorded in California.

Both long-term and short-term trends have combined to constrain the growth in taxable sales, relative to income. The long-term trends are the more rapid growth in spending on non-taxable items, such as housing, medical care and other services. E-commerce sales are a relatively small but growing part of this trend.

During the 1990s, the share of income spent on taxable items stabilized mainly as a result of strong growth in business to business sales. However, since 2000 the tech downturn has resulted in a sharp decline in this component of taxable sales.

strong pressures to expand the taxable sales base by taxing more e-commerce sales **and** by including a portion of currently untaxed services in the tax base.

In the baseline projections, CCSCE is assuming that 37% of personal income will be spent on taxable items in 2012. The low (35%) and high (38%) share assumptions show the implications, respectively, of either a continued drop in the sales/income share, or of no decline from current levels.

California Taxable Sales 1990-2012 (Billions of 2003$)	
Year	**Taxable Sales**
1990	$396.9
1994	$360.3
2000	$483.1
2003	$454.0
2012	$646.0
Low Projection	$559.6
High Projection	$693.1
Average Annual Growth Rates	
1994-2000	5.0%
2000-2003	-2.0%
2003-2012	4.0%
Low Projection	2.4%
High Projection	4.8%

Sources: 1990 - 2003 — California Board of Equalization (Taxable Sales) adjusted to 2003$ by CCSCE; 2012 — CCSCE

As a result, CCSCE projects that taxable sales in California will grow by 4.0% per year, reaching $646.0 billion in 2012 (measured in 2003$).

Progress in raising real wages (through productivity increases) will make a substantial difference in the size of the California market in the years ahead. Spending gains could average between 2.4% and 4.8% annually, resulting in a $135 billion difference in the size of the California market in 2012.

Taxable Sales as % of Personal Income in California

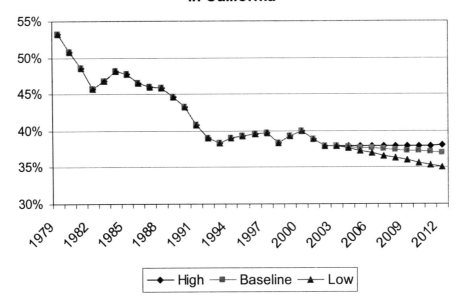

Construction Activity

Construction is a large and growing sector in the California economy. In 2003, construction related activities accounted for 936,300 jobs and recorded $69.4 billion in new building permits.[2]

Construction markets are primarily regional markets. This California construction section focuses on a broad overview of statewide trends and the **danger warning** CCSCE is issuing regarding residential market trends.

Short-Term Trends

The big story about construction activity during the recession was what **didn't happen** – there was no big decline. Residential construction levels rose in both 2001, 2002 and 2003, aided by low mortgage rates, and public construction remained at high levels, fueled by record levels of state and local bond approvals. Nonresidential building fell as vacancy rates rose and job growth stalled. Real construction levels (measured in 2003$) fell by 30% in the Bay Area (a loss of over $5 billion) but rose slightly throughout the rest of the state. Construction activity mirrored the general economy where the Bay Area experienced severe job losses and the rest of the state showed small, positive job growth.

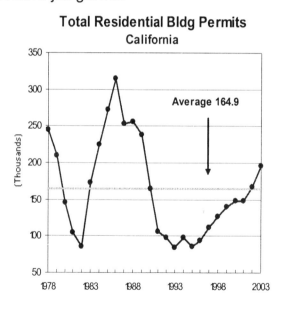

---

[2] This includes the $60.2 billion shown on the table and graph and $9.2 billion for public buildings – primarily schools. The public building data is not included in the graphs because there is no consistent data prior to 1997.

Residential building was up more that 16% statewide in 2003, following a gain of 10% in 2002. Permit levels are up again so far in 2004. The value of residential construction (in 2003$) last year was the second highest on record as more than 195,000 residential permits were issued — the largest number since 1989. Non-residential construction fell for the third straight year in response to slow job growth and high vacancy rates.

	California Construction Trends (Billions of 2003$)							
	New Construction				Residential Permits (Thousands)			
	1989	1993	2002	2003	1989	1993	2002	2003
Los Angeles Basin	$35.1	$14.6	$22.7	$24.6	116.4	28.8	68.2	78.5
San Francisco Bay Area	11.8	9.3	13.9	12.0	35.6	15.1	22.6	28.5
San Diego	6.1	2.6	5.3	5.8	18.7	5.6	15.7	18.3
Sacramento	4.7	2.6	6.2	6.4	21.2	9.4	24.4	24.3
San Joaquin Valley	4.8	3.8	6.0	7.0	27.3	16.4	23.5	30.8
Other	3.6	2.9	4.0	4.4	18.5	9.4	13.3	15.3
California	$66.1	$35.8	$58.1	$60.2	237.7	84.6	167.8	195.7

Source: Construction Industry Research Board

Long-Term Trends

Long-term construction spending depends on: 1) the growth in jobs, population and households, and 2) public decisions to support spending on infrastructure construction, repair and modernization. In both cases, the outlook is for **increased construction spending in future years.**

1) Annual job growth between 2003 and 2012 will average 391,000 per year — far higher than the 210,000 average gains in the 1990s. However, future growth levels will be slightly below the 400,000-per-year job gains between 1994 and 2000, and far below in terms of the annual growth percentage rate.

2) Household growth will be nearly double the average of the 1990s — 202,600 for 2004-2012 compared with 112,000 for the 1990s.

3) Population growth will average 540,700 annually to 2010 — more than 30% above the 411,000 per growth in the 1990s.

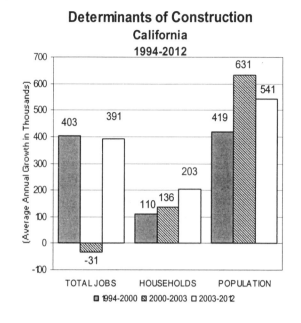

Determinants of Construction
California
1994-2012

Total Residential Bldg Permits
California
1980-2012

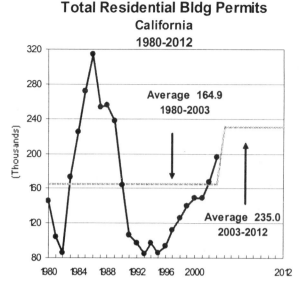

Housing Markets: Danger Signs Ahead

We now know why the housing market imbalance in the late 1990s was not as bad as previously feared.

1) Population growth in the 1990s was far below earlier estimates. As a result, the number of new households created in the 1990s can be explained by the low population growth and early 90s recession.

2) Housing affordability, while always far below national levels, actually improved in California during most of the years since 1994. Affordability ratios currently remain above the danger levels of the early 90s although California is, once again, falling further behind the nation.

3) Median household income growth kept pace with median resale price growth throughout the decade.

   — The relationship differs dramatically by region with the Bay Area showing a large escalation in prices even relative to the region's strong income growth.

   — However, by the end of the decade, median housing prices were, once again, rising faster than median incomes.

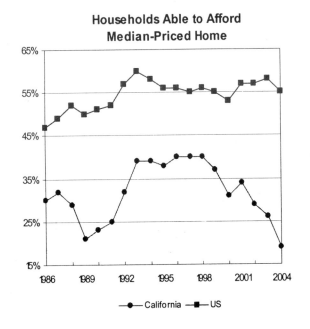

Households Able to Afford Median-Priced Home

California — US

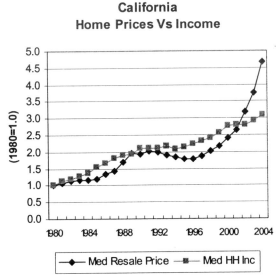

California Home Prices Vs Income

(1980=1.0)

Med Resale Price — Med HH Inc

Looking ahead, **household growth is about to surge.** Housing prices are, once again, growing faster than in the nation and faster than in most competing western market areas. Housing prices are rising much faster than overall prices and, in many regional markets, are rising faster than incomes. Affordability ratios are held up by historically low mortgage rates, rates which may rise as the economy enters a new strong growth era.

These are the early danger signs we see for California's housing markets. Unless the level of housing production rises in the coming years, the state residents could face the same kind of affordability crisis experienced in the late 1980s when housing markets and prices got out of balance.

A severe affordability crisis has been avoided so far only because mortgage rates fell in 2002 and the economy was weak. In 2002, California's median resale house price was $315,870 or 100% above the $158,300 national average. As shown below, California's median price has moved from 50% higher than the national average in 1997 to 100% last year. **The only other years in which the state/nation ratio was above 100% was during the housing market bubble and collapse of the late 1980s and early 1990s.**

Housing price increases are racing ahead of overall price growth as shown on the chart below. Again, the last time this "gap" was observed was in the late 80s/early 90s housing market correction. Today's "gap" is the largest on record and cannot be sustained as mortgage rates level off and then rise.

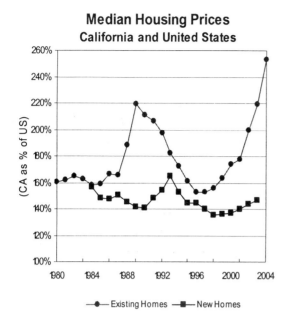

Median Housing Prices
California and United States

— Existing Homes   — New Homes

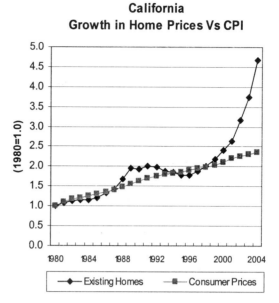

California
Growth in Home Prices Vs CPI

— Existing Homes   — Consumer Prices

Housing prices in California are also surging ahead of prices in other western markets. In the early and mid-1990s, housing prices in western regional markets like Denver, Las Vegas, Portland, Salt Lake City and Seattle got much closer to price levels in California. As shown on the following pages, prices in representative areas such as Denver, Portland and Salt Lake City grew steadily throughout the 1990s.

Prices in California markets dipped in the mid-1990s and didn't start rising again until 1996, 1997 or even as late as 1998 – depending on the market area. By 1997, median prices in most California markets were competitive with other areas, and markets like Sacramento and the Inland Empire were comparatively a bargain! For example, median resale prices in Sacramento were $116,100 — compared to $140,600 in Denver, $152,400 in. Portland and $128,600 in Salt Lake City.

Median Resale Housing Prices		
	Q3 1997	**Q1 2004**
Denver	$140,600	$231,800
Los Angeles	176,500	387,700
Portland	152,400	195,100
Riv-SB	114,300	258,900
Sacramento	116,100	277,900
Salt Lake City	128,600	148,000
San Diego	185,200	483,200

Source: National Association of Realtors

However, as shown in the following charts, prices in formerly less-expensive California markets have surged during the past three years. And prices in the most expensive state markets – Orange County and the Bay Area – are much higher, as shown above.

So housing in California is becoming less affordable in comparison to other markets, and less affordable compared to income and consumer price trends. Affordability ratios have been temporarily supported by the drop in mortgage rates from around 8% in late 2000 to near 7% at the beginning of 2002 and below 6% in early 2003. As long-term rates trend higher, affordability ratios will drop.

The bottom line is this: Unless Californians can significantly increase housing production and keep the cost of new housing affordable, housing markets in many California regions are headed for the price/affordability crisis of the early 1990s.

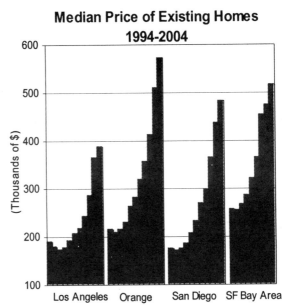

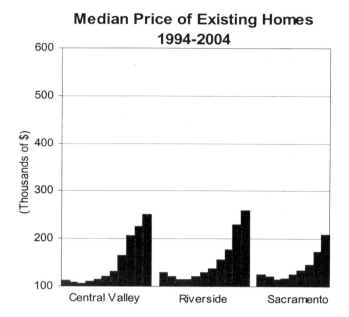

Median Price of Existing Homes 1994-2004

(Thousands of $)

Central Valley   Riverside   Sacramento

Nonresidential Construction

Nonresidential construction depends on regional growth and market conditions. The charts and tables below give a very brief overview of statewide trends.

Commercial, industrial and other nonresidential construction fluctuate with the level of job growth. The late 1990s, a period of strong job gains, saw a surge in commercial and industrial building, though still below the levels of the mid-1980s.

The slowdown in 2001 and 2002 will be followed by continuing weakness for a year or two. Then, renewed job growth should push commercial and industrial building levels higher (measured in constant dollars) although it is unlikely that the peak levels of the mid-1980s will be reached.

Two categories of nonresidential construction – additions and alterations and public works – have upward growth trends that should continue. Alterations and additions should grow as the size of the nonresidential capital stock increases over time. Moreover, as land becomes more limited and expensive, remodeling looks more attractive. The graph shows a steady increase in real (i.e., inflation adjusted) alterations and additions spending between 1980 and 2000, followed a sharp (and temporary) decline in 2001 and 2002.

Public works is now the largest component of nonresidential construction. The $9.1 billion spent in 2002 includes $3.8 billion for roads and bridges, $1.9 billion for water and sewer work, and $3.4 billion for other projects. In addition, there was $7.5 billion in public building construction – $4.2 billion for schools and colleges, $2.1 billion for cities and $1.2 billion for other jurisdictions.

Public works and public building construction reached record levels in 2002, despite a decline of $1.1 billion in power plant construction.

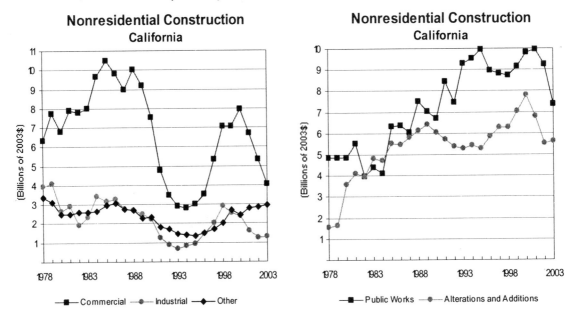

California Nonresidential Construction (Billions of 2003$)				
	1989	1993	2002	2003
Commercial	$9.2	$2.9	$5.4	$4.0
Industrial	2.5	0.7	1.3	1.3
Other Nonresidential	2.3	1.5	2.9	3.0
Alterations-Additions	6.4	5.3	5.6	5.5
Public Works	7.0	9.3	9.3	7.3
Public Buildings			7.4	9.2

Source: Construction Industry Research Board

There is widespread recognition of California's infrastructure shortage. Record levels of public bond issues are being proposed and approved, as further evidenced by the March 2002, November 2002, and March 2004 bond approvals. Public works spending should rise steadily in the years ahead and, with rising levels of home construction, push total construction spending higher.

The current state and local budget difficulties could restrain state public works spending in the short term. However, local communities continue to approve bonds for schools and public facilities, and to approve sales taxes devoted to local transportation projects.

Construction and Related Jobs

There are nearly 1 million construction-related jobs in California in 2003. The number of construction and related jobs increased each year from 1993 through 2001, dropped slightly in 2002 and rebounded in 2003

The need for skilled construction workers poses both a challenge and an opportunity for the state's workforce investment partners. With surging demand for housing and infrastructure, California will need more skilled construction workers during the next ten years.

Construction-Related Jobs
California

California Construction-Related Jobs (Thousands)				
	1990	**1993**	**2000**	**2003**
Construction	644.5	458.9	731.0	758.8
Wood Products Manufacturing	46.2	35.5	44.4	39.6
Furniture	73.7	57.0	76.7	62.9
Nonmetallic Mineral Products	54.4	40.8	48.1	45.0
Total Construction Related Jobs	818.8	592.2	900.2	936.3

Source: EDD

KEY ISSUES FACING
CALIFORNIA

KEY ISSUES FACING CALIFORNIA

Issues and challenges for the California economy are now addressed on a continuing basis with memos that are posted on CCSCE's website, www.ccsce.com.

This year's issues and challenges are related to three questions: 1) what makes a good business climate, 2) what is going on with the state budget, and 3) what role do state budget decisions play in creating a good business climate.

CCSCE and its non-profit affiliate, the Institute of Regional and Urban Studies, have been awarded a series of grants and contracts to write about key economic policy challenges facing California. This work is all in the public domain and is posted on our website as each memo is completed.

REGIONAL ECONOMIC GROWTH

REGIONAL ECONOMIC GROWTH

This chapter presents a more detailed examination of the economic trends in five major economic regions in California. These regions are the six-county Los Angeles Basin, the nine-county San Francisco Bay Area, the single-county San Diego Region, the six-county Sacramento Region and the eight-county San Joaquin Valley.

In 2003, CCSCE added the San Joaquin Valley to the major regions covered in *California Economic Growth — 2004 Edition*. The San Joaquin Valley is different from the other four regions because it is not a true labor market or commuting region. For example, workers in Kern County do not commute to San Joaquin County. The rationale for including the Valley is based on the following facts: 1) counties in the region have similar economic bases and face similar challenges, 2) the region is large **and** fast-growing, and 3) readers have expressed an interest in having the Valley included.

In the 2004 edition, CCSCE has modified the definition of the Sacramento region to include Sutter and Yuba counties. This makes the regional definition the same as that used by the Sacramento Area Council of Governments (SACOG).

This chapter begins with a comparison of economic growth rates among the regions. The main questions CCSCE looks at are as follows: Which regions have led the state since 1990, and where will the growth occur in the decade ahead?

After the comparison, each regional economy is examined separately. The analysis for each region includes:

- Examination of recent and current economic trends

- Description of the present and projected economic base

- Long-term trends in job growth

- Long-term trends in income and spending

- Analysis of construction activity—past, current, and projected

The counties included in each region are listed on the following page.

Los Angeles Basin

Imperial
Los Angeles
Orange

Riverside
San Bernardino
Ventura

CCSCE uses the same regional definition as the Southern California Association of Governments (SCAG). Some analysts include Imperial County in the San Diego region.

San Francisco Bay Area

Alameda
Contra Costa
Marin
Napa
San Francisco

San Mateo
Santa Clara
Solano
Sonoma

CCSCE uses the same regional definition as the Association of Bay Area Governments (ABAG). Some analysts include Santa Cruz County in the Bay Area, and there is increasing commuting between the Bay Area and the northern San Joaquin Valley. The full amount of detail on industry trends is lacking for these other counties compared to the nine-county region.

San Diego

San Diego

CCSCE uses the same regional definition as the San Diego Association of Governments (SANDAG).

Sacramento

El Dorado
Placer
Sacramento

Sutter
Yolo
Yuba

CCSCE now uses the same regional definition as the Sacramento Area Council of Governments (SACOG).

San Joaquin Valley

Fresno
Kern
Kings
Madera

Merced
San Joaquin
Stanislaus
Tulare

Comparison of Economic Regions

Economic Base

Each region in California has a different economic base. For example, the Bay Area economic base has a comparatively large share of California's high tech jobs, the Sacramento region economic base is heavily weighted toward state government jobs, the Los Angeles Basin has the highest concentration in diversified manufacturing and the Valley region is concentrated in resource-based industries.

Overall job growth in each region is determined by how much the region's economic base will grow. A more detailed analysis of each regional economic base is presented in Chapters 8–12. This chapter provides a summary comparison of the five major regions.

In analyzing the regional economic bases, CCSCE uses the eight categories of basic industry jobs described in Chapter 5. **The regional definition of economic base differs from the state definition in one respect: some industries are considered basic at the regional level, but local/population-serving from the state perspective.** Therefore, the regional economic bases contain more jobs in most categories as compared to the state definitions used for the table on page 5-9. Specific differences between the state and regional economic bases are described on page 7-18 and in Appendix tables A-1 and A-2.

California Jobs By Major Basic Industry Group Regional Definition 1994-2012 (Thousands)					Numerical Change		
	1994	2000	2003	2012	1994-2000	2000-2003	2003-2012
High Tech Manufacturing	519.6	558.1	438.3	439.3	38.5	-119.8	1.0
Diversified Manufacturing	1,118.4	1,259.7	1,072.0	1,177.7	141.3	-187.7	105.7
Wholesale Trade & Transportation	902.4	1,070.4	1,041.8	1,332.6	168.0	-28.6	290.8
Information	201.4	336.1	274.5	390.2	134.7	-61.6	115.7
Professional & Business Services	1,170.4	1,744.7	1,596.6	2,269.6	574.3	-148.1	673.0
Tourism & Entertainment	481.1	582.5	560.7	712.1	101.4	-21.8	151.4
Government	720.7	716.3	730.3	825.3	-4.4	14.0	95.0
Resource Based	452.8	474.8	431.8	392.3	22.0	-43.0	-39.5
Total Basic Jobs	**5,566.8**	**6,742.6**	**6,146.0**	**7,539.2**	**1,175.8**	**-596.6**	**1,393.2**

Sources: 1990, 2003 — EDD, CCSCE; 2012 — CCSCE

The regions had very different economic-base growth rates during the past ten years, as shown below. The Bay Area led all regions in basic job growth between 1994 and 2000 and then had, by far, the worst performance between 2000 and 2003. The Sacramento region and the San Joaquin Valley had below-average basic job growth rates in the 1994–2000 period, but did better than average after 2000. The San Diego and Rest of State regions did better than average during both periods.

California and Economic Regions Total Basic Jobs 1994-2012 (Thousands)					Percent Change		
	1994	2000	2003	2012	1994-2000	2000-2003	2003-2012
Los Angeles Basin	2,618.9	3,040.5	2,826.5	3,396.5	16.1%	-7.0%	20.2%
San Francisco Bay Area	1,312.6	1,696.5	1,359.5	1,755.2	29.2%	-19.9%	29.1%
San Diego Region	394.6	499.5	492.7	630.5	26.6%	-1.3%	28.0%
Sacramento Region	295.7	353.2	342.4	433.6	19.4%	-3.1%	26.6%
San Joaquin Valley	490.6	551.6	526.0	608.8	12.4%	-4.6%	15.7%
Rest of State	454.4	601.4	598.9	714.7	32.4%	-0.4%	19.3%
California	5,566.8	6,742.6	6,146.0	7,539.2	21.1%	-8.8%	22.7%

Future regional basic job growth depends on two factors: 1) which sectors are growing fast statewide, and 2) which regions have a high share of the fast-growing industries.

As shown in the table on the previous page, the largest basic industry job growth is projected for Professional and Business Services (+673,000 jobs) and Wholesale Trade and Transportation (+290,800 jobs). The Bay Area has an above-average concentration in both these sectors and therefore has the highest projected regional basic industry growth rate between 2003 and 2012.

California and Economic Regions
Profile of Economic Base
2003
(Percent of Total Basic Jobs)

	California	Los Angeles Basin	San Francisco Bay Area	San Diego	Sac'to Region	San Joaquin Valley
High Tech Mfg.	7.1%	6.7%	13.2%	7.2%	3.8%	0.9%
Diversified Mfg.	17.4%	22.5%	13.4%	14.3%	9.8%	16.4%
Whsl. Trade & Transp.	17.0%	19.8%	15.3%	12.1%	13.7%	14.6%
Information	4.5%	3.7%	6.7%	5.6%	4.8%	1.7%
Prof. & Business Serv.	26.0%	25.3%	30.1%	31.9%	21.3%	12.6%
Tourism & Ent.	9.1%	11.4%	7.6%	10.0%	6.8%	3.7%
Government	11.9%	8.1%	11.6%	16.4%	35.3%	12.3%
Resource Based	7.0%	2.5%	2.0%	2.4%	4.6%	37.7%
Total Basic Jobs	100.0%	100.0%	100.0%	100.0%	100.0%	100.0%

Source: EDD, CCSCE

After trailing other regions in the 1990s, Los Angeles Basin basic industry job growth is projected to be near the state average to 2012. The Basin will benefit from foreign trade–related job growth and will participate in the growth of professional services, entertainment and tourism jobs. Diversified manufacturing will grow modestly.

The San Francisco Bay Area economic base looks like a roller coaster. The region has been hard hit by high tech and professional services job losses since 2000. A strong rebound is projected in most sectors, but not in high tech jobs. As a result, the Bay Area has the highest projected basic job growth rate starting in 2003, **but the lowest growth rate starting from 2000, as shown on the next page.** Most job growth recaptures jobs lost since 2000.

The San Diego and Sacramento regions have done well since 2000, and that performance is projected to continue. San Diego has the highest concentration of professional services jobs and has gained share in most basic industry sectors. Sacramento has also gained share in many sectors. Future growth in the region assumes a renewal of job growth in state government and professional services sectors that are related to activities in the state capitol.

The San Joaquin Valley economic base has avoided the ups and downs of the other regions because the region does not have a high concentration in cyclical industries. The long-term challenge for the Valley is to find growth sectors to replace the job losses in the region's large resource-based sectors. Some relocation of activities from coastal regions has occurred, but as yet there is no clear sector to lead the region's economic base into the future.

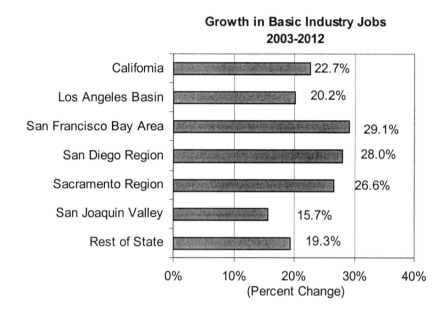

Growth in Basic Industry Jobs
2003-2012

Region	Percent Change
California	22.7%
Los Angeles Basin	20.2%
San Francisco Bay Area	29.1%
San Diego Region	28.0%
Sacramento Region	26.6%
San Joaquin Valley	15.7%
Rest of State	19.3%

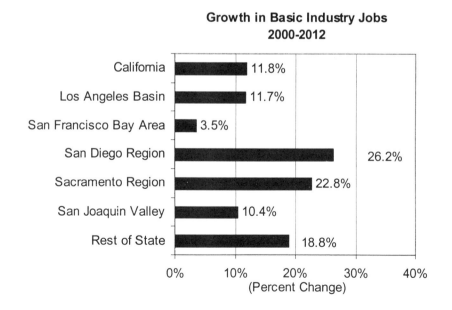

Growth in Basic Industry Jobs
2000-2012

Region	Percent Change
California	11.8%
Los Angeles Basin	11.7%
San Francisco Bay Area	3.5%
San Diego Region	26.2%
Sacramento Region	22.8%
San Joaquin Valley	10.4%
Rest of State	18.8%

Total Jobs

- California is projected to add 3.5 million jobs between 2003 and 2012, —an average gain of 391,000 jobs per year. The state will have an overall job increase of 21.8%—outpacing the nation's projected 15.0% gain.

  These job projections include an assumed "rebound" from the low recent job growth rates. Measured from 2000, annual job growth rates in the state and nation are lower than if measured from 2003. California outpaces the nation using either 2000 or 2003 as the starting date.

  Since 2000, the Bay Area and Los Angeles Basin have reversed their positions of a decade ago. In the early 1990s, it was the Basin (the site of aerospace job losses) that accounted for nearly all of the state's job losses, and it was the Basin that ended the 1990s with the lowest job growth rate. Now it is the Bay Area that has been hard hit by tech job losses and will end the decade with the state's lowest job growth rate measured from 2000.

  The projected annual gain of 391,000 jobs is in comparison with the annual increase of 210,000 in the 1990s, and 403,300 per year between 1994 and 2000.

California and Economic Regions Total Jobs 1994-2010 (Thousands)					Average Annual Growth		
	1994	**2000**	**2003**	**2012**	**1994-2000**	**2000-2003**	**2003-2012**
Los Angeles Basin	6,457.1	7,389.1	7,460.0	8,976.2	155.3	23.7	168.5
San Francisco Bay Area	3,186.7	3,847.0	3,523.4	4,383.4	110.1	-107.9	95.6
San Diego Region	1,072.9	1,317.2	1,366.8	1,716.1	40.7	16.5	38.8
Sacramento Region	759.0	921.1	966.3	1,190.9	27.0	15.1	25.0
San Joaquin Valley	1,144.0	1,300.4	1,336.5	1,586.2	26.1	12.0	27.7
Rest of State	1,193.4	1,458.1	1,487.6	1,806.7	44.1	9.8	35.5
California	**13,813.1**	**16,232.9**	**16,140.5**	**19,659.5**	**403.3**	**-30.8**	**391.0**

Sources: 1990, 2000 and 2003 — BLS, EDD, CCSCE; 2012 — United States: BLS; CCSCE; California and regions: CCSCE

- The Los Angeles Basin is participating in the current economic slowdown but has not suffered the significant job losses experienced in the Bay Area or in the Basin a decade ago.

- The Basin is projected to add 1.5 million jobs between 2003 and 2012. The average annual increase of 168,300 jobs is slightly above the annual gains experienced in the 1994–2000 period. Basin jobs are expected to grow by 20.3%, close to the state average.

   The Basin economy will benefit from growth in foreign trade, motion pictures, tourism, diversified manufacturing and professional services. The strong projected growth in foreign trade is expected to add jobs if the region maintains the aggressive expansion of port-related infrastructure. Housing costs and supply and regional infrastructure shortages are the most serious economic challenges facing the region.

- The Bay Area is currently the state's weakest regional economy, after being a star performer between 1994 and 2000. Tech losses, accentuated by a large drop in exports, continue to create significant job declines. **The Bay Area has accounted for more than the state's total job losses since 2000. All other regions have added some jobs and have outpaced the national growth rate.**

   The Bay Area economy is projected to recover, with new gains in tech-related professional services, exports and start-ups reversing recent job losses. While the region should experience significant growth from 2003 forward, the region's job growth rate from 2000 forward will be the lowest in California—barely matching the national average.

- San Diego began a strong economic recovery in 1994 and has experienced continuing job growth through the recent recession. The region is expected to be one of the state's leaders in job growth in the decade ahead. It is expected to have a 25.6% job increase from 2003 through 2012—38,700 added jobs per year.

   The region's economic strength comes from proximity to Mexico (trade and maquiladora activity), from continuing opportunities in telecommunications and biotech, and from growth in professional services. Housing prices have surged since 2000, and housing costs and availability could constrain growth. Like most California regions, San Diego faces challenges for expanding airport and other infrastructure capacity.

- The Sacramento region is projected to add approximately 25,000 jobs per year and to grow by 23.2% between 2003 and 2012. The Sacramento region has grown as a competitive location for activities seeking a California alternative to the higher-cost coastal regions. The growth of professional services related to state government is critical to continuing high rates of overall job growth. The region still has a large amount of vacant land, but faces challenges in accommodating the projected growth while maintaining a high quality of life.

- The San Joaquin Valley is projected to add 28,200 jobs per year and to grow by 18.7% between 2003 and 2012. The traditional resource base (agriculture, mining, timber) will see job declines in the decade ahead. Regional growth will be driven by relocation of firms and workers from the big urban areas of California, based on cost and quality-of-life considerations. The new UC campus in Merced and the long-term potential for households to live in the Valley and work in the coastal urban centers will boost the region's growth.

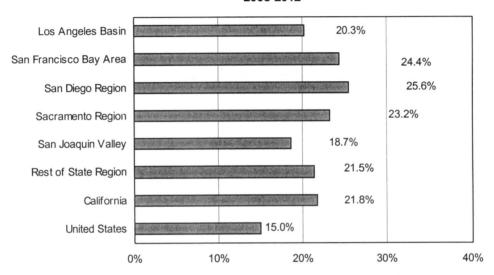

Projected Job Growth
Regions, California, and U.S.
2003-2012

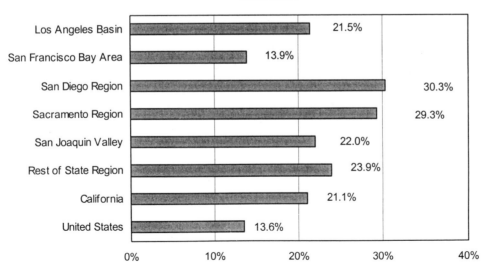

Projected Job Growth
Regions, California, and U.S.
2000-2012

Total Personal Income

- Total personal income (adjusted for inflation) is expected to grow by 4.3% annually between 2003 and 2012—outpacing the projected 3.8% national growth rate. All regions of California will have income growth rates above the national average, ranging from a 5.3% annual increase in the San Joaquin Valley to a 4.0% annual growth rate in the Bay Area. A portion of the future growth represents a recovery from three years of slow growth.

- The Bay Area experienced sharp income losses after 2000 as tech salaries and stock options fell. Other regions (except for San Diego) posted income gains above the national average during the past three years.

- The Los Angeles Basin is the state's largest market and will represent a buying pool of near $800 billion (in 2003$) in 2012. In 2003, the Los Angeles market was larger than all states except New York and Texas. The Bay Area market ($312.5 billion in 2003) exceeded the incomes of all but eight states, despite the sharp drop in income after 2000.

- The Sacramento, San Joaquin Valley, and San Diego regions will have the highest income growth rates in the state, but the Los Angeles and Bay Area markets will still account for 71% of the state's $1.7 trillion income pool in 2012.

California and Economic Regions
Total Personal Income
1994-2012
(Billions of 2003$)

	1994	2000	2003	2012	Average Annual Growth Rate		
					1994-2000	2000-2003	2003-2012
Los Angeles Basin	$426.1	$531.5	$552.6	$799.6	3.8%	1.3%	4.2%
San Francisco Bay Area	$242.4	$352.9	$312.5	$445.7	6.5%	-4.0%	4.0%
San Diego Region	$78.8	$105.1	$106.0	$154.6	4.9%	0.3%	4.3%
Sacramento Region	$48.4	$62.4	$66.1	$103.8	4.3%	1.9%	5.1%
San Joaquin Valley	$65.1	$78.0	$83.5	$132.5	3.1%	2.3%	5.3%
Rest of State Region	$57.3	$72.3	$76.8	$110.0	4.0%	2.0%	4.1%
California	$918.1	$1,202.4	$1,197.6	$1,746.1	4.6%	-0.1%	4.3%
United States	$7,243.2	$8,999.2	$9,199.0	$12,882.0	3.7%	0.7%	3.8%

Sources: 1994 and 2000 — U.S. Department of Commerce, California Department of Finance; CCSCE; 2003 and 2012 — CCSCE

Per Capita Income

- Per capita income varies significantly among the economic regions in California. The San Francisco Bay Area has the highest regional per capita income in the nation. In 2003, Bay Area per capita income averaged $44,688—41% above the national average—despite falling by 13.7% from 2000 levels.

- Real per capita income (i.e., adjusted for inflation) is projected to grow by 2.8% per year between 2003 and 2012 throughout the regions of California. This is slower than the 3.3% annual growth rate for the booming 1994–2000 period, but similar to the 2.9% projected national growth rate.

- By 2012, only the San Joaquin Valley region will significantly trail the nation. Per capita income in the Los Angeles Basin and Sacramento regions will be near the national average. The San Diego region will have per capita income 10% above the national average.

- Per capita income fell throughout the state after 2000. Strong population growth outpaced income growth and pushed real per capita income down, especially in the Bay Area. The best performance was in the San Joaquin Valley and Rest of State region.

California and Economic Regions
Per Capita Personal Income
1994-2012
(Billions of 2003$)

| | 1994 | 2000 | 2003 | 2012 | Average Annual Growth Rate | | |
					1994-2000	2000-2003	2003-2012
Los Angeles Basin	$27,607	$32,042	$31,345	$40,159	2.5%	-0.8%	2.8%
San Francisco Bay Area	$38,381	$51,754	$44,688	$58,412	5.1%	-4.5%	3.0%
San Diego Region	$30,189	$37,119	$35,473	$45,098	3.5%	-1.3%	2.7%
Sacramento Region	$27,672	$32,056	$31,213	$40,373	2.5%	-0.8%	2.9%
San Joaquin Valley	$21,401	$23,499	$23,292	$30,924	1.6%	-0.3%	3.2%
Rest of State Region	$24,166	$28,556	$29,317	$36,937	2.8%	0.9%	2.6%
California	**$29,125**	**$35,322**	**$33,326**	**$42,796**	**3.3%**	**-1.8%**	**2.8%**
United States	**$27,643**	**$31,892**	**$31,632**	**$40,921**	**2.4%**	**-0.3%**	**2.9%**

Sources: 1994 and 2000 — U.S. Department of Commerce, California Department of Finance, CCSCE; 2003 and 2012 — CCSCE

Average Household Income

- In 2003, California's average household income was $100,923—20.1% above the national average.

- After strong growth during the late 1990s, real household income turned down in California during the past three years, primarily as a result of Bay Area income losses. Other regions have real household incomes in 2003 that are similar to 2000 levels. After underperforming in the 1990s, the San Joaquin Valley and Rest of State regions did better than average after 2000.

- The measure of average household income shown below is total personal income per household. The Census Bureau uses a **money** income measure that produces lower household income estimates and also reports median incomes that are considerably lower than average household income estimates.

- The Bay Area has the highest average household personal income—$123,503 in 2003, or 47% above the national average. Average household income in the Los Angeles Basin was 19% above the national average. In the San Joaquin Valley, average household income was 8% below the national average.

- Real (i.e., inflation-adjusted) household income is projected to grow by 2.5% annually in California. This is in comparison to the projected 3.0% annual gain nationally.

California and Economic Regions Average Household Income 1994-2012 (2003$)					Average Annual Growth Rate		
	1994	**2000**	**2003**	**2012**	**1994-2000**	**2000-2003**	**2003-2012**
Los Angeles Basin	$83,445	$98,674	$100,087	$126,337	2.8%	0.5%	2.6%
San Francisco Bay Area	$104,805	$143,119	$123,503	$154,715	5.3%	-4.8%	2.5%
San Diego Region	$85,228	$105,699	$103,031	$124,005	3.7%	-0.8%	2.1%
Sacramento Region	$75,039	$87,598	$88,945	$108,601	2.6%	0.5%	2.2%
San Joaquin Valley	$67,302	$75,509	$77,108	$99,647	1.9%	0.7%	2.9%
Rest of State	$66,697	$79,500	$81,791	$99,299	3.0%	1.0%	2.2%
California	**$84,890**	**$104,526**	**$100,923**	**$126,081**	**3.5%**	**-1.2%**	**2.5%**
United States	**$75,459**	**$85,317**	**$84,009**	**$109,652**	**2.1%**	**-0.5%**	**3.0%**

Sources: 1994 and 2000 — U.S. Department of Commerce, California Department of Finance, CCSCE; 2003 and 2012 — CCSCE

Total Taxable Sales

- Real taxable sales (i.e., adjusted for inflation) will grow between 3.8% and 4.9% per year among regions. The projected statewide growth rate is 4.0%. It includes a rebound from three years of falling real taxable spending.

- Spending in the Los Angeles and Bay Area markets will increase by a combined $125 billion (in 2003$) between 2003 and 2012. These two regions will still account for nearly 70% of the state's taxable sales in 2012.

- Real taxable sales fell by $29 billion (6.0%) between 2000 and 2003. Nearly 90% of the statewide decline ($26 billion) was in the Bay Area as business-to-business sales plummeted during the tech downturn. The Los Angeles and San Diego regions posted modest sales declines, while Sacramento and the San Joaquin Valley showed slight gains.

The 2000-2003 losses came after six years during which California averaged 5.0% real (i.e., after taking inflation into account) annual gains.

California and Economic Regions Total Taxable Sales 1994-2012 (Billions of 2003$)							
					Average Annual Growth Rate		
	1994	2000	2003	2012	1994-2000	2000-2003	2003-2010
Los Angeles Basin	$164.4	$215.2	$213.4	$298.2	4.6%	-0.3%	3.8%
San Francisco Bay Area	$91.0	$129.4	$102.9	$144.8	6.0%	-7.4%	3.9%
San Diego Region	$29.7	$41.1	$40.1	$56.4	5.6%	-0.9%	3.9%
Sacramento Region	$21.0	$28.9	$29.5	$45.1	5.5%	0.8%	4.8%
San Joaquin Valley	$28.6	$37.0	$38.6	$59.6	4.4%	1.5%	4.9%
Rest of State Region	$25.6	$31.5	$29.5	$41.8	3.6%	-2.2%	3.9%
California	**$360.3**	**$483.1**	**$454.0**	**$646.0**	**5.0%**	**-2.0%**	**4.0%**

Sources: 1994 and 2000 — California Board of Equalization, CCSCE; 2003 and 2012 — CCSCE

Population

- California's population is projected to increase by nearly 5 million between 2003 and 2012, averaging just under 550,000 added residents a year. The state will account for 13.0% of the nation's population in 2012—up from 12.4% in 2003.

- California's population growth slowed temporarily in the early '90s, but has rebounded to over 600,000 per year since 2000. The California Department of Finance estimate for July 1, 2003 shows 35.9 million residents in California—an increase of 631,300 per year since July 1, 2000. The level of population growth is expected to slow modestly in future years.

- The Los Angeles Basin is projected to add nearly 2.3 million new residents (253,400 annually), reaching a population of 19.9 million in 2012. The Basin will then be home to more people than any state except Texas and, possibly, New York. Population growth between 2000 and 2003 was 347,200 per year.

- The Bay Area is projected to add more than 600,000 residents by 2012. Other workers will choose to live in adjacent counties outside the region. An increasing number of Bay Area workers are seeking lower home prices in adjacent counties. Housing is a serious challenge for the Bay Area.

California and Economic Regions Population 1994-2012 (Thousands)					Average Annual Growth		
	1994	2000	2003	2012	1994-2000	2000-2003	2003-2012
Los Angeles Basin	15,435.9	16,587.8	17,629.4	19,910.4	192.0	347.2	253.4
San Francisco Bay Area	6,314.9	6,819.4	6,993.8	7,629.6	84.1	58.1	70.6
San Diego Region	2,611.0	2,832.5	2,989.3	3,427.2	36.9	52.3	48.7
Sacramento Region	1,748.2	1,948.0	2,117.4	2,570.4	33.3	56.5	50.3
San Joaquin Valley	3,041.8	3,319.6	3,583.8	4,284.0	46.3	88.1	77.8
Rest of State	2,371.2	2,532.7	2,620.3	2,978.4	26.9	29.2	39.8
California	31,523.0	34,040.0	35,934.0	40,800.0	419.5	631.3	540.7
United States	262,026.4	282,178.0	290,810.0	314,800.0	3,358.6	2,877.3	2,665.6

Source: Historical — U.S. Census Bureau and California Department for Finance for July 1, 1994, 2000 and 2003; Projections — CCSCE for July 1, 2012

- San Diego experienced a return to strong population growth after 1996, averaging more than 50,000 new residents per year and reversing a pattern of low annual gains in the early 1990s. The strong economy will continue to attract residents, and annual gains in the decade ahead should be nearly 50,000 annually, as has been the case since 2000.

- The Sacramento region is experiencing and will continue to experience substantial population growth. Annual growth has averaged 56,500 since 2000—far above the 33,300-per-year gains between 1994 and 2000. Sacramento is projected to be the state's fastest-growing region (+21.4%) between 2003 and 2012.

- Population growth is surging again in the San Joaquin Valley. Annual gains will average 77,800 to 2012, far above the 46,300 annual growth between 1994 and 2000. The Valley's 20% population growth will be more than 2 times the national growth rate to 2012.

- Despite high growth rates in the Sacramento and San Joaquin Valley regions, the overall pattern of population shares will remain quite stable. As of 2003, the Los Angeles and San Francisco regions contained 68.5% of the state's population. By 2012, these regions will still house more than two of every three Californians (67.5%).

- Each region in California will grow faster than the nation in the period to 2012. Even the slowest-growing Bay Area region will have population gains of 9.1%. The projected national gain will be 8.2%.

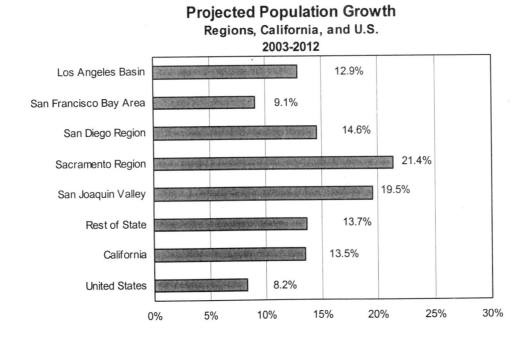

Projected Population Growth
Regions, California, and U.S.
2003-2012

Los Angeles Basin	12.9%
San Francisco Bay Area	9.1%
San Diego Region	14.6%
Sacramento Region	21.4%
San Joaquin Valley	19.5%
Rest of State	13.7%
California	13.5%
United States	8.2%

Households

- These projections incorporate household estimates and household formation rates from the 2000 Census. The household projection trends follow the pattern of the population projection trend.

- As explained on page 5-71, California is projected to add more than 1.7 million households by the year 2012—an increase of 202,600 per year. This growth is below record levels (e.g., 1985–1989) but it is higher than the average growth in the 1980s, and much higher than the household growth between 1990 and 2000.

- Household size has continued to increase in the Los Angeles Basin between 2000 and 2003. This has restricted household growth. Household size has leveled out in other regions of the state. CCSCE expects household size to begin declining as 1) fertility rates drop, and 2) aging pushes more residents into the 55+ age bracket (where household sizes start to fall).

- There is widespread agreement that housing construction needs to increase to meet the demands of projected job growth. The complicated issues linking housing, land use and economic competitiveness are discussed throughout this report.

California and Economic Regions Households 1994-2012 (Thousands)					Average Annual Growth		
	1994	2000	2004	2012	1994-2000	2000-2004	2004-2012
Los Angeles Basin	5,106.8	5,386.5	5,579.9	6,278.4	44.8	51.4	82.2
San Francisco Bay Area	2,312.6	2,466.0	2,551.1	2,857.5	24.5	22.6	36.1
San Diego Region	924.9	994.7	1,043.2	1,236.4	11.2	12.9	22.7
Sacramento Region	644.7	712.9	784.5	947.9	10.9	19.1	19.2
San Joaquin Valley	967.2	1,033.1	1,107.1	1,318.9	10.5	19.7	24.9
Rest of State	859.2	909.7	950.0	1,099.1	8.1	10.7	17.5
California	**10,815.3**	**11,502.9**	**12,015.8**	**13,738.2**	**110.0**	**136.4**	**202.6**
United States	**95,988.4**	**105,480.1**	**110,927.1**	**121,000.0**	**1,518.7**	**1,449.1**	**1,185.0**

Sources: Historical, U.S. Census Bureau and DOF for January 1, 2004; Projections — CCSCE as of July 1

Definition of Regional Economic Base

The data in *California Economic Growth — 2004 Edition* are based on the 2002 NAICS Code industry definitions. The classification of industries as *basic* or *population serving* changes as the analysis area moves from the state to the regional level. Once again, eight categories of basic industries are used:

> High Tech Manufacturing
> Diversified Manufacturing
> Wholesale Trade & Transportation
> Information
> Professional and Business Services
> Tourism & Entertainment
> Government
> Resource Based

However, in some cases, the industries in each category are different at the regional level, because the regional economic bases are broader in definition than the state economic base.

The regional economic bases generally include all industries classified as basic for California, plus additional industries that are population serving at the state level but for which the regions compete for location. The best example is state government, which is population serving at the state level of analysis (i.e., these jobs serve state residents). State government jobs are clearly basic (or open to competition) at the regional level, as Sacramento's uniquely high share attests.

Major differences between the state and regional economic base definitions occur in the following categories:

Diversified Manufacturing — the regional definition includes about 250,000 jobs more that the state definition in 2003. Many of these jobs are in food processing and nonmetallic minerals (related to nearby construction).

Wholesale Trade and Transportation — Trucking, Couriers and Warehousing are included in the regional basic industry category, but are excluded at the state level.

Government — State government is included in the regional basic industry category, but is excluded at the state level.

The regional definition is used in the remainder of this report, and comparisons of each regional economic base to California should use the California economic base table on page 7-4. Since the regional and state definitions of economic base do differ, it is necessary to use one California table when comparing to the U.S. and another when comparing to the regions.

LOS ANGELES BASIN

LOS ANGELES BASIN

The Bottom Line

What a difference a decade makes! In the early 1990s, the Los Angeles Basin lost more than 500,000 jobs while the rest of the state was saying "what recession?" Since 1994, however, the region has added jobs at a faster pace than the nation. Although the region's growth has slowed since 2000, it has not slowed as much as that of the state and the nation.

The Los Angeles Basin had 17.6 million residents and nearly 7.5 million jobs in 2003. This accounted for approximately 50% of the state's jobs and population. The region represented a market of more than $550 billion in personal income in 2003, and it ranked as the world's 10th largest economy.

The region has a strong and diversified economic base. It is built around the nation's largest port complex, the nation's largest entertainment and tourism sector, the nation's largest diversified manufacturing center and participation in the fast-growing professional services, biotech and design markets. **The region's ports are posting double-digit volume gains in 2004, driven by a surge in trade with China. They recently added 3,000 jobs at the docks in order to process the volume of trade.**

CCSCE projects that the Los Angeles Basin will outpace the nation in job growth to 2012. The region's projected 20.3% job growth for 2003-2012 compares to a projected national increase of 15.0%. The Basin is projected to grow more slowly than the state, however, and should mirror the performance between 1994 and 2000.

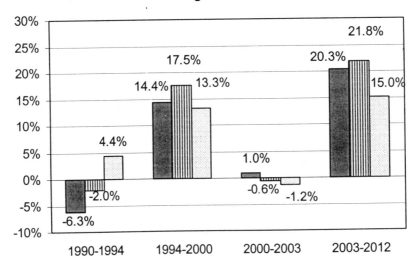

Past and Future Job Growth
Los Angeles Basin

■ Los Angeles Basin ▥ California ☐ United States

Housing availability and affordability remain serious challenges for the long-term economic growth of the region. Housing production has increased in recent years and new construction levels are beginning to approach long-term needs, but more still must be done. Some communities are welcoming new housing, and adaptive reuse of older commercial and hotel properties is providing new residential building opportunities that do not require more land.

Housing prices reached record highs in all regional submarkets in 2004, while affordability reached record lows.

The Southern California Association of Governments (SCAG) has identified a set of land use, infrastructure and housing policies to accommodate the growth and to plan for future economic needs. There is no consensus as yet as individual communities have very different perspectives on growth. SCAG's projections and the Compass process can be followed at www.scag.ca.gov.

More than 50% of the Basin's population was Hispanic in 2003, and Hispanic residents will account for more than three quarters of the region's population growth in the next 20 years. These demographic changes offer enormous opportunities and challenges for the region.

The Los Angeles Basin labor force will continue growing, even while retirements slow labor force growth throughout most of the nation. The Basin's population will be at least five years younger on average than in the rest of the nation. Its future economy will depend on the education and occupational progress of the children and grandchildren of recent immigrants. The region possesses a large competitive advantage if these children get a good education, including the opportunity to attend college for those who are academically able.

Early '90s, the 1994-2000 Period and the Period Since 2000

The Los Angeles Basin lost more than 500,000 jobs between 1990 and 1994. All of the job losses occurred in Los Angeles and Orange counties, where the aerospace complex was centered. Los Angeles County alone lost more than 400,000 jobs.

The Inland Empire (Riverside and San Bernardino counties) added jobs in the early '90s as a result of population growth and movement of some manufacturing activities from Los Angeles County to the Inland Empire.

Since the bottom of the early 1990s recession, the Basin has outpaced the nation in job growth, led by strong gains in Orange County and the Inland Empire and by a recovery in Los Angeles County. Between November 1993 and March 2001, the region added more than 1.1 million non-farm jobs, including nearly 500,000 jobs in Los Angeles County. As shown on page 8-5, Orange County and the Inland Empire outpaced the state and the nation in job growth rate during this period.

Los Angeles Basin Non-Farm Wage & Salary Jobs (Thousands)				
Metro Area	**March 1990**	**Nov 1993**	**March 2001**	**July 2004**
Los Angeles	4,192	3,675	4,128	4,009
Orange	1,182	1,113	1,424	1,444
Riverside-San Bernardino	710	736	1,024	1,114
Ventura	229	227	279	286
Los Angeles Basin	6,313	5,751	6,855	6,854

Source: EDD, seasonally adjusted by CCSCE

By July 2004 the Basin had recovered all jobs lost during the region's brief recession. The loss of 119,000 jobs in Los Angeles County was offset by continued job gains in Riverside and San Bernardino counties. Orange and Ventura posted small job gains during this period.

The region has grown faster than the nation since the mid 1990s, despite aerospace job losses that continued into 2003. The Basin now has 5.2% of U.S. jobs (down from a peak of 5.7%) and it has 5.7% of U.S. manufacturing jobs (down from a peak of 6.5%). Both shares have increased since 1996 and are projected to increase in the decade ahead.

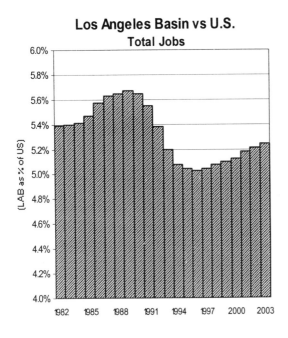

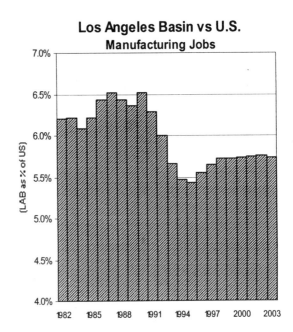

Growth in Non-Farm Jobs
Los Angeles Basin
July 1994-July 2004

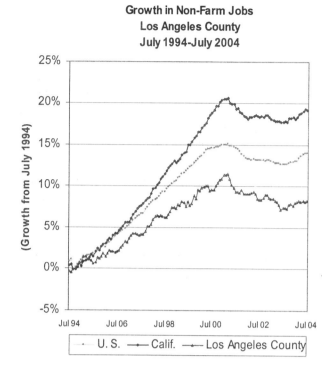

U. S. — Calif. — Los Angeles Basin

Growth in Non-Farm Jobs
Los Angeles County
July 1994-July 2004

U. S. — Calif. — Los Angeles County

Growth in Non-Farm Jobs
Orange County
July 1994-July 2004

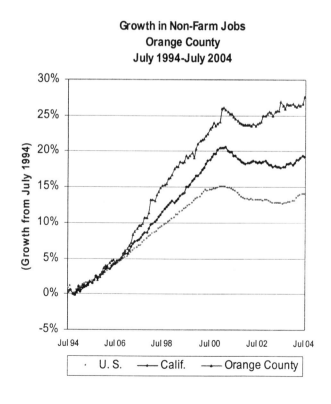

U. S. — Calif. — Orange County

Growth in Non-Farm Jobs
Riverside-San Bernardino
July 1994-July 2004

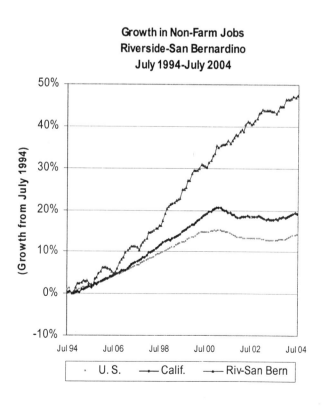

U. S. — Calif. — Riv-San Bern

The Region's Economic Base

The Los Angeles Basin economic base possesses formidable long-term strengths, as evidenced in the strong recovery after 1994:

- A large, diverse manufacturing base—despite permanent loss of some aerospace jobs. The region's great strength in design and fashion has led to gains in apparel and toy manufacturing, as well as in other sectors such as textiles and furniture.

- The nation's largest tourism and entertainment complex. More than half of the nation's films are made in Los Angeles. The region possesses attractions for visitors from the state, nation and world.

- The nation's largest port and airport complex. These are located next to two fast growing market areas—Mexico and the Pacific Rim.

- The nation's second-largest high tech and biotech complex. This is built around Southern California's educational institutions, large pool of skilled labor and growing pool of venture capital funding.

- A large financial services complex that serves both domestic and international markets.

- A growing number of new, small and medium-sized businesses. The region has been attractive to immigrant entrepreneurs, who are bringing energy, innovation and international connections to the Basin's economic base.

The region has another great advantage: diversity of locations for living and working. As one part of the region sees prices for housing and workspace surge ahead, activity shifts to less expensive areas. The Los Angeles Basin has been able to offer alternative locations within its own regional boundaries.

Decentralization has allowed the region to accommodate substantial job and population growth. Whereas most jobs used to be located in Los Angeles County and northern Orange County, job nodes have been established in the Antelope Valley, western San Bernardino County around Ontario, and the Irvine area in Orange County. As population growth has shifted north and east to find affordable housing, new areas (such as the Ontario area) are now centrally located to large numbers of potential workers.

In 2003 there were 2.8 million jobs in the region's economic base, as shown on page 8-7. The largest sectors in the Basin's economic base were Professional and Business Services (715,100 jobs); Diversified Manufacturing (636,600 jobs); Wholesale Trade and Transportation (559,000 jobs); and Tourism and Entertainment (322,000 jobs).

Los Angeles Basin
Major Sectors in Economic Base
2003
(Thousands)

	Jobs	
High Tech Manufacturing	188.5	
Semiconductor and Electronic Component Manufacturing		30.1
Electronic Instrument Manufacturing		59.1
Aerospace Product and Parts Manufacturing		53.9
Pharmaceutical and Medicine Manufacturing		18.7
Diversified Manufacturing	636.6	
Fabricated Metal Product Mfg		90.0
Machinery Manufacturing		43.7
Electrical Equipment and Appliance Manufacturing		24.9
Transportation Equipment (except Aerospace)		31.8
Furniture and Related Product Manufacturing		44.0
Miscellaneous Manufacturing		50.4
Food Manufacturing		51.8
Apparel Manufacturing		78.3
Chemicals (except Pharmaceuticals)		25.4
Plastics and Rubber Products Manufacturing		44.2
Professional and Business Services	715.1	
Legal Services		72.0
Accounting, Tax Preparation and Bookkeeping Services		52.8
Architectural, Engineering and Related Services		60.0
Computer Systems Design and Related Services		48.1
Management and Consulting Services		48.4
Management of Companies and Enterprises		127.4
Employment Services		212.2
Information	105.7	
Software Publishers		9.6
Telecommunications		52.4
Internet Service Providers and Related Services		22.2
Wholesale Trade and Transportation	559.0	
Wholesale Trade		354.0
Air Transportation		26.4
Truck Transportation		54.2
Support Activities for Transportation		48.4
Couriers and Messengers		36.7
Warehousing and Storage		28.5
Tourism and Entertainment	322.0	
Motion Pictures and Sound Recording		122.6
Arts, Entertainment, and Recreation		123.9
Accommodation		75.5
Government	228.5	
Federal Government		92.2
State Government		136.3
Resource Based	71.1	
Total Basic Jobs	2,826.5	

Source: EDD

The Basin's economic base is different from that of other regions in California: the Basin is the only region where Diversified Manufacturing is the second-largest sector, and it is the only region where Tourism and Entertainment had more basic jobs than Government.

Profile of Economic Base in 2003

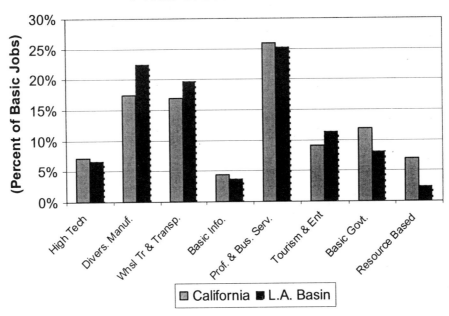

Los Angeles Basin Jobs By Major Basic Industry Group 1994-2012 (Thousands)							
					Numerical Change		
	1994	**2000**	**2003**	**2012**	**1994-2000**	**2000-2003**	**2003-2012**
High Tech Manufacturing	245.4	228.7	188.5	182.1	-16.7	-40.3	-6.4
Diversified Manufacturing	675.1	751.6	636.6	674.8	76.4	-115.0	38.2
Wholesale Trade & Transportation	477.3	565.6	559.0	684.0	88.4	-6.7	125.0
Basic Information	84.1	129.7	105.7	139.4	45.7	-24.0	33.7
Professional & Business Services	566.8	734.9	715.1	997.9	168.1	-19.8	282.8
Tourism & Entertainment	272.9	333.1	322.0	402.4	60.2	-11.1	80.4
Basic Government	223.9	225.1	228.5	252.5	1.2	3.4	24.0
Resource Based	73.4	71.6	71.1	63.5	-1.7	-0.5	-7.7
Total Basic Jobs	**2,618.9**	**3,040.5**	**2,826.5**	**3,396.5**	**421.6**	**-214.0**	**570.0**

Diversified Manufacturing

Between 1994 and 2003, the number of Diversified Manufacturing jobs in the Basin showed the now-familiar roller coaster pattern of up, then down. Job levels went from 675,100 in 1994 to 751,800 in 2000, and then down to 636,600 in 2003.

The 1990-94 declines were associated with the loss of aerospace jobs. The 1994-2000 gains were broad-based and reestablished Southern California as the nation's leading Diversified Manufacturing center. The losses subsequent to 2000 were the result of the national recession, export declines and the continuing strong productivity gains that have allowed firms to produce more with fewer workers.

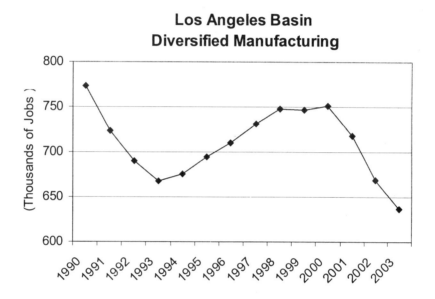

Los Angeles Basin
Diversified Manufacturing

The Basin's share of national Diversified Manufacturing jobs rose during the aerospace boom, plummeted in the early '90s aerospace declines and rose again throughout the later 1990s, driven by gains in apparel job shares and by smaller gains in other Diversified Manufacturing sectors.

Large losses in apparel jobs are projected in the years ahead, due to national and international trends. Nevertheless, the Basin's share of national Diversified Manufacturing jobs is expected to remain near the current level—topped only by the aerospace-driven high of the late 1980s.

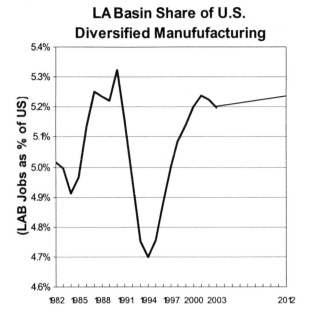

**LA Basin Share of U.S.
Diversified Manufufacturing**

The region is projected to add only 38,200 jobs in the Diversified Manufacturing sector between 2003 and 2012. However, relatively stable job levels will support rising production, exports and jobs related to Diversified Manufacturing production. **Even if direct job levels rise only modestly, maintaining competitiveness in the sector is important for the region's economic base.**

Locations in the Inland Empire are attracting a growing number of manufacturing jobs, even as the regional total has shrunk. As a result, the Inland Empire is rapidly becoming a key part of the Basin's Diversified Manufacturing sector and a significant participant in the future growth of the region's Diversified Manufacturing base. Manufacturing job levels in the Inland Empire (nearly all in Diversified Manufacturing) have risen from 77,900 in 1990 to 113,500 in 2003.The Inland Empire has avoided the steep manufacturing job losses seen in other California areas.

Fabricated metal products accounted for the largest number of jobs (90,000) in 2003 in the region's Diversified Manufacturing base. Job levels fell by 20,000 in the early '90s, were regained by 2000, and then fell back to 1994 levels by 2003. Machinery manufacturing showed the same pattern of job growth and accounted for 43,700 jobs in 2003.

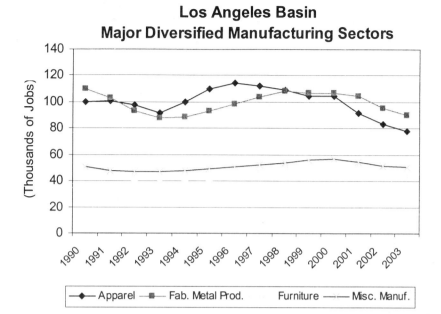

Los Angeles Basin
Major Diversified Manufacturing Sectors

Nationally, both the fabricated metal products and the machinery manufacturing sectors are projected to have steady sales growth and a modest rebound in job levels to 2012. As shown on page 5-41, there has been a slow increase in California's share of national jobs in both these sectors, and this share growth is projected to continue. Both industries are projected to regain most of the jobs lost since 2000 in the Basin.

Given the region's location advantages, the challenge for local firms is to keep in a leadership position in terms of the technological training of the local workforce. The region's competitiveness is supported by the efforts in Gateway Cities, where industry and local community colleges partner to upgrade the technological skills of the new generation of machinists, and to open up career opportunities for the Basin's younger workers.

Another segment of the Basin's Diversified Manufacturing base **builds on the region's leadership position in applying design skills to manufacturing products.** Industries where this applies include apparel, furniture, and toys (included in miscellaneous manufacturing). In all of these industries, sales of California firms (most of which are located in the Basin) have risen **and** California's share of national production has risen even faster.

The region's competitive advantage in each industry is a combination of world-class design centers and schools, energetic small business entrepreneurs and the growing application of technology. California now has nearly 30% of the nation's apparel manufacturing jobs. Basin apparel jobs peaked at 114,100 in 1996, and then fell to 78,300, even as the region's share of national jobs was surging.

California retains a design advantage in women's wear, but the ability to keep production in the region will depend increasingly on the application of technology to reduce costs. Programs like the fashion design center at Los Angeles Trade and Technical College, which trains local workers to use computers in design and production activities, raise the competitive position of the region in an industry that is under constant cost pressures.

Apparel job levels are projected to continue falling, despite the region's competitive edge in design.

In 2003 the Basin had 44,000 furniture jobs and 50,400 jobs in miscellaneous manufacturing—two other design-intensive sectors. Both sectors are projected to see modest job gains to 2012.

Food manufacturing, with 51,800 jobs in 2003, is projected to add more than 8,000 jobs by 2012. Bolstered by the large and growing regional and worldwide markets for ethnic specialty foods, regional firms are developing a center for ethnic food production and distribution.

High Technology Manufacturing

The Los Angeles Basin had 188,500 high tech manufacturing jobs in 2003—more than in the Bay Area. High tech manufacturing includes aerospace, defense electronic, civilian high tech and pharmaceuticals. The Basin lost nearly half of its high tech manufacturing base in the 1990s, when aerospace jobs disappeared.

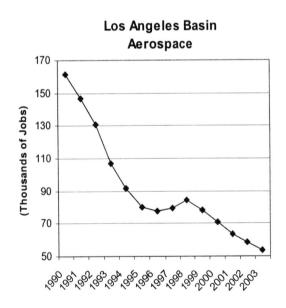

Los Angeles Basin
Aerospace

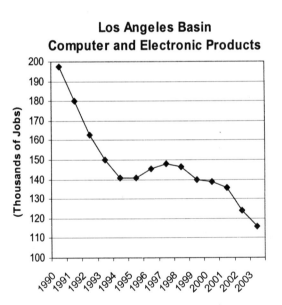

Los Angeles Basin
Computer and Electronic Products

Aerospace manufacturing jobs fell from 161,300 in 1990 to 91,500 in 1994. But aerospace job losses did not stop after 1994. Instead, they continued, and aerospace jobs in the Basin reached a low of 53,900 in 2003—one third of the 1990 level.

Job levels in computer and electronic products fell from approximately 197,600 in 1990 to 115,900 in 2003. More than 60% of these losses were in search and navigational equipment (included in the new NAICS electronic instruments category) and were directly related to defense spending.

No growth is projected for high tech jobs in the region, even though production levels will increase substantially.

Wholesale Trade and Transportation

The Wholesale Trade and Transportation sector has strong ties to the region's foreign trade and Diversified Manufacturing activities. Wholesale trade accounted for 354,000 of the sector's overall job total of 559,000 in 2003. Truck transportation had 54,200 jobs, followed by support activities for transportation with 48,400 jobs, couriers and messengers with 36,700 jobs, and warehousing and storage with 28,500 jobs.

**Los Angeles Basin
Wholesale Trade & Transportation**

Foreign Trade

The region's ports and airports have posted a twenty-five year record of double-digit gains in the volume of trade handled. Between 1977 and 2003, trade volume grew by 10.2% annually. As reported in Chapter 3, trade growth is forecast to top 10% in the Basin in 2004.

The growth in foreign trade supports job gains in Professional Services (such as construction design and engineering), as well as in financial services, wholesale trade, manufacturing, and tourism and entertainment.

Trade volumes grew from $18.7 billion in 1977 to $230.0 billion in 2000. They then fell to $212.5 in 2001. Trade volumes rebounded to a record $235.0 billion in 2003.

Los Angeles Basin Foreign Trade Value of Exports and Imports 1990-2003 ($Billions)			
	Exports	**Imports**	**Total**
1990	$42.1	$64.6	$106.7
2000	$77.6	$152.4	$230.0
2003	$67.7	$167.2	$235.1
Average Annual Growth Rate 1990-2003			
Los Angeles	3.7%	7.6%	6.3%
California	5.1%	7.1%	5.9%
United States	5.2%	7.8%	6.7%

Source: U.S. Department of Commerce

Trade in services is important to the regional economy. Travel, the largest category of service exports, directly supports jobs in the Basin's large tourist cluster. Much of the nation's film and entertainment exports originate in the region, and film export volumes have surged as discussed on page 5-58.

The region has handled between 11.0% and 12.5% of the nation's trade for the past decade. The Basin's share, currently at the low end of the range as a result of Asian economic weakness, has started to rise again. Port expansions and the strong growth of Chinese trade are spurring Basin trade volumes.

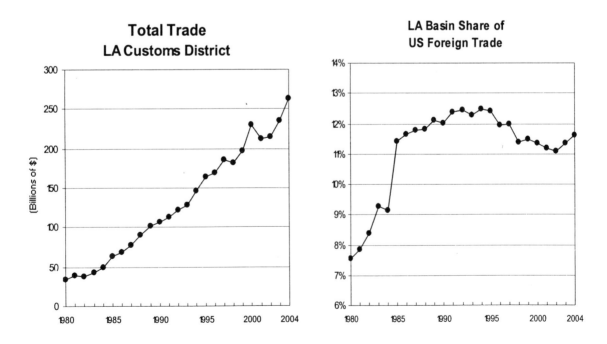

Total Trade
LA Customs District

LA Basin Share of
US Foreign Trade

China has surged into the lead as the region's top trading partner. Two-way trade with China totaled $68.2 billion in 2003, well ahead of the $41.5 billion with Japan. Imports from China were $60.2 billion, accounting for the vast majority of total trade.

Five Pacific Rim countries headed the list of two-way trade partners. After China and Japan came South Korea ($16.2 billion), Taiwan ($14.2 billion), and Malaysia ($11.3 billion). Germany ($7.5 billion) was the highest-ranking non-Asian country, and was followed by Singapore ($7.1 billion) and Thailand $6.7 billion).

The future for trade continues to be bright. Pacific Rim markets remain the world's growth leaders, and approximately 40% of the nation's Pacific Rim trade goes through California ports and airports. National and international trade agreements of recent years support the continued growth in this trade. The growing volume of trade with China is a strong positive factor for the region's trade activity. The opening of Pacific Rim markets for financial and professional services will help Southern California firms.

The Los Angeles Customs District (Los Angeles and Long Beach ports) is the largest port complex in the United States. The Los Angeles Customs District is the third-largest container complex in the world. It ranks behind Hong Kong and Singapore, but ahead of Rotterdam and the major port complex in South Korea. The ports handled a record 7.2 million containerized shipments in 2003, up from 6.5 million in 2000 and behind only Singapore and Hong Kong.

Los Angeles increased its lead over New York in foreign trade volume for the nation. The top five trade centers in 2003 were Los Angeles ($235.0 billion), New York ($219.6 billion), Detroit ($186.5 billion), Laredo ($115.43 billion) and New Orleans ($95.1 billion). San Francisco dropped from 4th place in 2000 to 7th place in 2003.

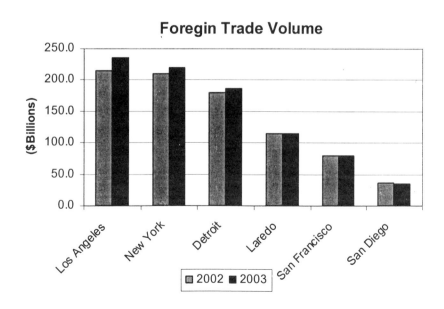

The Alameda Corridor was opened on schedule in April 2002 and now allows faster transfer of cargo from the port complex to eastern destinations. Both the Los Angeles and San Pedro ports are continuing to invest for future expansions. The labor agreement between the ILWU and shippers will allow technological advances in processing cargo.

However, significant infrastructure issues remain. The region has not made progress on expanding air cargo capacity. Additionally, there are still problems with truck traffic from the ports because the 710 freeway expansion is meeting with intense community conflicts. It now appears that specialized facilities for trucks heading to the Inland Empire and east will be needed in addition to the Alameda corridor.

For more information on trade trends and issues, see the Los Angeles Economic Development website, www.laedc.org. For information on trade infrastructure issues, see the SCAG website, www.scag.ca.gov.

Professional and Business Services

The basic industry component of Professional and Business Services is the largest basic industry group in the Los Angeles Basin with 715,100 jobs in 2003. The sector added 168,100 jobs between 1994 and 2000 and has held on to most of the job gains during the current downturn.

**Los Angeles Basin
Basic Prof. & Business Services**

This sector includes professional, scientific and technical services and the new NAICS "Management of Companies" category, as well as employment services (which includes temporary help agencies).

In the Basin, this sector is more heavily oriented to legal, accounting and engineering services. By contrast, the Bay Area sector is more concentrated in computer and technical/scientific services. Employment services (including temporary help agencies) had 212,200 jobs in 2003. Management of companies had 127,400 jobs, and was followed by legal services (72,000 jobs), architectural and engineering services (60,000 jobs) and accounting services (52,800 jobs).

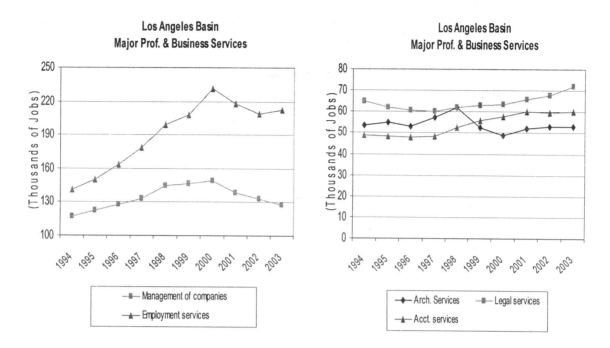

The auto industry plays a small but interesting role in the professional, scientific, technical and management services category for three reasons. First, Los Angeles is a major auto design center. There are currently 16 design studios in the region representing all of the major companies. The Art Center College Design in Pasadena has an internationally recognized curriculum in auto design. Second, Los Angeles is a center for advertising services, including for automobiles. Third, the region is a center for auto research and publications.

The design advantage carries over to other manufactured goods, including furniture and apparel. Industrial design services is a small, but growing, segment of the professional, scientific, technical and management services sector.

The Los Angeles Basin has a remarkable concentration of top design firms. The *Engineering News-Record* reports that five of the top 10 design firms in the country (measured by revenue) are located in the Basin. These include Flour (2nd), Jacobs (3rd), AECOM Technology (4th), Earth Tech (5th), Parsons (6th) and Tetra Tech (10th). Four of the top 20 international design firms (companies doing business outside their own country) are in the Basin.

CCSCE projects that basic Professional and Business Services sectors will account for half of the Los Angeles Basin basic industry job growth between 2003 and 2012. They will add nearly 300,000 jobs, reaching a total of 997,900 jobs in 2012. Leading growth sectors include computer and scientific R&D services, management of companies and employment services.

Tourism and Entertainment

Tourism and entertainment accounted for 322,000 jobs in 2003, led by motion picture, video and sound recording with 122,600 jobs. After substantial job growth in the mid '90s, job levels have fallen recently. With the expansion of cable stations and made-for-TV content, television is becoming a more important industry segment in terms of production days.

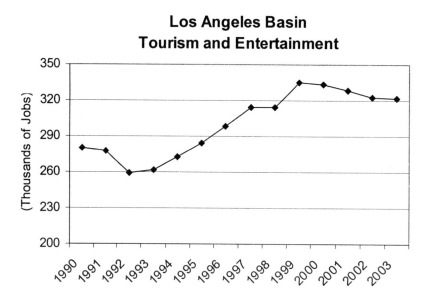

Los Angeles Basin
Tourism and Entertainment

Job levels grew steadily in the mid '90s and have fallen by approximately 15,000 jobs since the peak in 2000. Domestic and foreign box office receipts continue to grow, and exports of American films reach record levels each year.

The Entertainment Industry Development Corporation, www.eidc.com, is involved in a number of projects to understand and improve labor force needs and skills in the industry. There is no question about the long-term growth in motion picture and video production. The challenge for the Los Angeles Basin is to maintain a competitive position through proactive location and workforce policies.

The arts, entertainment and recreation segment has shown steady job growth as the region's major amusement complexes, including Disneyland and Universal Studios, continue to open new attractions. Although the last two years have been relatively due to a result of a decrease in foreign visitors, the long-term growth outlook for tourism remains positive.

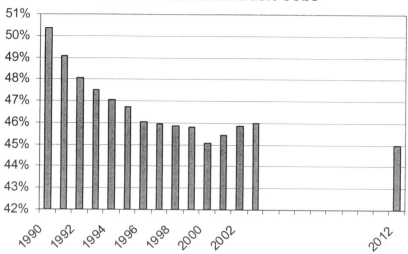

Los Angeles Basin
Share of California Basic Jobs

Job Projections

After poor economic performance in the early 1990s, the Los Angeles Basin has surpassed the state and the nation in job growth since 1994. CCSCE expects that the region will grow faster than the nation to 2012, and will nearly keep pace with projected statewide job growth.

Jobs in the region are projected to grow by 20.3% between 2003 and 2012, or by a little over 1.5 million jobs. The driving factors are growth in foreign trade, entertainment and tourism, professional and design services and the growth in production for diversified manufacturing and high tech manufacturing.

Los Angeles Basin **Total Jobs** **1994-2012** **(Thousands)**					**Percent Change**		
	1994	**2000**	**2003**	**2012**	**1994-2000**	**2000-2003**	**2003-2012**
Los Angeles Basin	6,457.4	7,389.4	7,460.0	8,976.2	14.4%	1.0%	20.3%
California	13,813.1	16,232.9	16,140.5	19,659.5	17.5%	-0.6%	21.8%
United States	127,233.7	144,132.4	142,336.9	163,756.8	13.3%	-1.2%	15.0%

Source: EDD, BLS and CCSCE (Projections)

In 2012, the Los Angeles Basin is projected to account for 45.7% of California's jobs, up from 45.5% in 2000 but down from 46.7% in 1994.

Jobs by Major NAICS Industry Sector

Measured by total jobs, Government is still the largest sector in the Los Angeles Basin. With 1 million of the region's 7.5 million jobs in 2003, Government is still slightly larger than Professional and Business Services, which will be the region's largest job category in 2012.

Manufacturing was the largest sector in 1994, but has since lost nearly 100,000 jobs. With 832,700 jobs in 2003, Manufacturing is now the third-largest sector in terms of total jobs. Retail Trade is now the Basin's fourth-largest sector, with 730,300 jobs in 2003.

<table>
<tr><th colspan="8">Los Angeles Basin
Jobs By Major Industry Group
1994-2012
(Thousands)</th></tr>
<tr><th></th><th colspan="4"></th><th colspan="3">Numerical Change</th></tr>
<tr><th></th><th>1994</th><th>2000</th><th>2003</th><th>2012</th><th>1994-
2000</th><th>2000-
2003</th><th>2003-
2012</th></tr>
<tr><td>Agriculture, Forestry, Fishing, Hunting</td><td>54.8</td><td>56.4</td><td>55.7</td><td>52.4</td><td>1.6</td><td>-0.7</td><td>-3.3</td></tr>
<tr><td>Mining</td><td>8.1</td><td>6.0</td><td>6.2</td><td>4.0</td><td>-2.1</td><td>0.2</td><td>-2.2</td></tr>
<tr><td>Construction</td><td>209.9</td><td>304.3</td><td>330.1</td><td>392.8</td><td>94.3</td><td>25.8</td><td>62.7</td></tr>
<tr><td>Manufacturing</td><td>930.9</td><td>989.5</td><td>832.7</td><td>863.9</td><td>58.6</td><td>-156.8</td><td>31.2</td></tr>
<tr><td>Wholesale Trade</td><td>299.0</td><td>348.6</td><td>354.0</td><td>415.6</td><td>49.6</td><td>5.4</td><td>61.6</td></tr>
<tr><td>Retail Trade</td><td>617.3</td><td>700.3</td><td>730.3</td><td>901.3</td><td>83.0</td><td>30.0</td><td>171.0</td></tr>
<tr><td>Transp., Warehousing & Utilities</td><td>219.8</td><td>256.7</td><td>244.8</td><td>315.6</td><td>36.9</td><td>-11.9</td><td>70.8</td></tr>
<tr><td>Information</td><td>224.8</td><td>304.9</td><td>254.5</td><td>321.7</td><td>80.1</td><td>-50.4</td><td>67.2</td></tr>
<tr><td>Financial Activities</td><td>373.5</td><td>371.0</td><td>426.3</td><td>486.0</td><td>-2.5</td><td>55.3</td><td>59.7</td></tr>
<tr><td>Professional & Business Services</td><td>777.0</td><td>983.6</td><td>971.8</td><td>1,336.6</td><td>206.6</td><td>-11.8</td><td>364.8</td></tr>
<tr><td>Educational & Health Services</td><td>567.1</td><td>655.4</td><td>728.5</td><td>1,010.4</td><td>88.3</td><td>73.1</td><td>281.9</td></tr>
<tr><td>Leisure & Hospitality</td><td>524.7</td><td>611.0</td><td>657.4</td><td>805.2</td><td>86.3</td><td>46.4</td><td>147.8</td></tr>
<tr><td>Other Services</td><td>197.7</td><td>228.6</td><td>241.6</td><td>303.0</td><td>30.8</td><td>13.1</td><td>61.4</td></tr>
<tr><td>Government</td><td>863.4</td><td>964.3</td><td>1,009.3</td><td>1,130.9</td><td>100.9</td><td>45.0</td><td>121.6</td></tr>
<tr><td>Self-Employed</td><td>590.1</td><td>608.7</td><td>617.4</td><td>636.7</td><td>18.5</td><td>8.8</td><td>19.3</td></tr>
<tr><td>Total Jobs</td><td>6,457.4</td><td>7,389.4</td><td>7,460.0</td><td>8,976.2</td><td>931.9</td><td>70.7</td><td>1,516.1</td></tr>
</table>

Sources: 1990-2003 — EDD with CCSCE estimate of self-employed; 2012 — CCSCE

Professional and Business Services jobs accounted for the largest numerical increase among the region's major industry sectors. Jobs increased by slightly more than 190,000 (+25%) between 1990 and 2003. Professional and Business Services is projected to add the most jobs (+364,800) of any major industry sector to 2012, and to be the largest Basin major industry sector in 2012, with more than 1.3 million jobs.

Educational and Health Services accounted for a gain of more than 160,000 jobs between 1994 and 2003. This is second only to the 195,000 jobs added in Professional and Business Services. By 2012 Educational and Health Services is projected to be the region's third-largest major industry group, with 1 million jobs—up 281,900 from 2003 levels.

Two other primarily population-serving sectors, Retail Trade and Leisure and Hospitality, are projected to continue the steady and substantial job gains of the past decade as the region's population and income grow in the decade ahead.

Retail Trade is projected to add 171,000 jobs, reaching a total of 901,300 in 2012. This follows a gain of 113,000 jobs since 1994. Leisure and Hospitality is projected to add 147,800 jobs by 2012. This follows a gain of 132,700 jobs between 1994 and 2003.

The Government sector contributed approximately 150,000 added jobs between 1994 and 2003. Growth in state and local government jobs (including education) kept pace with population and enrollment increases. State government and education jobs grew by nearly 20%, reaching 136,300 in 2003. Local government and education jobs increased by more than 150,000, reaching 780,700 in 2003.

Federal government jobs declined, due to a combination of base closures and other federal job reductions.

Los Angeles Basin Government Jobs (Thousands)			
	1990	**2003**	**Change**
Federal Government	121.4	92.3	-29.1
Defense	32.5	15.3	-17.2
Other	88.9	76.9	-12.0
State Government	113.2	136.3	23.1
Local Government	625.7	780.7	155.0
Total Government	860.3	1,009.3	149.0

Source: EDD; Excludes Imperial County

The Construction sector was hard hit by the collapse in regional construction in the early '90s. Since 1994, job levels have increased by more than 50%, reaching 330,100 in 2003. The Basin's construction job levels kept rising during the recent downturn, as increases in housing and public works offset a slowdown in nonresidential construction.

Construction will be a source of continuing job growth as regional housing and public works spending move even higher in the years ahead. CCSCE projects that Construction will add another 62,700 jobs by 2012, and that more will be added if the region is able to fund and implement all of the planned infrastructure investments.

Financial Activities was one of the region's leading growth sectors between 2000 and 2003. It gained 55,300 jobs as real estate markets heated up and the economy grew modestly. Financial Activities (including banking, insurance and real estate) are projected to add nearly 60,000 jobs between 2003 and 2012.

Income and Spending

The Los Angeles Basin represents nearly half of the California market—and over 6% of the national market—in terms of income and spending. In 2003, the income earned by Basin residents reached $552.6 billion. The region ranks as the world's 10th largest economy when measured in terms of total output and income. It has more income than all other states except New York ($701.9 billion) and Texas ($649.7 billion).

All data shown below are in 2003 dollars (2003$).

Following six years of strong real (i.e., inflation-adjusted) growth in income and spending, the region experienced slowing growth in 2001, 2002 and 2003. Real personal income grew by 1.3% per year, after having risen by 3.8% annually between 1994 and 2000. However, in the three years after 2000, the Basin still outperformed the state (-0.1% per year), the nation (+0.7% per year) and the Bay Area (-4.0% per year).

Real taxable sales fell by 0.3% per year, from $215.2 billion in 2000 to $213.4 billion in 2002. Still, the region did better than the state (-2.0% per year) and the Bay Area (-7.4% per year). The better-than-average results for the region are in sharp contrast to the 1990-94 recession, where the Los Angeles region lagged behind the state average.

Los Angeles Basin Income and Taxable Sales 1990-2012 (2003$)				
	Per Capita Income	Average HH Income	Total Personal Income (Billions)	Taxable Sales (Billions)
1990	$29,885	$88,875	$438.5	$186.3
1994	$27,607	$83,445	$426.1	$164.4
2000	$32,042	$98,674	$531.5	$215.2
2003	$31,345	$100,087	$552.6	$213.4
2012	$40,159	$126,337	$799.6	$298.2
Average Annual Growth Rates				
1994-2000	2.5%	2.8%	3.8%	4.6%
2000-2003	-0.8%	0.5%	1.3%	-0.3%
2003-2012	2.8%	2.6%	4.2%	3.8%
California	2.8%	2.5%	4.3%	4.0%
United States	2.9%	3.0%	3.8%	

Sources: U.S. Department of Commerce; California Board of Equalization; CCSCE

Per capita income gains in the 1990s were much higher than previously estimated. With the surge in total income in 2000 and the downward revision of the region's estimated population, per capita income in 2000 is estimated at **$32,042, just above the national average ($31,892)**. Following the next three years of large population gains, real per capita income fell slightly below the national average in 2003.

Strong gains in income and spending will return in the decade ahead. Total real personal income is projected to rise by 4.2% per year in the Basin between 2003 and 2012. This is above the 3.8% annual growth anticipated for the nation. The reason for the Basin's lead is that its total market size (measured by population) is projected to grow significantly faster than the national average (see page 7-11).

If the national economy produces productivity gains in the decade ahead as projected, real per capita income in the Los Angeles Basin will grow by 2.8% per year, reaching $40,159 by 2012 (in 2003$). This is up from $31,345 in 2003.

Average household income in the Basin was $100,087 in 2003—198% above the national average.[1] The Basin has larger households and more workers per household than does the nation.

Average household income will increase by 2.6% per year and will reach $126,337 in 2012. This will be 15% above the national average.

Because the share of income spent on taxable items declined in relation to spending non-taxable items (housing and services), spending growth for taxable sales has lagged behind income gains. Internet sales are not yet a major factor in the slowing of taxable sales, although Internet sales will rise steadily as a share of spending.

Spending on taxable sales will continue to lag behind income growth in the decade ahead. Regional spending on taxable items by households is projected to grow from $213.4 billion in 2003 to $298.2 billion in 2012 (all measured in 2003$). This represents an annual spending growth of 3.8%, slower than the growth rate for total personal income.

In general, income and spending in the Basin will keep pace with statewide growth rates and will grow faster than the projected national rates.

---

[1] See page 5-72 for an explanation of CCSCE's measure of household income.

Construction Activity

In 2003, construction valuations in the Basin rose to their highest levels since the late 1980s. Housing prices in Basin markets reached record levels in 2003 and again in 2004. Residential permits reached their highest level since 1989.

The fundamental determinants of long-term construction growth—jobs, population, and households—continue to look solid in the decade ahead. Public construction should post strong gains also, as Californians support more infrastructure investment. The Basin, like other regions in the state, is struggling to build enough housing to keep pace with growth and to maintain housing affordability for Basin residents.

Construction: A Large and Cyclical Industry

The value of new construction activity (including public works) in the Los Angeles Basin averaged $21.6 billion per year between 1978 and 2003, measured in 2003$.[2]

An average of 70,200 new homes was built each year since 1978. The peak year was 1986, with 161,300 units. Residential building has increased for the last seven straight years, reaching 78,500 units in 2003.

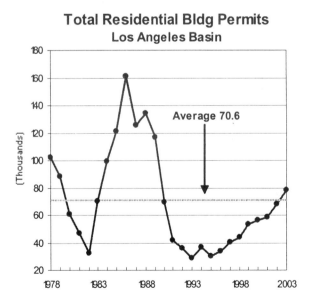

---

[2] Total construction spending in 2003 was $28.6 billion. That figure includes the $24.6 billion shown on the table and graph on these pages, plus $4.08 billion for public buildings. The public building data is not included in the graphs because there is no consistent data prior to 1997.

Recent Construction Market Trends

There was a sharp decline in construction activity throughout California after 1989. In the early '90s, the Los Angeles Basin construction market sustained the sharpest declines in the state.

Total annual new construction in 2003 ($24.6 billion) showed a 68% increase from 1993 levels, but remained 30% below 1989 levels. Los Angeles County has recovered the least, with 2003 construction levels barely one-half of their 1989 valuation. Orange County construction levels are also well below 1989 levels.

The Inland Empire counties (Riverside and San Bernardino) posted strong gains in building since 1996, also led by increases in nonresidential construction. Construction spending in both counties combined, however, has finally reached the $10 billion mark, slightly exceeding the 1989 spending levels.

The Los Angeles Basin shows a construction pattern opposite to the Bay Area. Recent construction levels in the Basin are up and continuing strong in 2004, although well below their 1989 peaks. By contrast, recent construction spending in the Bay Area is down sharply, but is still ahead of 1989 levels in many markets.

	Los Angeles Basin **Construction Trends** **(Billions of 2003$)**							
	New Construction				**Residential Permits** **(Thousands)**			
	1989	**1993**	**2002**	**2003**	**1989**	**1993**	**2002**	**2003**
Imperial	$0.1	$0.2	$0.2	$0.2	0.8	0.6	1.1	1.2
Los Angeles	16.7	7.0	8.9	9.5	48.3	7.3	19.4	21.3
Orange	6.1	2.7	4.0	3.5	16.6	6.4	12.0	9.3
Riverside	5.2	2.0	5.1	6.6	25.7	7.3	22.7	30.4
San Bernardino	4.6	1.6	3.1	3.4	20.0	5.9	10.6	12.6
Ventura	1.4	0.8	1.3	1.3	5.0	1.4	2.5	3.6
Los Angeles Basin	**$35.1**	**$14.6**	**$22.7**	**$24.6**	**116.4**	**28.8**	**68.2**	**78.5**

Source: Construction Industry Research Board

The amount of new residential permits has risen rapidly in recent years, but the region is still far below 1989 building levels. The Inland Empire counties had 43,000 permits in 2003—the highest number since the 45,700 permits issued in 1989. Los Angeles County had 21,300 permits—down more than 50% from the 48,300 residential permits issued in 1989.

Orange County, aided by strong job growth, saw increased residential construction in the late 1990s. Permit levels fell back to 9,300 in 2003, however, after several years near 12,000.

In recent years, rising residential building valuation levels have offset declining nonresidential building. Public works spending, unlike the gains in other regions, has remained relatively flat.

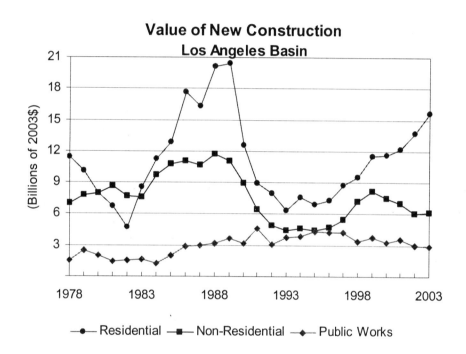

Affordability and Household Growth: Foundations for Housing Recovery

Housing prices have surged, and housing affordability has re-emerged as a major challenge in the region. Measured housing affordability rose in 2001, but this was based on historically low mortgage rates and strong income gains the year before. Housing affordability turned down in 2002, despite low interest rates. **It reached record lows in mid-2004.**

As discussed in Chapters 3 and 5, prices in the Basin have reached record levels each year since 2002. Even the Inland Empire, traditionally the region's main source of moderately priced housing, now has prices higher than in many competing markets, including Portland, Salt Lake City and Las Vegas.

Moreover, housing prices have reached historically high levels in relationship to regional household income and regional price trends. As shown on the next page, the last time housing prices raced far ahead of annual consumer price trends was in 1989, just before housing prices and construction collapsed.

Housing prices in Orange and Ventura counties, in particular, have increased well beyond gains in regional household income and the CPI. Median resale prices in Los Angeles County are now near $400,000, and the county's affordability ratio is nearing an all-time low. Continued sharp gains in the Inland Empire are sending danger signs for the region's currently most affordable housing market.

The long-term outlook will be heavily influenced by whether communities in the region have incentives to approve higher levels of housing construction, especially for moderately priced housing and apartments. Household income growth will continue, and mortgage rates should remain below 7½%, even with the current upturn in rates.

Households Able to Afford
Median Priced Home

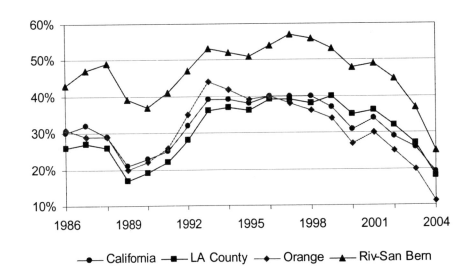

Los Angeles Basin
Median Resale Prices vs. HH Income

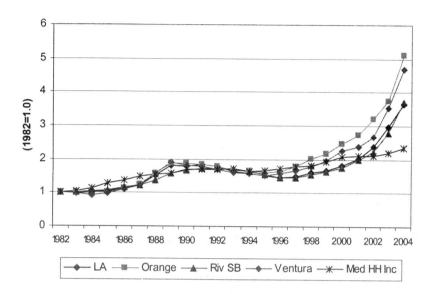

Los Angeles Basin
Median Resale Prices vs. CPI

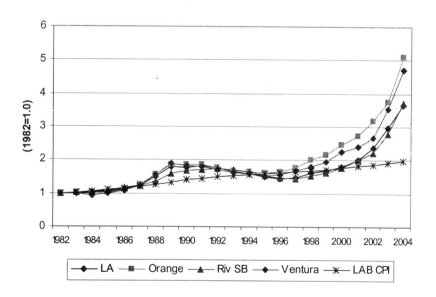

Job growth and demographic trends point to higher household formation in the region. Annual job growth is projected to average 168,300 between 2003 and 2012, slightly above the 155,300 average for the 1994-2000 period. As a result, household growth is projected to average 82,200 per year between 2003 and 2012.

The projected household growth will support new residential construction averaging 92,500 units per year from 2003 to 2012. The demographic projections point to a strong residential market in the Los Angeles Basin in the years ahead.

Land use availability and affordability pose substantial challenges to meeting the demographic demand for housing. The region has recently adopted a new land use/transportation goal called the "2% solution," where changes in land use in 2% of the region's land can allow significantly more housing to be built. More information on the region's planning efforts can be found on the website of the Southern California Association of Governments – www.scag.ca.gov.

Nonresidential Construction: Analysis and Outlook

Commercial, industrial and other nonresidential construction fluctuate with the level of job growth. The late 1990s, a period of strong job growth, saw a surge in these construction activities, although they were still below the level of the mid-1980s.

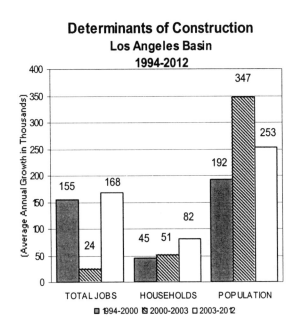

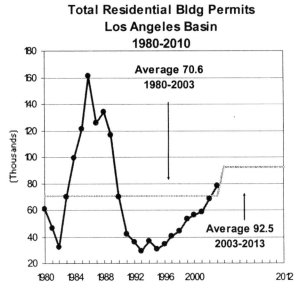

Since 1999, commercial and industrial building has slowed. There will be continuing weakness until vacancy rates are reduced. When this occurs, renewed job growth will support higher construction levels, although it is unlikely that the peak levels of the 1980s (for commercial building) will be reached.

Los Angeles Basin Nonresidential Construction (Billions of 2003$)				
	1989	1993	2002	2003
Commercial	$5.4	$1.3	$2.1	$1.7
Industrial	1.4	0.2	0.7	0.7
Other Nonresidential	1.1	0.6	1.0	1.2
Alterations/Additions	3.2	2.3	2.3	2.3
Public Works	3.7	3.8	2.9	2.9
Public Buildings			2.8	4.0

Source: Construction Industry Research Board

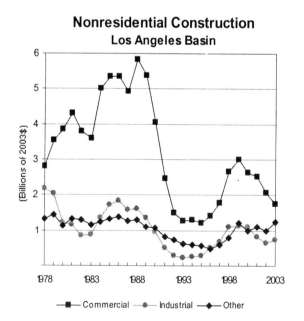

Two categories of nonresidential construction were stronger in the 1990s than in the 1980s: Alterations and Additions, and Public Works. The value of Alterations and Additions grew steadily to 1989, and then plateaued at $2.5 billion per year since then. This is the second-largest category of nonresidential building in the 1990s. (Alterations and additions are related to upgrading the existing stock of buildings. They have always grown, even when new construction slows down.)

Heavy construction (Public Works) has grown to where it is now the largest category of nonresidential building in the Los Angeles Basin. It averaged over $3 billion per year in the 1990s. Public buildings are a second large component of public construction.

In 2003, Public Works valuation ($2.9 billion) and public building ($4.0 billion) were the top two categories of nonresidential construction in the Basin.

The outlook for public construction and alterations and additions is very strong in the decade ahead. California is moving toward reversing its decades-old downturn in infrastructure investments. A growing wave of dollar commitments to infrastructure has been unleashed by the following factors:

- The majority required to pass school bonds has been reduced to 50%.

- Recent state and local elections have provided financing for schools and transportation.

- There has been a growing recognition of the critical contribution of infrastructure to the economy.

The Los Angeles Basin faces substantial challenges and opportunities:

- A massive backlog of school repair and construction needs.

- Regional airport capacity expansion and related ground infrastructure temporarily delayed by the events of 9/11 but looming large in the decade ahead.

- Continued port expansion and upgrading of the linkages between the ports and the region's rail and truck distribution networks.

- The growing need for transportation investment for maintenance and expansion of system capacity.

SAN FRANCISCO BAY AREA

SAN FRANCISCO BAY AREA

The Bay Area Recession

The depth and length of the Bay Area's recession has been far greater than CCSCE and other economists expected. Job levels are rising slowly but remain no higher than a year ago. They are currently 380,000 jobs below the region's peak in 2000.

There were five major contributing factors:

- A decline in domestic business capital spending (a major market for the region's technology base)

- A simultaneous and sharp decline in exports of technology manufacturing products

- A decline in business and international travel and resulting reductions in airline travel and business spending

- The continuation of strong productivity growth, which has allowed technology firms to produce more with fewer employees

- The large buildup in employment in 1999 and 2000, fueled by rising venture capital and corporate investment, which far exceeded the growth of market demand.

The result was that the Bay Area suffered a greater loss of jobs and income between 2000 and early 2004 than did the Los Angeles Basin during the early '90s aerospace-led recession.

The Bay Area economy was hit by several negative **external economic** forces, most of which will eventually be reversed. **However, much of the severity of the current downturn was the result of companies being formed and then going bankrupt because there was no market demand to support their business plans.**

The downturn appears to have ended but the short-term recovery is slow and it will take many years to recover the jobs lost since 2000.

The Bay Area lost approximately 380,000 jobs between the peak in December 2000 and July 2004. This is equal to a decline of approximately 10% of the region's job base. The Los Angeles Basin lost 8.8% of its non-farm jobs that existed at the peak in the early '90s.

The Bay Area's job losses were concentrated in Silicon Valley and San Francisco. Silicon Valley lost nearly 20% of the non-farm job base since the peak in December 2000. The San Francisco metro area lost nearly 13% of its non-farm jobs. In comparison, Los Angeles County lost 12.2% of the county's jobs at the peak in the early 1990s.

San Francisco Bay Area Non-Farm Wage & Salary Jobs (Thousands)				
Metro Area	July 1994	July 2000	December 2000	July 2004
Oakland	873	1,048	1,063	1,030
San Francisco	905	1,091	1,100	958
San Jose	802	1,047	1,055	851
Santa Rosa	146	185	189	178
Vallejo-Napa	143	175	173	186
Bay Area	**2,868**	**3,546**	**3,580**	**3,203**

Source: EDD, with CCSCE seasonal adjustment to EDD data

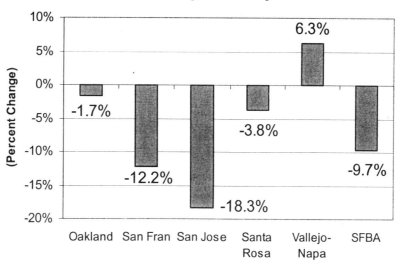

Nonfarm Job Change
July 2000-July 2004

The region's job losses were concentrated in technology and in related high-wage service sectors.

San Francisco Bay Area Sectors with Greatest Job Loss December 2000-July 2004 (Thousands)				
Job Sector	Dec. 2000	July 2004	Numerical Change	Percent Change
Manufacturing	485.5	346.9	-138.6	-28.5%
Computer & Electronic Products	235.4	151.9	-83.5	-35.5%
Information	160.4	114.4	-46.0	-28.7%
Professional & Business Services	698.8	519.6	-179.2	-25.6%

Source: EDD

The Bay Area lost approximately 25% of the region's job base in Manufacturing, Information and Professional and Business Services. Nearly all of the region's job losses came in these three high-wage sectors.

More than 80,000 of the 138,500 losses in manufacturing jobs came in one sector— Computer and Electronic Products. 80% of the high tech job losses occurred in Silicon Valley. These job losses came as market demand fell, many companies started in 1999 and 2000 did not survive **and** venture capital funding for new companies plummeted.

Venture capital funding in the Bay Area fell by more than 80% between 2000 and 2003, from a level of $35.1 billion to just $6.1 billion. **However, there was no loss of competitive share for Bay Area venture capital funding.** The decline in Bay Area venture capital funding mirrored national and state trends. The Bay Area maintained a relatively steady 75% share of state venture capital funding, and state funding followed the national pattern.

California Venture Capital Funding 1995-2003 ($Billions)							
	1995	1997	1998	1999	2000	2001	2003
Los Angeles/Orange	$.5	$.8	$1.4	$3.7	$6.5	$2.2	$1.0
Sacramento/N. Calif.	.0	.0	.1	.1	.3	.2	.1
San Diego	.3	.5	.6	1.3	2.3	1.6	.8
San Francisco Bay Area	1.9	4.8	6.3	18.9	35.1	12.9	6.1
California	**$2.7**	**$6.1**	**$8.4**	**$24.0**	**$44.2**	**$16.9**	**$8.0**
Calif. Share of U.S.	**34.2%**	**39.6%**	**38.4%**	**42.7%**	**41.0%**	**39.4%**	**42.6%**

Source: Price Waterhouse Coopers

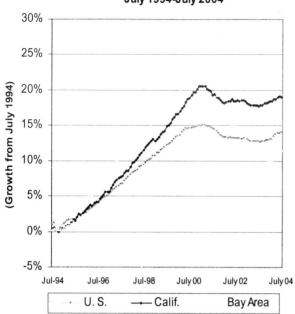

Growth in Non-Farm Jobs
San Francisco Bay Area
July 1994-July 2004

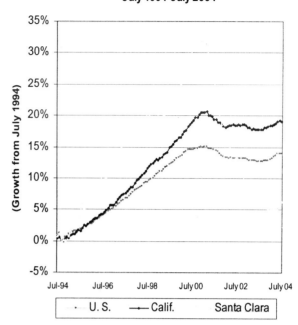

Growth in Non-Farm Jobs
Santa Clara County
July 1994-July 2004

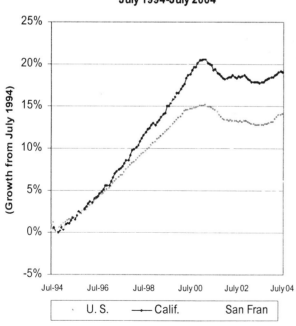

Growth in Non-Farm Jobs
San Francisco Metro Area
July 1994-July 2004

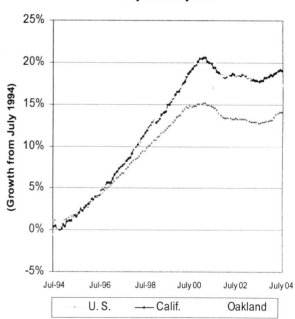

Growth in Non-Farm Jobs
Oakland Metro Area
July 1994-July 2004

Wage levels fell and unemployment rates rose in the region—and both trends were much more sharply felt in the Bay Area than elsewhere.

Average Wages			
Metro Area	**1994**	**2000**	**2002**
Oakland (East Bay)	$32,157	$44,207	$46,877
San Francisco	36,510	59,288	56,602
San Jose	39,123	76,252	63,056
Santa Rosa (Sonoma)	25,232	35,742	36,494
Vallejo-Napa	26,181	32,156	34,543
Bay Area	34,475	56,546	54,182
United States	26,939	35,320	36,214

Source: U.S. Bureau of Labor Statistics

Unemployment rates rose throughout the region. For example, the unemployment rate in Santa Clara County rose from 1.3% in December 2000 to 8.3% in April 2003. It later rose as high as 8.9% before falling back to 6.3% in July 2004.

As with the wage trends, two points stand out: 1) the severe impact of the economic downturn and 2) the fact that even after three bad years, Bay Area wage levels and unemployment rates are much better than are normally associated with such sharp job losses.

San Francisco Bay Area Unemployment Rates			
County	**December 2000**	**April 2003**	**July 2004**
Alameda	2.3%	6.7%	6.2%
Contra Costa	2.2%	5.5%	5.3%
San Francisco	2.5%	6.8%	6.3%
San Mateo	1.2%	5.1%	4.1%
Santa Clara	1.3%	8.3%	6.3%

Source: EDD

The Bottom Line

The Bay Area will come back. Key indicators are turning up in 2004. Technology manufacturing exports in California rose 21% in the first six months of 2004. Venture capital funding in the Bay Area rose 26% during this same time period. Wage levels are rising again, and a small recovery in job levels is underway.

The questions for Bay Area economic growth are: How much, how quickly and for how long? The Bay Area has gone from being one of the state's fastest-growing economies to its slowest in the past four years. What will the future bring?

CCSCE expects that the Bay Area economy **will rebound from 2003 levels and post strong growth between 2003 and 2012. However, measured from 2000 levels, Bay Area growth will lag behind the state average to 2012.**

Three of the five factors contributing to the downturn are being reversed. The national economy has begun to grow, although not yet as rapidly as hoped. Business capital investment is rising, based on rising profits, the need to keep up with new technology and a growing national economy. Exports of technology products are growing as the world economy enters a new period of growth.

The remaining two factors—rapid productivity growth and the large buildup of excess capacity—are placing continuing pressure on Bay Area job growth. Moreover, the Bay Area has additional challenges in the high cost of housing and low rate of housing production within the region.

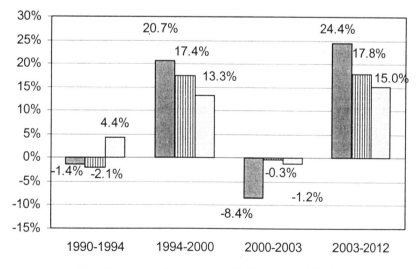

Past and Future Job Growth
San Francisco Bay Area

□ San Francisco Bay Area ▥ California □ United States

The Bay Area economy still possesses some long-term positives. Technology remains the leading high-wage growth sector in the world economy. Although the past two years have brought losses in jobs, income, profits and tax revenues, the competitive position of the region in technology remains strong.

While the drop in venture capital funding was dramatic, California and the Bay Area did not lose in terms of the share of national activity.

The region retains the country's most highly educated, productive and well-paid workforce. Even with a large drop in stock option income in 2001 and 2002, average wages in the region were more than 40% above the national average and are now rising again.

While the main recovery in the region will come from a rebound in existing technology areas, other sectors will bring additional growth over time—including biotechnology, possibly stem cell research, nanotechnology, domestic security and the next round of defense technology.

Measuring the Bay Area economic progress is a "tale of two cities." Technology sales can and will grow. Companies can and will record rising profit levels. Wages can and will rise, including some renewed growth in stock option income. **But all of this can happen without producing the high levels of job growth seen in the late 1990s.** Productivity growth allows companies and workers to prosper **without requiring many additional workers.**

The regional economy is not solely dependent on technology production. The East Bay and North Bay subregions have not been hurt as badly as San Francisco and Silicon Valley. The region's competitive strength as an international financial center, headquarters region and tourism center are intact.

CCSCE's projection is for the Bay Area economy to recover and have job growth comparable to the national average between 2000 and 2012. This projection requires a strong recovery starting in 2004 to recover the ground lost between 2000 and 2004. CCSCE projects job growth of 24.4% (above the state average) between 2003 and 2012. However, job growth measured from 2000 is projected to be 13.9%, the lowest among California's major economic regions.

By 2012, the Bay Area will still have the highest per capita and average household income of any region in the United States. Per capita income is projected to rise from $44,688 in 2003 to $58,412 in 2012 (measured in 2003$), and to be 43% higher than the national average.

The challenges of housing availability and affordability and of traffic congestion still remain for this region as it tries to retain the world's leadership as a center for technology innovation and growth.

The Region's Economic Base

The San Francisco Bay Area has an economic base concentrated in high tech manufacturing and the basic industry components of information and professional and business services. In 2003, the Bay Area had nearly 1.4 million jobs in this economic base, as shown on page 9-10, including the state's largest concentrations in each of the above three sectors.

Profile of Economic Base in 2003

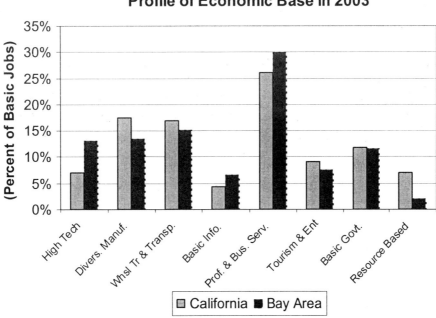

The concentration in high-wage technology products and services helped push the Bay Area economy ahead in the late 1990s. It also caused the current downturn to be so severe in the region. The San Francisco Bay Area possesses a number of strengths that will be the foundation for job growth in the decade ahead:

- A large and highly skilled labor force. The Bay Area has one of the nation's largest concentrations of scientific, professional and managerial talent. It also has the state's most highly educated workforce.

- Leading educational institutions, such as Stanford University and the University of California, Berkeley, with world-class programs in science and engineering.

- The nation's largest concentrations of technology and related venture capital firms.

- A leading position in the new growth sectors—biotech, nanotech, applying technology to domestic security **and** a strong position in older technology markets.

- A highly attractive quality of life, including outstanding climate and proximity to unique environmental and outdoor recreation opportunities.

High Technology

The Bay Area is well known for its high technology manufacturing companies. In 2003, the major high tech manufacturing industries accounted for 179,300 jobs, down from a high of 245,900 in 2000. Most of the industry is located in Santa Clara County, although recent trends have pushed more high tech manufacturing into the East Bay. New industries such as biotechnology, nanotechnology, advanced telecommunications and the application of technology to domestic and defense security are being added to the region's base in computers, semiconductors and instruments.

Semiconductors and electronic component manufacturing is the largest job center within high tech manufacturing, with 62,600 jobs in 2003—down from a high of 90,100 in 2000. Computer manufacturing is next, with 44,000 jobs—down form a high of 58,000. Next is electronic instruments (which under the NAICS structure includes measuring and controlling instruments), with 34,600 jobs, and then communications equipment, with 11,500 jobs.

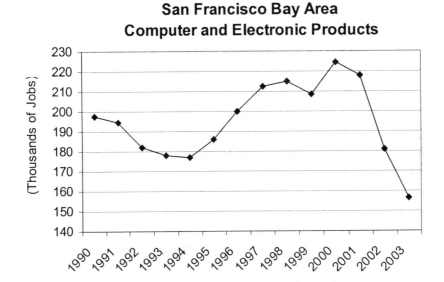

San Francisco Bay Area
Computer and Electronic Products

Pharmaceutical manufacturing (a portion of the biotech complex) had 13,400 jobs in 2003. It was the only high tech sector to add jobs since 2000.

The volume of high tech exports influences high tech manufacturing job levels. The surge in Bay Area export volume (most of which is high tech related) was matched by a surge in high tech job levels. Since 2000, Bay Area export volumes have plummeted—from $58.3 billion to $33.0 billion in 2003.

San Francisco Bay Area
Major Sectors in Economic Base
2003
(Thousands)

	Jobs	
High Tech Manufacturing	**179.3**	
Computer & Peripheral Equipment Manufacturing		44.0
Communications Equipment Mfg.		11.5
Semiconductor & Electronic Component Mfg.		62.6
Electronic Instrument Mfg.		34.6
Aerospace Product & Parts Mfg.		9.2
Pharmaceutical & Medicine Mfg.		13.4
Diversified Manufacturing	**182.6**	
Fabricated Metal Product Manufacturing		21.1
Machinery Mfg.		23.0
Miscellaneous Manufacturing		19.2
Beverage & Tobacco Product Mfg.		16.3
Apparel Manufacturing		6.9
Chemicals (except Pharmaceuticals)		7.6
Printing & related Support Activities		10.9
Professional and Business Services	**409.1**	
Legal Services		35.7
Accounting, Tax Preparation & Bookkeeping Services		20.5
Architectural, Engineering & Related Services		43.5
Computer Systems Design & Related Services		80.6
Management, Scientific & Technical Consulting Services		27.9
Scientific Research & Development Services		39.9
Management of Companies & Enterprises		68.2
Employment Services		64.0
Information	**91.5**	
Software Publishers		27.3
Telecommunications		28.6
Internet Service Providers & Related Services		26.3
Wholesale Trade and Transportation	**208.1**	
Wholesale Trade		124.0
Air Transportation		23.8
Support Activities for Transportation		14.2
Couriers and Messengers		18.3
Tourism and Entertainment	**103.5**	
Arts, Entertainment, & Recreation		48.7
Accommodation		45.4
Government	**157.7**	
Federal Government		57.2
State Government		100.4
Resource Based	**27.7**	
Total Basic Jobs	**1,359.5**	

Source: EDD

San Francisco Foreign Trade Value of Exports and Imports 1990-2003 ($Billions)			
Year	Exports	Imports	Total
1990	$23.1	$28.1	$51.3
2000	$58.3	$68.9	$127.2
2003	$33.0	$46.5	$79.6
Average Annual Growth Rate 1990 – 2003			
San Francisco	2.8%	3.9%	3.4%
California	4.0%	7.1%	5.9%
United States	5.1%	7.8%	6.7%

Source: U.S. Department of Commerce

The Bay Area had 7.82% of U.S. high tech manufacturing jobs in 1990 and 8.3% in 1994, at the beginning of the high tech boom in the region. The Bay Area share rose to a high of 9.5% in 2000. The region's share of national high tech jobs held steady in 2001 but fell sharply in 2002 and 2003, ending slightly above the 1994 share.

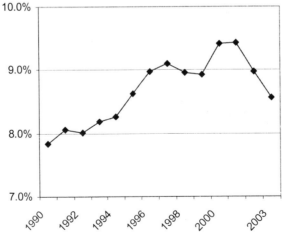

Bay Area Share of U.S. High Technology Jobs

Most of the growth in high tech jobs since 1990 came from the formation of new companies. The level of future gains in high tech production and exports will depend on the attractiveness of the Bay Area for new company formation and investment. So far, the Bay Area has not lost any share of national venture capital investments and is participating in the expansion of funding in 2004.

The Bay Area remains well placed to participate in the next wave of innovation. The most recent regional patent data released by the U.S. Patent Office is for 1999. As shown below, the Bay Area (led by Silicon Valley) was the nation's leading patent center. Patent data by state of origin is available through 2001. The number of patents issued to California firms rose from 16,773 in 1999 to 17,492 in 2000 and 18,598 in 2001.

Patents in 1999	
Northern California	
San Jose	5,664
San Francisco	1,700
Oakland	1,589
Southern California	
Los Angeles	2,348
Orange County	1,473
Boston	3,806
Chicago	2,929
Minneapolis - St. Paul	2,181
Detroit	1,964

The biotech sector continues to grow, as discussed on pages 5-40 and 5-42. The Bay Area leads in the number of public biotech firms.

Public Biotechnology Industry in 2002 Number of Firms	
San Francisco Bay Area	62
New England	52
San Diego	28
New Jersey	24
Mid-Atlantic	20
Los Angeles/Orange County (11th)	13

Source: Ernst & Young

Although the number of Bay Area biotech firms and employees declined from 2001 to 2002, the level of sales and research and development spending reached record levels.

Public Biotech Companies
($Billions)

	Employees		Product Sales		R & D	
	2001	2002	2001	2002	2001	2002
Bay Area	34,983	31,844	$7.4	$9.0	$3.3	$3.6
Los Angeles/Orange	25,976	27,091	5.5	7.2	1.1	4.2
New England	24,452	24,447	3.9	4.8	2.7	2.8
San Diego	7,534	8,569	1.4	1.6	.8	.8
Total for U.S.	141,238	142,878	$25.3	$30.3	$11.5	$16.3

Source: Ernst & Young

High tech manufacturing job levels will probably recover some from the current depressed levels, but direct manufacturing jobs will not be a growth sector in the Bay Area. The most likely scenario is for job creation in new companies to slightly exceed continuing layoffs in some existing companies. A new wave of high tech job growth will occur only if the region attracts a large wave of new venture capital investments.

High tech–related job growth will come in the Professional, and Business Services, Information and Wholesale Trade and Transportation sectors.

San Francisco Bay Area
Jobs By Major Basic Industry Group
1994-2012
(Thousands)

	1994	2000	2003	2012	Numerical Change 1994-2000	Numerical Change 2000-2003	Numerical Change 2003-2012
High Tech Manufacturing	201.0	245.9	179.3	181.2	44.9	-66.7	1.9
Diversified Manufacturing	198.3	231.1	182.6	204.3	32.8	-48.5	21.7
Wholesale Trade & Transportation	209.7	239.3	208.1	279.3	29.6	-31.3	71.3
Basic Information	63.5	123.3	91.5	138.0	59.8	-31.8	46.5
Professional & Business Services	346.1	558.3	409.1	616.7	212.2	-149.2	207.6
Tourism & Entertainment	89.4	107.3	103.5	132.5	17.9	-3.8	29.0
Basic Government	171.9	158.7	157.7	177.8	-13.2	-1.0	20.1
Resource-Based	32.7	32.6	27.7	25.4	-0.2	-4.8	-2.4
Total Basic Jobs	**1,312.6**	**1,696.5**	**1,359.5**	**1,755.2**	**383.8**	**-337.0**	**395.7**

Source: EDD; projections — CCSCE

Professional and Business Services

Professional and Business Services was the largest component of the region's economic base, with 409,100 jobs in 2003. The Bay Area accounts for more than 25% of the state's jobs in this sector, even after large job losses since 2000.

Job levels grew by nearly 225,000 between 1994 and 2000, reaching a peak of 568,300 in 2000. The region lost nearly 150,000 basic Professional and Business Services jobs between 2000 and 2003.

CCSCE projects a gain of nearly 50% in sector jobs between 2003 and 2012, based on strong projected national job growth in Professional and Business Services. Even with this large job growth, however, the sector will still have only approximately 60,000 more jobs than in 2000.

The largest component of this sector is computer systems design, with 80,600 jobs in 2003. Job levels surged from approximately 38,000 in 1994 to more than 111,100 in 2000. The tech downturn and bankruptcy of many new firms wiped out more than 30,000 jobs in the following three years.

Management jobs (classified in the new NAICS industry standard under "Management of Companies") were especially hard hit since 2000. Job levels rose from 83,600 in 1994 to more than 112,800 in 2000, and then fell back to 68,200 in 2003. On the other hand, scientific research service jobs, at 39,900 in 2003, remain near the sector's highest levels.

Employment services (including temporary help agencies) serve many Bay Area high tech companies. Employment levels were like a roller coaster, rising from 59,900 in 1994 to 118,700 in 2000, and then falling back down to 64,000 in 2003.

Information

Among all California regions, the Bay Area has the highest concentration of jobs in basic information services. In 2003, the Bay Area had 91,500 basic information jobs, or 6.7% of total basic jobs. In comparison, 4.5% of the state's basic jobs were in this sector.

Three industries—software publishing, telecommunications and Internet service providers (ISPs)—account for nearly all of the region's information jobs.

Software publishing jobs have maintained most of the 1990s growth during the past three years, as shown on the graph below. Software publishing jobs rose from 14,100 in 1994 to a high of 30,900 in 2001, and then fell back slightly to 27,500 in 2003. ISP jobs, web portal jobs and related jobs showed the roller coaster pattern between 1994 and 2003, rising from 9,500 to 38,400 and then declining to 26,300 in 2003.

Telecommunications jobs have fallen sharply since 2000 and are now below 1994 levels.

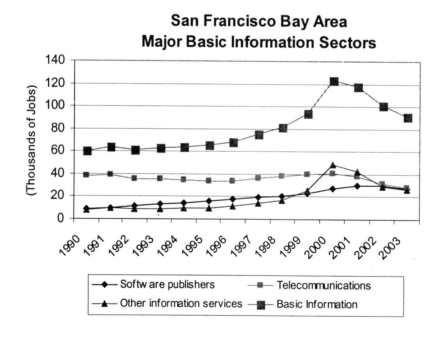

Jobs in information services are projected to recover and grow. Total sector jobs are projected to increase from 91,500 in 2003 to 138,000 in 2012. The largest projected gains are in software publishing and ISPs/web portals.

Diversified Manufacturing

In 2003, the Bay Area had **more** Diversified Manufacturing jobs than high tech manufacturing jobs by a small amount. Bay Area firms had 182,600 Diversified Manufacturing jobs, spread among a large number of industries.

The largest industries are machinery manufacturing (23,000 jobs) and fabricated metal products (21,100 jobs). These industries are partially connected to high tech manufacturing. As a result, Diversified Manufacturing jobs in the Bay Area rose and fell with high tech manufacturing jobs since 1990. Job levels rose from 198,100 in 1994 to 231,100 in 2000, before falling by nearly 50,000 over the next three years.

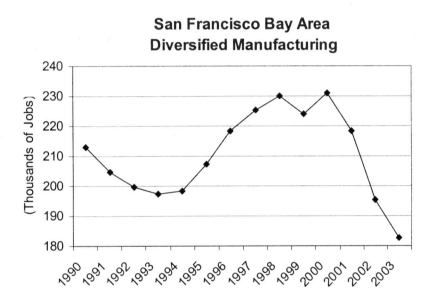

**San Francisco Bay Area
Diversified Manufacturing**

A large portion of Diversified Manufacturing jobs have nothing to do with high tech. These include printing, chemicals, apparel, food and beverage manufacturing and industries that support construction activities.

Jobs in Diversified Manufacturing are projected to recover from current depressed levels, but the sector will not produce many new jobs in the decade ahead. Job levels are projected to rise from 182,600 in 2003 to 204,300 in 2012. This is in comparison to the 191,200 jobs projected for high tech manufacturing.

Wholesale Trade and Transportation

Wholesale Trade and Transportation is the second largest sector in the Bay Area's economic base. The sector's 208,100 jobs in 2003 are more than either Diversified Manufacturing (182,600) or high tech manufacturing (179,300).

Sector job levels rose by 30,000 between 1994 and 2000 and then fell by a like amount during the following three years.

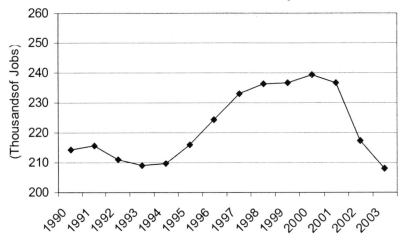

San Francisco Bay Area
Wholesale Trade & Transportation

Wholesale trade accounts for more than half of the sector's total jobs, with 124,000 jobs in 2003. In recent years, wholesale trade job levels have followed the trend of technology and foreign trade: falling in the early '90s, rising sharply between 1994 and 2000, and then falling again in the current downturn. Wholesale trade jobs are projected to increase by approximately 40,000 between 2003 and 2012 as the Bay Area economy and foreign trade levels improve.

Air transportation has been the second-largest component of Wholesale Trade and Transportation, with 23,800 jobs in 2003. Job levels have fallen with the slowdown in air travel and the financial difficulties at United Airlines, which used to have a larger presence in the region.

One positive sign is the recent decision by Virgin Airlines to locate part of their new United States operations in the Bay Area.

Total Basic Jobs

As shown on page 9-14, basic industry job levels are projected to increase by nearly 400,000 jobs, or 29.1%, between 2003 and 2012. While this is a strong growth rate going forward, the gains will mostly replace jobs lost since 2000. Most of the basic industry job growth is projected in Professional and Business Services, Information and Wholesale Trade and Transportation.

At the peak in 2000, the Bay Area had 25.2% of the state's basic industry jobs. That share fell to 22.1% by 2003. Although projected to rise back to 23.5% in 2012, this is still below the Bay Area's share throughout most of the 1990s.

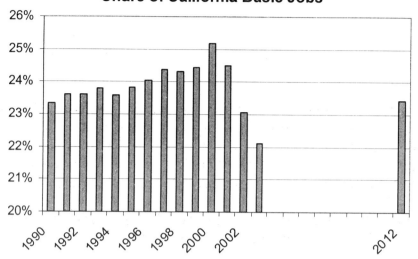

San Francisco Bay Area
Share of California Basic Jobs

Job Projections

The San Francisco Bay Area outpaced the state and the nation in job growth in the late 1990s. However, CCSCE expects that the region will grow no faster than the nation to 2012.

					Percent Change		
San Francisco Bay Area **Total Jobs** **1994-2012** **(Thousands)**							
	1994	**2000**	**2003**	**2012**	**1994-2000**	**2000-2003**	**2003-2012**
San Francisco Bay Area	3,184.0	3,843.8	3,522.1	4,383.4	20.7%	-8.4%	24.4%
California	13,813.1	16,232.9	16,140.5	19,659.5	17.5%	-0.6%	21.8%
United States	127,233.7	144,132.4	142,336.9	163,756.8	13.3%	-1.2%	15.0%

Source: EDD, BLS and CCSCE (Projections)

Jobs in the region are projected to grow by 24.4% between 2003 and 2012, a little over 850,000 jobs. The driving factors are a rebound in technology manufacturing and foreign trade, combined with the region's continuing attraction as an international financial center and tourism locale.

However, measured from 2000, the region's job growth will trail the state average because much of the projected growth merely replaces jobs lost since 2000. By 2012, the Bay Area will account for 22.3% of California's jobs, down from 23.7% in 2000 and 23.1% in 1994.

Jobs by Major NAICS Industry Sector

Professional and Business Services (a new NAICS industry category) is the largest major industry sector in the Bay Area with 520,500 jobs in 2003. Professional and Business Services includes the professional, scientific, technical and management services sectors from the region's economic base **and** administrative and support services jobs.

Out of all major industry sectors, Professional and Business Services accounted for the most job growth in the Bay Area. Between 1994 and 2000, Professional and Business Services added 230,500 jobs, more than a third of the region's total job gains. Subsequent sharp job losses (-155,400) occurred as the region's high tech sector and overall economy faltered between 2000 and 2003.

Professional and Business Services is projected to account for 248,100 added jobs by 2012, nearly 30% of the region's overall job growth.

Manufacturing accounted for 364,500 jobs in 2003, or 10.4% of total jobs. Even with the large loss in manufacturing jobs since 2000, the Bay Area still has a higher share of jobs in manufacturing than the state, which has an average of 9.6% of total jobs in manufacturing.

Manufacturing jobs in the region increased by nearly 20% (75,000 jobs) during the 1994-2000 high tech boom. Since 2000, more than 155,000 manufacturing jobs were lost, and no significant recovery is underway yet. CCSCE projects that the Bay Area will add only 23,400 manufacturing jobs by 2012, even though manufacturing output, profits and wages may rise substantially during this period.

The new NAICS Information major industry category is relatively small (116,900 jobs in 2003) but has shown high growth rates since 1994. Job levels rose from 89,200 in 1994 to 151,460 in 2000. They then fell to 116,900 in 2003. A gain of 50,700 jobs is projected to 2012. This gain will mainly recover the jobs lost since 2000.

San Francisco Bay Area
Jobs By Major Industry Group
1994-2012
(Thousands)

	1994	2000	2003	2012	Numerical Change 1994-2000	Numerical Change 2000-2003	Numerical Change 2003-2012
Agriculture, Forestry, Fishing, Hunting	22.6	25.8	23.0	22.2	3.2	-2.8	-0.8
Mining	4.2	3.5	1.7	0.8	-0.7	-1.8	-0.9
Construction	109.2	185.2	177.9	220.9	76.1	-7.3	43.0
Manufacturing	405.3	480.4	364.5	387.9	75.1	-115.9	23.4
Wholesale Trade	118.4	138.6	124.0	164.7	20.3	-14.6	40.7
Retail Trade	300.1	350.0	334.2	419.7	49.8	-15.8	85.5
Transp., Warehousing & Utilities	115.3	125.4	105.9	140.9	10.2	-19.5	35.0
Information	89.2	151.4	116.9	167.6	62.3	-34.5	50.7
Financial Activities	193.4	198.5	212.3	247.9	5.1	13.8	35.6
Professional & Business Services	445.4	675.9	520.5	768.6	230.5	-155.4	248.1
Educational & Health Services	294.0	334.1	354.1	486.4	40.1	20.0	132.3
Leisure & Hospitality	250.0	297.5	300.9	371.4	47.5	3.4	70.5
Other Services	100.0	110.7	112.3	142.8	10.7	1.6	30.5
Government	444.5	463.8	470.2	523.6	19.3	6.4	53.4
Self-Employed	290.6	299.5	304.0	318.0	9.0	4.4	14.1
Total Jobs	**3,184.0**	**3,843.8**	**3,522.1**	**4,383.4**	**659.8**	**-321.7**	**861.4**

Sources: 1990-2003 — EDD, with CCSCE estimate of self-employed; 2012 — CCSCE

Four major population-serving industries showed sustained job growth since 1994. The largest gains were in Educational and Health Services, which grew from 294,000 jobs in 1994 to 354,100 jobs in 2003—a 20% increase. Leisure and Hospitality (which now includes food service) also posted a 20% job gain, ending with 300,900 jobs in 2003. Retail Trade and Other Services showed smaller job gains.

These four sectors are projected to add more than 320,000 jobs between 2003 and 2012, as population and incomes rise in the region.

Construction jobs increased by 75,000 between 1994 and 2000, and construction job levels did not fall much after 2000, as large public works spending offset declines in nonresidential building. The region had 177,900 construction jobs in 2003, a number projected to increase to 220,900 in 2012.

Government is the second-largest major industry sector, with 470,200 jobs in 2003, or 13.3% of total jobs in the region.

Government job levels were affected by the loss of nearly all the Bay Area's civilian government jobs at military bases. Federal government jobs fell by 38,700 between 1990 and 2003, with 27,900 of the job losses associated with base closures. State government jobs increased slightly; and local government jobs increased by 39,500.

The government sector will provide more job growth in the decade ahead. CCSCE projects that the region will add 53,400 government jobs between 2003 and 2012, with the majority of added jobs coming in the local government sector.

San Francisco Bay Area Government Jobs (Thousands)			
	1990	**2003**	**Change**
Federal Government	96.1	57.4	-38.7
Defense	31.8	3.9	-27.9
Other	64.1	53.4	-10.7
State Government	89.4	100.4	+11.0
Local Government	272.9	312.4	+39.5
Total Government	**458.4**	**470.2**	**+11.8**

Source: EDD

Income and Spending

The San Francisco Bay Area represents 25% of the California market and over 3% of the national market in terms of income and spending. In 2003, total personal income in the Bay Area was $312.5 billion.

The Bay Area is the nation's wealthiest region of comparable size. Per capita and average household incomes in the region are far above the national average, as shown in Chapter 7. The Bay Area has the highest average wages in the nation, even after the recent sharp decline.

Between 1994 and 2000, real income and spending surged. Total income (in 2003$) grew by 6.5% annually. Taxable sales, led by business spending, increased by 6.0% annually.

By contrast, Bay Area income and spending fell substantially between 2000 and 2003. Wage levels fell partly from the reductions in stock option income, and partly as a result of salary reductions. Real per capita and household income fell by nearly 15%. Total personal income (in 2003$) fell from $352.9 billion in 2000 to $312.5 billion in 2003.

	Per Capita Income	Average HH Income	Total Personal Income (Billions)	Taxable Sales (Billions)
San Francisco Bay Area Income and Taxable Sales 1990-2012 (2003$)				
1990	$38,954	$104,450	$234.6	$96.1
1994	$38,301	$104,805	$242.4	$91.0
2000	$51,754	$143,119	$352.9	$129.4
2003	$44,688	$123,503	$312.5	$102.9
2012	$58,412	$154,715	$445.7	$144.8
Average Annual Growth Rates				
1994-2000	5.1%	5.3%	6.5%	6.0%
2000-2003	-4.5%	-4.8%	-4.0%	-7.4%
2003-2012	3.0%	2.5%	4.0%	3.9%
California	2.8%	2.5%	4.3%	4.0%
United States	2.9%	3.0%	3.8%	

Source: U.S. Department of Commerce, California Board of Equalization, CCSCE

Taxable sales fell even more rapidly. This created very difficult budget conditions for cities and transit agencies in the Bay Area. Real taxable sales fell from $129.4 billion in 2000 to $102.9 billion in 2003—a decline of 22%. In addition to the declines in retail spending, business-to-business spending also fell sharply.

Income growth is expected to begin again in 2004. Total real personal income is projected to rise by 4.0% per year in the region between 2003 and 2012. This annual growth rate is below that anticipated for the state (4.3%) and slightly above that projected for the nation (3.8%).

However, the venture capital/Internet crash of 2001 and 2002 will keep income growth (measured from its peak in 2000) well below the state average. Between 2000 and 2012, Bay Area real (i.e., inflation-adjusted) personal income is projected to increase by only 26%. This is in sharp contrast to the statewide projected gain of 69%

If the national economy produces productivity gains in the decade ahead as projected, real per capita income in the Bay Area will grow by 3.0% per year and will reach $58,412 by 2012 (in 2003$).

Average household income in the Bay Area was $123,503 in 2003, or 47% above the national average. Real average household income is projected to increase by 2.5% per year and reach $154,715 in the Bay Area in 2012[1]. This will be 41% above the national average.

Total income and spending growth in the Bay Area will trail the state and national averages to 2012 as a result of slowing rates of job and population growth.

The region will remain the nation's wealthiest area of more than 1 million people throughout the next decade.

Spending on taxable items will rise more slowly than income in the decade ahead. Regional spending on taxable items by households is projected to grow from $102.9 billion in 2003 to $144.8 billion in 2012 (measured in 2003$). This represents an annual real spending growth of 3.9%.

Income and spending projections are below those projected last year because job and wage levels are below those anticipated a year ago.

---

[1] See page 5-72 for an explanation of CCSCE's measure of average household income.

Construction Activity

Nonresidential construction spending has plunged since 2000 as Bay Area job levels have fallen and vacancies have surged. In 2003, public construction also fell, leading to a sharp drop in overall construction spending. Total spending fell from $19.3 billion in 2000 to $13.8 billion in 2003.[2]

Bay Area housing markets are still among the tightest in California, and demand for single-family housing remained strong in 2003 despite the large job losses. The Bay Area has the highest housing prices and rents in the nation, although other market areas (including Orange and San Diego counties) are fast closing the gap. The Bay Area is facing major public policy challenges in creating conditions to support residential building.

The long-term outlook is more mixed than in other regions of California. Housing affordability is approaching all-time low levels. While job losses have taken some pressure off residential markets, the region's long-term underproduction of housing will again be evident as soon as economic recovery begins.

Nonresidential construction may take several years to recover from current vacancy levels. On the other hand, Bay Area residents continue to approve higher levels of public construction funding.

Value of New Construction
San Francisco Bay Area

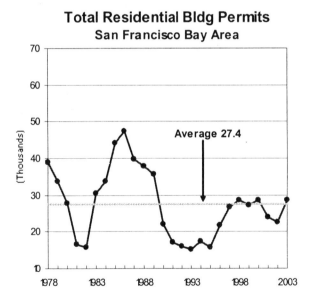

Total Residential Bldg Permits
San Francisco Bay Area

---

[2] The $12.0 billion in new construction in 2003 shown on the graph above excludes $1.8 billion for public buildings, primarily schools. The public building data is not included in the graphs because there is no consistent data prior to 1997.

Construction: A Large and Cyclical Industry

The value of new building construction (including public works) in the San Francisco Bay Area averaged $11.3 billion a year between 1978 and 2003, measured in 2003 prices. Even with the drop, 2003 was above the long-term average for construction spending.

An average of 27,400 new homes was built each year since 1978. Residential building levels rebounded in 2003 to 28,500 units, but are still below what is required to keep pace with the region's future job growth, especially if residents desire to reduce the need for long commutes.

Recent Construction Market Trends

The Bay Area experienced a sharp drop in new construction in each of the past three years. The major declines were in nonresidential building and were related to job losses and rising vacancy rates. As shown below, new nonresidential valuation fell from nearly $8 billion 2000 to just over $3 billion in 2003.

Both public works and public building spending reached record levels in 2002, but public works spending fell sharply in 2003. These long-term gains, which should continue, offset some of the declines in other sectors.

Even with the recent declines, construction spending in most Bay Area counties, including Santa Clara and San Francisco, is above 1989 levels (adjusted for inflation). Residential building levels remain below those of the late 1980s.

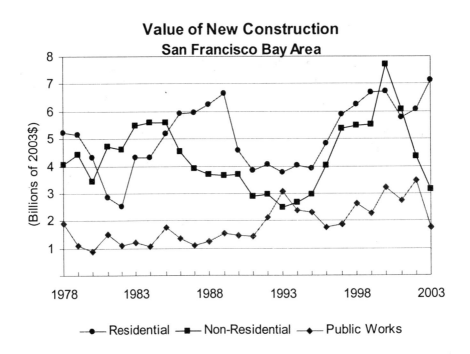

Value of New Construction
San Francisco Bay Area

—●— Residential —■— Non-Residential —◆— Public Works

San Francisco Bay Area
Construction Trends
(Billions of 2003$)

	New Construction				Residential Permits (Thousands)			
	1989	1993	2002	2003	1989	1993	2002	2003
Alameda	$2.2	$1.6	$2.7	$2.1	6.0	2.6	3.6	4.5
Contra Costa	1.8	2.5	2.2	2.3	7.7	3.4	5.8	6.9
Marin	.5	.3	.3	.5	1.4	.3	.4	.7
Napa	.3	.2	.4	.4	1.0	.4	1.2	.9
San Francisco	1.1	1.1	2.0	1.4	1.5	1.0	1.3	1.6
San Mateo	1.1	.7	1.4	1.0	2.4	.5	1.4	1.3
Santa Clara	2.3	1.8	3.0	2.7	4.9	3.4	4.5	7.5
Solano	1.3	.5	.8	.7	6.2	1.5	2.5	2.7
Sonoma	.9	.5	.7	.8	4.5	1.9	1.8	2.3
Total	**$11.8**	**$9.3**	**$13.9**	**$12.0**	**35.6**	**15.1**	**22.6**	**28.5**

Source: Construction Industry Research Board

San Francisco Bay Area
Median Resale Prices vs. CPI and Income

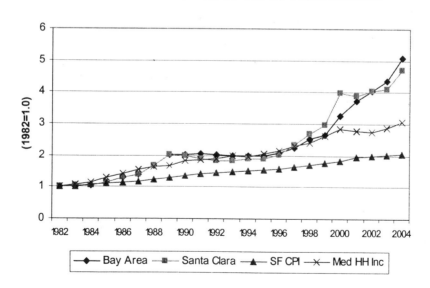

The Outlook for Housing

The long economic slump has had some effect on the Bay Area housing market. Apartment rents have fallen each year since 2000 and have continued to decline in many regional submarkets in the second quarter of 2004. Housing prices stopped rising throughout much of 2001 and 2002. As shown below, affordability did not fall in the region and actually rose in Santa Clara County for a brief period.

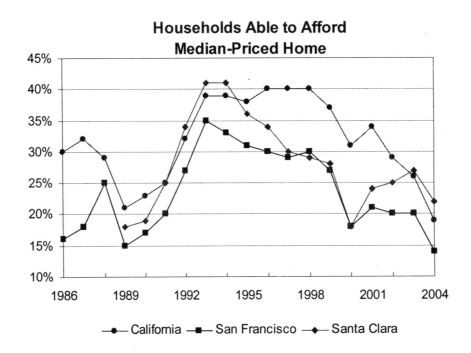

Households Able to Afford Median-Priced Home

— California — San Francisco — Santa Clara

However, the rise in measured affordability during 2001 and 2002 was temporary. Household incomes have fallen and median housing prices are rising again, driven by record low mortgage rates. In May 2004, the percent of regional households able to afford a median-priced home fell to an all-time low. Affordability in Santa Clara County is falling sharply again.

Moreover, median prices are racing far ahead of gains in income and much faster than overall consumer prices. As shown on the graph above, housing prices are much farther out of line with income and consumer price trends than they were even in 1989.

Future job and population growth will provide a foundation for increased housing demand in the Bay Area. Annual job growth is projected at 95,600 between 2003 and 2012. This is lower than the 110,000 annual gains during the 1994-2000 period. Population growth will average 70,600 annually, even with many workers and their families living outside the region.

The projected job and population growth will support approximately 40,000 new residential units per year between 2003 and 2012, both to meet new demand and to make up for recent low levels of housing production.

These projections of housing demand far exceed recent levels of residential construction. Since housing availability and affordability are key economic competitiveness issues for Bay Area employees, failure to meet the region's housing challenges will eventually reduce future job growth.

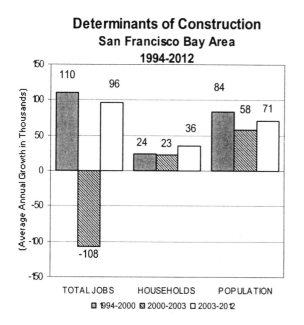

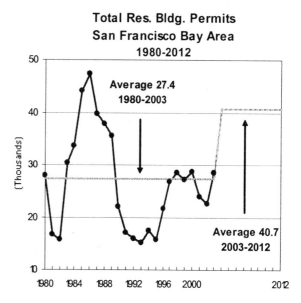

A fierce struggle about housing is going on in most communities. Many residents do not recognize the potential damage to economic competitiveness posed by low housing production. They instead mainly see the problems caused by new neighbors. On the other hand, landowners now see opportunities for building housing on sites previously reserved for new office buildings. This creates "new" land for housing in a scarce market. Hopefully, the economic and equity (fairness) arguments for housing will prevail, along with needed fiscal reform.

Some housing for the region's workers is being built in adjacent counties like San Joaquin (Stockton, Tracy), Stanislaus (Modesto) and San Benito. These trends are becoming stronger as housing price increases remain high in the region. While housing outside the region provides one answer as to how workers will get affordable housing, there may be an eventual limit to these long commutes through family choices and/or congestion.

On the other hand, a positive approach is to develop new communities in the San Joaquin Valley and bring jobs nearer to Valley residential communities. This offers a positive solution for creating a jobs/housing balance and reducing long commutes.

Nonresidential Construction — Analysis and Outlook

In response to the Bay Area's large job gains and the previous five years of low building levels, nonresidential building surged between 1995 and 2000—setting an all time record in 2000. Commercial construction, led by a surge in office building, reached $ 3.1 billion in the region in 2000. The surge was led by new construction in Silicon Valley, although San Mateo and San Francisco also posted substantial gains.

Since 2000, commercial and industrial building levels have fallen sharply and no turnaround is apparent so far in 2004. Regional job losses of more than 350,000 have left substantial vacant space and plummeting lease rates. Commercial construction valuation fell by more than 80% between 2000 and 2003. In addition, industrial construction has fallen to its lowest level in the past 25 years.

Public buildings and public works are now the largest components of nonresidential building in the Bay Area. They reached record levels in 2002. However, in 2003, public works spending fell by 50%, from $3.5 billion in 2002 to $1.8 billion in 2003. At the same time, spending on public buildings rose to a new record of $1.8 billion in 2003.

San Francisco Bay Area Nonresidential Construction (Billions of 2003$)				
	1985	**1993**	**2002**	**2003**
Commercial	$2.6	$0.5	$1.5	$0.7
Industrial	0.7	0.2	0.2	0.1
Other Nonresidential	0.4	0.2	0.7	0.6
Alterations/Additions	1.8	1.7	1.9	1.8
Public Works	1.7	3.1	3.5	1.8
Public Buildings			1.6	1.8

Source: Construction Industry Research Board

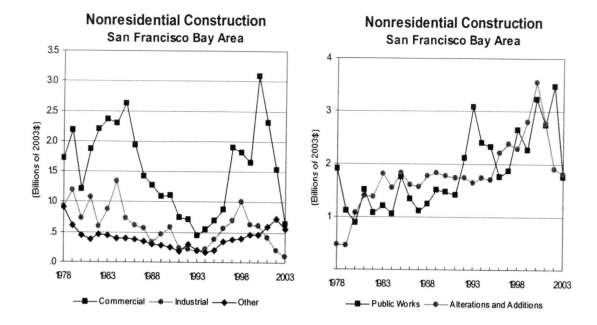

Nonresidential Construction
San Francisco Bay Area

Nonresidential Construction
San Francisco Bay Area

Outlook for Future Growth

The bright spot is public construction. Bay Area communities continue to fund public schools and transportation with new bonds, taxes and tolls. A $1 toll increase went into effect on July 1, 2004. Several Bay Area counties placed sales tax measures to fund transportation infrastructure on the November 2004 ballot. Domestic security concerns may further add to public construction funding.

There are active proposals for new rail and ferry services. The Caltrain "bullet train" project has been completed and initial passenger levels and customer satisfaction is very strong.

BART extensions and high-speed rail projects are longer-term possibilities. One near-term caveat is that most Bay Area public transit systems are facing declines in passenger levels and revenues, and are therefore instituting service cutbacks and delaying some construction projects.

The residential market could strengthen if cities approve the growing number of infill residential projects. Moreover, Bay Area landowners are starting to pursue housing projects on land previously designated for commercial/office uses.

A nonresidential building recovery is unlikely for a while.

SAN DIEGO REGION

SAN DIEGO REGION

The Bottom Line

The San Diego region included nearly 3 million residents and 1.4 million jobs in 2003. With a gross regional product of $129 billion, the region ranks as the world's 30th largest economy, approximately the size of Finland and Thailand. Moreover, the region's size expands significantly when considered in combination with the Tijuana area contiguous to San Diego across the Mexican border.

The region avoided recession after 2000, although the pace of economic growth slowed considerably. Still, the region managed to post a 3.8% job gain between 2000 and 2003 while both the state and the nation lost jobs.

San Diego has a strong economic base built around technology, foreign trade and business and professional services. The region draws on a labor force that stretches from Tijuana in the south to Temecula in the north. The region's manufacturing base has performed better than most big regions, despite the loss of significant numbers of defense-related jobs after 1990.

CCSCE projects that San Diego will be one of the fastest-growing regions in California. Between 2003 and 2012 job levels are projected to increase by 25.6% in the region. By comparison, job increases in California should be 21.8% and in the nation, 15.0%.

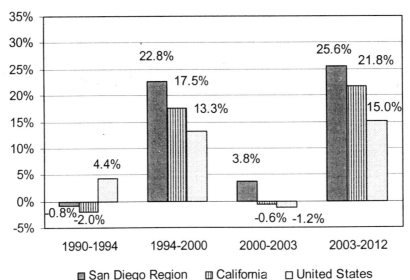

Past and Future Job Growth
San Diego Region

■ San Diego Region   ▥ California   ☐ United States

Foreign trade and the connection with Mexico are two of the region's economic strengths. The volume of foreign trade through San Diego has grown by 12.5% annually since 1990—nearly double the nation's 6.7% annual gains. In large part, this growth is the result of a nearly four-fold increase in trade with Mexico. Trade with Mexico accounts for more than 85% of San Diego's trade volume.

The region has successfully diversified its manufacturing base with telecommunications, biotech and light manufacturing replacing defense technology losses. An upturn in defense spending will help, but San Diego's future economic base growth will be driven by civilian technology sectors, professional services and information-related sectors.

Two looming challenges relate to housing. First, median home prices in the region surged past $550,000 in 2004. This makes San Diego one of the nation's five most expensive housing markets. Second, the region is rapidly using up the land presently zoned residential. Although the current economic growth has not yet been limited by land use constraints, the San Diego region (like the Bay Area) is now confronting the close connection between economic growth, land use and housing policies, and quality of life. The land use and growth debates in San Diego can be followed on the San Diego Association of Governments website, www.sandag.cog.ca.us.

The region has seen progress in the rise of per capita income. In 2003, per capita income in the San Diego region was $35,473, or 12% above the national average. Real (i.e., inflation-adjusted) per capita income in the region is projected by increase by 2.7% per year to 2012, reaching $45,000.

The Region's Economic Base—Existing Status and Future Prospects

The San Diego region has a diversified economic base. In 2003, the 492,700 jobs in San Diego's economic base were distributed throughout CCSCE's eight major new NAICS-based categories, as shown on page 10-5.

The San Diego region possesses a number of strengths that will be the foundation for job growth in the decade ahead:

- San Diego is located adjacent to the Mexican border and, as a result, continues to record double-digit foreign trade gains. This is far above the state and national averages. Benefits include:

    - Participation in Mexico's growing economy
    - Spin-offs from the maquiladora program
    - Access to the broader labor and retail market areas of the greater San Diego-Tijuana metro area

- San Diego has world-class university research programs. The U.C. campus at La Jolla is a world leader in biotech and other areas. The CSU system has multiple campuses in the region, and there are private universities and colleges as well. San Diego has the third-largest biotech complex in the nation.

- San Diego is a growing center for diversified manufacturing. The region added more than 10,700 jobs between 1994 and 2000, partly as a result of the ability to link to Tijuana's maquiladora center.

- San Diego has a broad base in technology, from computers and electronics to the developing telecommunications industry cluster. The region's businesses and labor force have a depth of talent and experience. San Diego ranked 5th in venture capital funding nationwide in the 2nd quarter of 2004, and accounted for 4% of U.S. venture capital funding in 2003. San Diego also ranked 8th as a center for receiving new patents in 1999, the last year for which regional data is available.

- San Diego is a major tourism site for state, national, and worldwide visitors. The convention business is an important and growing sector.

Foreign Trade

San Diego has one of the nation's fastest-growing foreign trade sectors. The volume of trade expanded by 12.5% per year between 1990 and 2003—far outpacing state and national growth rates. In 2003, trade volume reached $35.7 billion. This was up from $7.8 billion in 1990.

Trade with Mexico is the mainstay of San Diego's trade volume with Mexico. It accounts for 99% of all exports and 75% of imports. The San Diego–Baja California border is the busiest international crossing in the world (58 million crossings in 2002).

San Diego Customs District Value of Exports and Imports 1990-2003 ($Billions)			
Year	Exports	Imports	Total
1990	$3.4	$4.4	$7.8
2000	$12.7	$22.3	$35.0
2003	$12.7	$23.0	$35.7
Average Annual Growth Rate 1990-2003			
San Diego	10.8%	13.6%	12.5%
California	4.0%	7.1%	5.9%
United States	5.1%	7.8%	6.7%

Source: U.S. Department of Commerce

San Diego Region
Major Sectors in Economic Base
2003
(Thousands)

	Jobs
High Tech Manufacturing	**35.4**
Computers & Peripheral Equipment Mfg.	5.2
Communications Equipment Mfg.	4.8
Semiconductor & Electronic Component Mfg.	7.1
Electronic Instrument Mfg.	5.5
Aerospace Product & Parts Mfg.	5.4
Pharmaceutical & Medicine Mfg.	4.4
Diversified Manufacturing	**70.6**
Fabricated Metal Product Mfg.	8.8
Machinery Mfg.	9.3
Furniture & Related Product Mfg.	4.2
Miscellaneous Mfg.	11.3
Food Mfg.	4.8
Printing and Related Support Activities	4.7
Professional and Business Services	**157.0**
Legal Services	11.6
Architectural, Engineering & Related Services	19.4
Computer Systems Design & Related Services	14.4
Mgmt., Scientific & Technical Consulting Services	12.1
Scientific Research & Development Services	24.4
Management of Companies & Enterprises	19.2
Employment Services	35.5
Information	**27.7**
Software Publishers	4.1
Telecommunications	16.0
Wholesale Trade and Transportation	**59.8**
Wholesale Trade	41.3
Truck Transportation	4.8
Transportation Support Activities	4.2
Couriers & Messengers	4.1
Tourism and Entertainment	**49.5**
Arts, Entertainment, and Recreation	21.2
Accommodation	25.5
Government	**80.9**
Federal Government	42.7
State Government	38.2
Resource Based	**11.8**
Total Basic Jobs	**492.7**

Source: EDD

The volume of trade with Mexico grew from $2 billion in 1978 to approximately $10 billion in the early '90s. After the passage of the North American Free Trade Agreement (NAFTA), trade volumes with Mexico exploded and reached nearly $30 billion in 2003.

The basic industry components of Wholesale Trade and Transportation accounted for 59,800 jobs, or 12.1% of San Diego's economic base in 2003. About 2/3 of these jobs (41,300) were in wholesale trade. The remainder were mainly in trucking, warehousing and courier services.

The sector added 10,000 jobs between 1994 and 2000, before leveling off during the current state downturn. This growth is expected to continue. It relates directly to both the growing volume of foreign trade activity and the region's overall job gains. The San Diego Chamber of Commerce reports that approximately 52,000 jobs in San Diego are related to foreign trade activity.

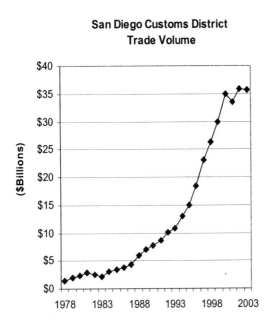

**San Diego Customs District
Trade Volume**

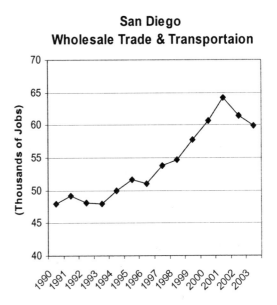

**San Diego
Wholesale Trade & Transportaion**

In converting the trade opportunities into actual gains for the region, the region faces infrastructure and foreign-trade negotiation issues. The U.S. is still negotiating agreements about the conditions under which Mexican truckers will have free access into the United States.

The continuing expansion of trade under NAFTA is important for the San Diego region, as are adequate border-crossing facilities to handle the expected growth in travel. The possible creation of Mexican port complexes in Baja California is another factor to monitor.

High Tech and Diversified Manufacturing

CCSCE splits regional manufacturing jobs into two segments—High Tech Manufacturing and Diversified Manufacturing. With the introduction of the new NAICS industry structure, CCSCE is including aerospace and defense electronics in the High Tech Manufacturing category, along with the pharmaceuticals component of chemical manufacturing.

High Tech Manufacturing accounts for the same share of basic industry jobs in San Diego as in California. The Diversified Manufacturing sector is comparatively smaller in the region.

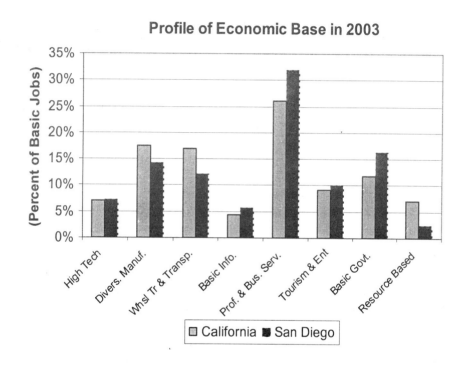

Profile of Economic Base in 2003

Both manufacturing segments added jobs between 1994 and 2000, and both have lost jobs in recent years. San Diego lost a large number of high tech aerospace jobs between 1990 and 1994. In 2003 the Diversified Manufacturing sector (with 70,600 jobs) had approximately twice as many jobs as the region's High Tech Manufacturing sector (35,400 jobs). Manufacturing job levels in the region, state and nation have fallen. This is primarily a result of rapid productivity gains that allow more production with fewer workers.

High Tech Manufacturing

The primarily civilian segment of high tech includes computers, electronic components, communications equipment and pharmaceuticals. These industries added jobs and facilities in the 1990s before falling victim to the current worldwide high tech slowdown.

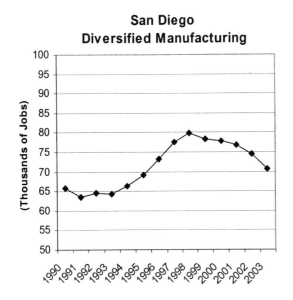

San Diego Diversified Manufacturing

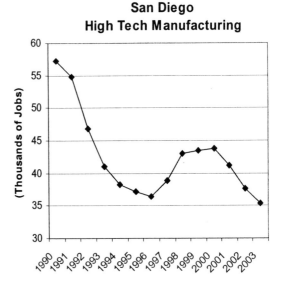

San Diego High Tech Manufacturing

These industries accounted for 21,500 jobs in 2003. They were split between computers (5,200), communications equipment (4,800), semiconductor and electronic components (7,100) and pharmaceuticals (4,400). Recent tech job losses have been less severe than in other regions of the state.

The aerospace/defense segments of high tech manufacturing have experienced continuing job losses. Aerospace manufacturing accounted for 22,900 jobs in 1990. By 1994, this level had fallen to 8,700, and a new low of 5,400 jobs was reported in 2003. Electronic instrument manufacturing (which includes search and navigation equipment) fell from 11,100 jobs in 1990 to 7,200 jobs in 1994 and a low of 5,500 jobs in 2003. Without the defense-related job losses, San Diego's manufacturing sector would have shown steady job gains until 2000.

The San Diego Regional Chamber of Commerce reports a recent increase in defense/aerospace employment. This is based on increases in non-manufacturing defense contracting activities in the areas of information management, telecommunications and surveillance systems. The nature of defense-related activity in the region has changed significantly since 1990.

San Diego has developed a presence in the venture capital world. Its presence is focused on telecommunications and biotech. Qualcomm is the telecommunications industry leader; it put San Diego in the center of telecommunications activity worldwide. Qualcomm has more than 6,000 jobs in the region and is planning for continuing leadership in innovation and providing services to the growing telecommunications industry.

Much of San Diego's technology activities take place at universities like the San Diego Supercomputer Center at U.C. San Diego and at non-profit institutions like the Salk and Scripps Institutes. It therefore does not show up in the traditional technology sectors used in compiling jobs data.

Venture capital funding in the region surged from $300 million in 1995 to $2.3 billion at the height of the venture capital boom. Funding levels fell below $1 billion in 2003, but were up 30% in the first half of 2004. A large share of San Diego venture capital funding is invested in biotechnology ventures.

California Venture Capital Funding 1995-2003 ($Billions)							
	1995	1997	1998	1999	2000	2001	2003
Los Angeles/Orange	$.5	$.8	$1.4	$3.7	$6.5	$2.2	$1.0
Sacramento/N. Calif.	.0	.0	.1	.1	.3	.2	.1
San Diego	.3	.5	.6	1.3	2.3	1.6	.8
San Francisco Bay Area	1.9	4.8	6.3	18.9	35.1	12.9	6.1
California	**$2.7**	**$6.1**	**$8.4**	**$24.0**	**$44.2**	**$16.9**	**$8.0**
Calif. Share of U.S.	**34.2%**	**39.6%**	**38.4%**	**42.7%**	**41.0%**	**39.4%**	**42.6%**

Source: Price Waterhouse Coopers/Venture Economics/NVCA

Many sources are available to provide detailed analyses of regional, state and national biotech prospects. Some of them are cited on page 5-36. The following section of this chapter draws heavily on these sources.

The San Diego region has the nation's third-largest concentration of public biotech firms, according to a recent Ernst & Young survey.

Public Biotechnology Industry in 2002 Number of Firms	
San Francisco Bay Area	62
New England	52
San Diego	28
New Jersey	24
Mid-Atlantic	20
Los Angeles/Orange County (11th)	13

Source: Ernst & Young

The San Diego biotech sector is made up of many smaller companies, and much activity takes places also in nonprofit institutions. As a result, the region ranks high in the number of companies, but relatively lower in total revenues. Even so, the region did rank fifth in the number of biotech jobs in public companies in 2002, according to the Ernst & Young tabulation.

Public Biotech Companies
($Billions)

	Employees		Product Sales		R & D	
	2001	2002	2001	2002	2001	2002
Bay Area	34,983	31,844	$7.4	$9.0	$3.3	$3.6
Los Angeles-Orange	25,976	27,091	5.5	7.2	1.1	4.2
New England	24,452	24,447	3.9	4.8	2.7	2.8
San Diego	7,534	8,569	1.4	1.6	.8	.8
Total U.S.	141,238	142,878	$25.3	$30.3	$11.5	$16.3

Source: Ernst & Young

According to San Diego Chamber of Commerce and *Business Journal* compilations, there are approximately 25 companies with at least 100 employees in the region. Large pharmaceutical companies including Pfizer, Merck, Johnson & Johnson and Novartis have established research facilities in the San Diego region.

Bioscience jobs nearly tripled from 1991 through 2003. They reached a level of more than 35,000, as compiled by the San Diego Regional Chamber of Commerce.

San Diego Bioscience Jobs

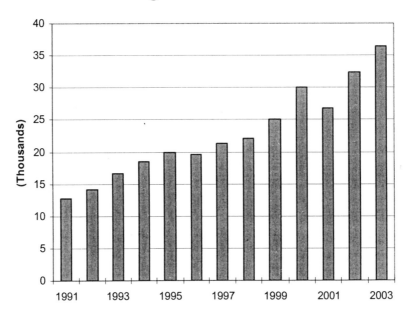

Diversified Manufacturing

Diversified Manufacturing accounted for 70,600 jobs in 2003, or 14.3% of the region's economic base. The largest sector is Miscellaneous Manufacturing, which, under the new NAICS industry structure, includes medical equipment along with most of the previous Miscellaneous Manufacturing sector; the latter portion of this in San Diego is tied to the maquiladora activity in Baja California.

In 2003, Miscellaneous Manufacturing accounted for 11,300 jobs, of which 4,600 were in medical equipment and supplies and the other 6,700 were in a range of activities. Both segments of this sector added jobs since 1990.

Other significant parts of the Diversified Manufacturing sector include machinery manufacturing (9,300 jobs in 2003), fabricated metal products (8,800), food manufacturing (4,800), printing (4,700) and furniture (4,200).

Until very recently, the maquiladora and related twin-plant activities were growing steadily and providing jobs to San Diego's Diversified Manufacturing base. Baja has become an international center for the assembly of color televisions, and Sony has been the region's largest diversified manufacturing firm, with 3,500 employees working in San Diego associated with the maquiladora activity.

The Baja California maquiladora activity, which takes advantage of lower labor costs in Mexico and favorable export terms to the United States, is under two pressures currently: the U.S. economic slowdown and foreign competition, particularly from China. Job levels have fallen, partly from reduced U.S. demand and partly from the closure and movement of facilities out of Mexico.

The cost of labor competition from China will force the maquiladora centers to focus more on higher-valued products, where labor costs make up a lower share of total costs. One positive note is Toyota's plan to open an assembly plant.

The largest maquiladoras in Tijuana in 2003 included Sony (4,500 employees), Matsushita (4,000) and Samsung (3,600)—all related to TV production; Hitachi (4,000) and Sanyo (2,700) in electronics assembly; Alaris (3,000) and Tyco (2,400) in medical products and Mattel (3,000) in toy assembly.

Projections

The number of Diversified Manufacturing jobs is projected to increase by nearly 20%, growing from 70,600 in 2003 to 84,500 in 2012, as shown in the table on the next page. The number of jobs in traditional high tech manufacturing is projected to increase, but only slightly, because productivity growth is constraining high tech job growth throughout the nation.

Professional and Business Services

Professional and Business Services is the largest and fastest-growing segment of San Diego's economic base. Job levels grew from 96,400 in 1994 to 157,000 in 2003, or 31.9% of the region's economic base.

San Diego Jobs By Major Basic Industry Group 1994-2012 (Thousands)					Numerical Change		
	1994	2000	2003	2012	1994-2000	2000-2003	2003-2012
High Tech Manufacturing	38.2	43.8	35.4	38.8	5.6	-8.5	3.4
Diversified Manufacturing	66.4	77.8	70.6	84.5	11.3	-7.2	13.9
Wholesale Trade & Transportation	49.9	60.7	59.8	79.8	10.8	-0.9	19.9
Basic Information	15.8	28.4	27.7	43.3	12.6	-0.6	15.6
Professional & Business Services	96.4	151.7	157.0	223.2	55.2	5.4	66.1
Tourism & Entertainment	40.5	47.4	49.5	61.4	6.9	2.1	12.0
Basic Government	75.6	77.0	80.9	88.3	1.4	3.9	7.4
Resource-Based	11.8	12.7	11.8	11.3	0.9	-0.9	-0.5
Total Basic Jobs	**394.6**	**499.5**	**492.7**	**630.5**	**104.8**	**-6.7**	**137.8**

Source: EDD; projections — CCSCE

The largest segment is scientific, research and development services, which provides services to the region's bioscience sector and other technology activities. Job levels increased from 16,600 in 1990 to 24,400 in 2003.

"Management of companies" jobs grew from 12,100 in 1990 to 19,200 in 2002. San Diego is one region where management jobs in 2003 exceed 2000 levels.

Architectural and engineering jobs are the third-largest component, with 19,400 jobs in 2002. This is up from 11,900 in 1990. Legal and computer service jobs have also grown steadily during this period.

Professional and Business Services jobs will be the largest segment of San Diego's economic base in future years. CCSCE projects that 66,100 jobs will be added between 2003 and 2012. This will account for approximately 50% of the region's basic industry job growth.

Information

Information is a new NAICS industry category. It is also a new basic industry segment in CCSCE's economic base categories. In 2003, there were 27,700 jobs in basic information services. By far, the largest number of jobs (16,000) was in telecommunications, up from 6,500 in 1990. Software publishing grew from 1,000 jobs in 1990 to 4,100 in 2003.

Information-related basic jobs are projected to increase by 15,600 jobs, for a gain of 56% between 2003 and 2012.

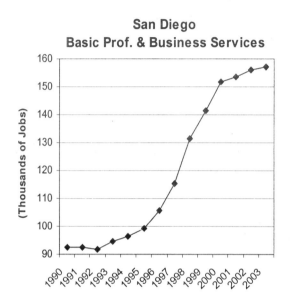

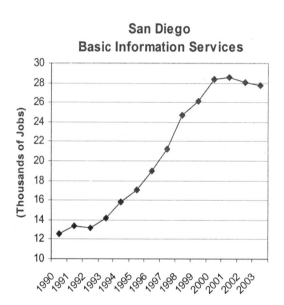

Tourism and Entertainment

The two major segments of the Tourism and Entertainment sector in the San Diego region are accommodations (with 25,500 jobs in 2003) and arts, entertainment and recreation (21,200 jobs). In addition, a portion of jobs in other sectors are related to tourism activity. Moreover, the jobs related to cruise ship activity, which is growing rapidly, are not included here.

Visitor revenue reached a record of $5.3 billion in 2003 as the tourism sector rebounded from the post–9/11 downturn. Airport and theme park traffic is nearing pre recession levels.

The region will remain a major national and international tourist center. Job levels (excluding the impact on restaurant business) are projected to increase from 49,500 in 2003 to 61,400 in 2012.

Government

Government is the second-largest segment of San Diego's economic base, with 80,900 jobs in 2003. Government jobs in the economic base have remained roughly level since 1994.

Federal government jobs (including civilian jobs at Navy bases) have declined from 45,400 in 1994 to 42,700 in 2003. This is in spite of the fact that San Diego has had fewer base cuts than other regions in the state. State government and education jobs increased from 30,200 in 1994 to 38,200 in 2003.

Basic government job levels are projected to increase by 7,400 to 2012, with all of the growth occurring in state government (including education).

Total Basic Jobs

Total basic jobs in the San Diego region are projected to increase by 137,800, or 28%, between 2003 and 2012, as shown on page 10-12. The region will outpace the state in basic job growth as San Diego's share of basic jobs rises from 8.0% in 2003 to 8.4% in 2012.

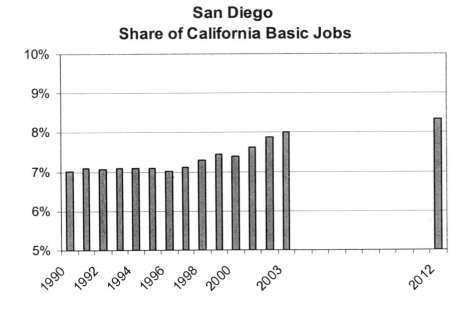

San Diego
Share of California Basic Jobs

Job Projections

The San Diego region has outpaced the state and the nation in job growth since 1990. CCSCE expects that the region will grow faster than the state and the nation to 2012.

San Diego Region
Total Jobs
1994-2012
(Thousands)

| | 1994 | 2000 | 2003 | 2012 | Percent Change | | |
					1994-2000	2000-2003	2003-2012
San Diego	1,072.9	1,317.2	1,366.8	1,716.1	22.8%	3.8%	25.6%
California	13,813.1	16,232.9	16,140.5	19,659.5	17.5%	-0.6%	21.8%
United States	127,233.7	144,132.4	142,336.9	163,756.8	13.3%	-1.2%	15.0%

Source: EDD, BLS and CCSCE (Projections)

Jobs in the region are projected to grow by 25.6% between 2003 and 2012, or by nearly 350,000 jobs. The driving factors are above-average growth in the region's economic base fueled by growing trade with Mexico, and a strong competitive position in biotech and technology manufacturing.

By 2012, San Diego will account for 8.7% of California's total jobs. This will be up from 8.5% in 2003, 8.1% in 2000 and 7.7% in 1990.

Job Trends by Major NAICS Industry Sector

Total jobs in the region grew by 27.4% between 1994 and 2003. They rose from 1,072,900 in 1994 to 1,366,800 in 2003. The region's growth rate was more than 60% higher than the state job growth rate during the same period. Jobs by major industry (using the new NAICS industry structure), are shown on the next page.

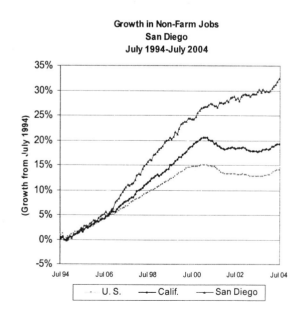

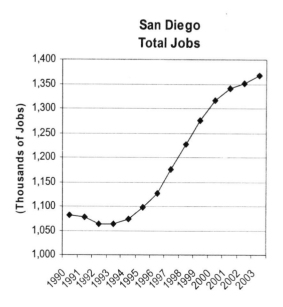

The largest sector in 2003 was Government. It accounted for 219,800 jobs, or 16.1% of the region's total jobs. Nearly all of the job gains in this sector came from local government, and most of those were in local education. The Government sector is projected to add 27,900 jobs to 2912, when it will be the region's second-largest major industry sector.

Professional and Business Services will soon be the largest sector, measured by jobs. More than 70,000 jobs (+54.8%) were added between 1994 and 2003. This sector includes the economic base sector of professional, scientific, technical and management services and administrative and support services. Both parts of the sector have grown rapidly since 1990. Professional and Business Services is projected to add 83,600 jobs by 2012, approximately 25% of total job gains in the region.

San Diego Area Jobs By Major Industry Group 1994-2012 (Thousands)					Numerical Change		
	1994	2000	2003	2012	1994-2000	2000-2003	2003-2012
Agriculture, Forestry, Fishing, Hunting	10.6	11.4	11.2	10.6	0.9	-0.2	-0.6
Mining	0.3	0.3	0.3	0.2	0.0	0.0	-0.1
Construction	41.8	69.7	79.6	96.4	28.0	9.9	16.8
Manufacturing	105.6	122.6	105.4	123.8	17.0	-17.2	18.4
Wholesale Trade	31.4	39.1	41.3	50.1	7.7	2.2	8.8
Retail Trade	113.9	133.7	140.0	179.3	19.8	6.3	39.3
Transp., Warehousing & Utilities	27.2	29.8	27.3	40.1	2.6	-2.5	12.8
Information	24.1	39.2	37.1	54.6	15.0	-2.1	17.5
Financial Activities	58.6	71.2	80.5	94.9	12.6	9.3	14.4
Professional & Business Services	130.2	195.2	201.6	285.2	65.0	6.4	83.6
Educational & Health Services	95.4	115.3	122.0	180.0	19.9	6.7	58.0
Leisure & Hospitality	109.9	129.0	139.9	173.7	19.1	10.9	33.8
Other Services	35.0	42.2	47.2	59.8	7.2	5.0	12.6
Government	181.5	206.6	219.8	247.7	25.1	13.2	27.9
Self Employed	107.4	112.0	113.7	119.6	4.6	1.7	5.9
Total Jobs	**1,072.9**	**1,317.2**	**1,366.8**	**1,716.1**	**244.3**	**49.5**	**349.3**

Sources: 1990-2003 — EDD with CCSCE estimate of self-employed; 2012 CCSCE

The next three largest sectors primarily serve the local population. All three posted moderate job growth as the region's population steadily increased. Retail Trade had 140,000 jobs in 2003, up by 26,100 from 1994. Leisure and Hospitality had 139,900 jobs in 2003, up 30,000 from 1994. Educational and Health Services had 122,000 jobs in 2003, up 26,600 from 1994.

These three sectors are projected to add more than 130,000 jobs between 2003 and 2012, with the largest gains occurring in Educational and Health Services.

Manufacturing accounted for 105,400 jobs in 2003, or 7.7% of the region's total jobs. The statewide manufacturing job share was 9.6% in 2003. Manufacturing did better in the San Diego region than statewide, as the region avoided net job losses since 1994. Manufacturing is projected to add 18,400 jobs by 2012 and to account for nearly 20% of the projected statewide manufacturing job gains.

Information is a new NAICS major industry category. It has grown rapidly since 1990. Job levels increased from 24,100 in 1994 to 37,100 in 2003, driven by gains in telecommunications and software publishing. The sector is projected to show strong job growth to 2012.

Income and Spending

The San Diego region represents 9% of the California market and 1% of the national market in terms of income and spending. In 2003 total personal income in the region reached $106.0 billion.

The San Diego market exceeded national income and spending growth rates in the 1990s, despite starting the decade with a long recession.

Real income and spending in the region remained roughly constant between 2000 and 2003. San Diego's losses were in line with the state average, and the region fared slightly worse than the nation since 2000. **Still, per capita income in 2003 ($35,473) was 12% above the national average.**

Year	Per Capita Income	Average HH Income	Total Personal Income (Billions)	Taxable Sales (Billions)
San Diego Region **Income and Taxable Sales** **1990-2012** (2003$)				
1990	$31,023	$87,569	$77.7	$32.3
1994	$30,189	$85,228	$78.8	$29.7
2000	$37,119	$105,699	$105.1	$41.1
2003	$35,473	$103,031	$106.0	$40.1
2012	$45,098	$124,005	$154.6	$56.4
Average Annual Growth Rates				
1994-2000	3.5%	3.7%	4.9%	5.6%
2000-2003	-1.3%	-0.8%	0.3%	-0.9%
2003-2012	2.7%	2.1%	4.3%	3.9%
California	2.8%	2.5%	4.3%	4.0%
United States	2.9%	3.0%	3.8%	

Sources: U.S. Department of Commerce, California Board of Equalization, CCSCE

Total real personal income is projected to rise by 4.3% per year in the San Diego region between 2003 and 2012. By comparison, 3.8% annual growth is anticipated for the nation. In the San Diego region, real personal income grew by 4.9% per year from 1994 through 2000.

If the national economy produces productivity gains in the decade ahead as projected, real per capita income in the region will grow by 2.7% per year and reach $45,098 in 2012 (in 2003$)—10% above the national average.

Average household income in the San Diego region was $103,031 in 2003—23% above the national average. Average household income (in 2003$) is projected to increase by 2.1% per year and reach $124,005 in 2012[1]—13% above the national average.

Spending on taxable items will rise more slowly than income in the decade ahead. Regional spending on taxable items is projected to grow from $40.1 billion in 2003 to $56.4 billion in 2012 (measured in 2003$). This represents an annual real spending growth of 3.9%.

In general, San Diego will keep pace with projected statewide growth rates in terms of income and spending growth, and will grow faster than projected national rates.

---

[1] See page 5-72 for an explanation of CCSCE's measure of average household income.

Construction Activity

In 2003, construction levels rose to their highest level since 1989 in San Diego, led by a rise in residential building. In 2003, private construction (residential and nonresidential combined) was $5.0 billion; another $900 million was spent on public works and $800 million on public buildings.

Median home prices reached record levels of $565,000 in mid-2004. The number of new units reached 18,300, the highest since 1989. Housing affordability fell to record low levels, even with historically low mortgage rates.

The longer-term fundamentals continue to look strong in San Diego. Growth in jobs, population and income should lead to continued growth in residential and nonresidential markets in the decade ahead. However, affordability, a shortage of land and NIMBY pressures raise challenges for getting enough housing built.

Construction: A Large and Cyclical Industry

The value of new building construction activity (including public works) in the San Diego region averaged $4.7 billion per year between 1978 and 2003, measured in 2003 prices[2]. At its peak in 1986, the new construction market reached nearly $8 billion. During the past five years, new construction has exceeded $5 billion—well above the long-term average.

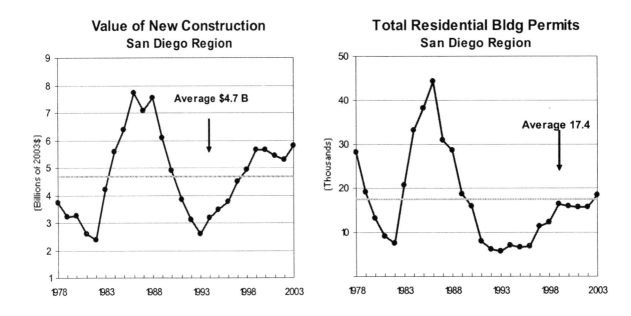

---

[2] The $5.9 billion in new construction shown on the graph for 2003 excludes $800 million for public buildings. The public building data is not included in the graphs because there is no consistent data prior to 1997.

An average of 17,400 new homes has been built each year since 1978. The peak year for units was 1986, with a record 44,300 units. In 2003, residential permits surpassed the long-term average for the first time since 1990.

Residential building valuation rebounded to over $3 billion since 1999 with the rise in new units. By contrast, residential building valuation was in the $4–5 billion range throughout the mid-1980s.

Nonresidential building remains above the levels of the early '90s recession, but it is well below the $2 billion-per-year average of the mid-1980s. Public works and public buildings now represent the largest nonresidential market in San Diego.

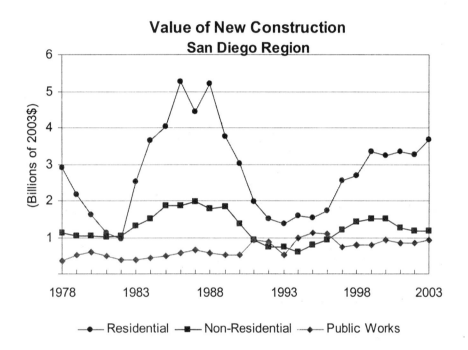

Value of New Construction
San Diego Region

—●— Residential —■— Non-Residential —◆— Public Works

The Outlook for Housing

Continuing job growth has led to a rebound in housing construction since 1996. Median resale prices rose to more than $350,000 in 2002, well above $400,000 in 2003. They are now above $550,000 in mid-2004.

The demographic fundamentals for continued residential building increases are good. Annual job gains are projected to average 38,700—near the levels of the 1994–2000 boom period. Population growth will average 48,700 per year—close to recent levels and well above the annual gains of the 1990s.

As a result, residential construction levels should average 25,100 units per year between 2003 and 2012, slightly above the yearly additions so far in the decade.

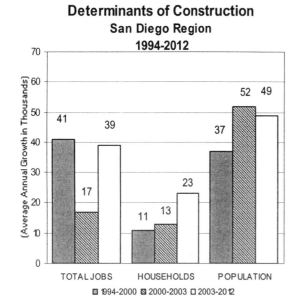

Determinants of Construction
San Diego Region
1994-2012

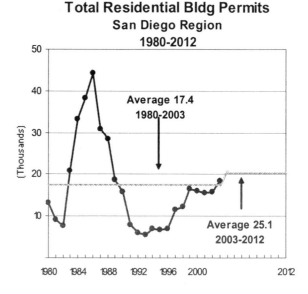

Total Residential Bldg Permits
San Diego Region
1980-2012

The affordability outlook in the region has reached record low levels. Income gains kept pace with housing price appreciation for most of the 1990s, but the recent housing price surges reversed this trend as shown on the bottom of page 10-23. As a result, only 10% of San Diego households can afford the current median resale housing price of over $550,000, as shown on the next page.

In addition, San Diego region resale prices became much less competitive with other regions after 1999, also shown on page 5-86.

One additional question mark is the availability of land zoned for residential building. However, local zoning decisions are not unchangeable, and the region does possess sufficient vacant land overall to support the projected housing gains and more.

San Diego is the site of active public discussion about the best way to support urban infill development and to promote "urban villages." This is one approach to increasing the supply of housing while providing exciting places for residents to live and work.

In San Diego, as in other regions, the surge in commercial vacancies is allowing landowners and communities to reevaluate the opportunities for infill housing to boost economic competitiveness **and** to address housing affordability.

Households Able to Afford
Median-Priced Home

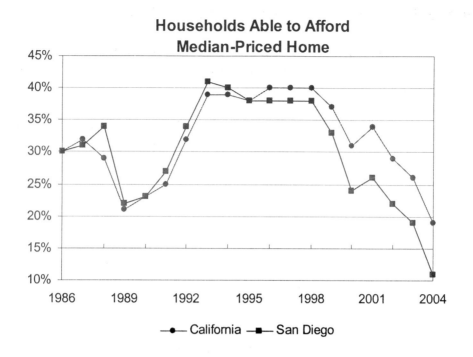

San Diego
Median Resale Prices Vs. CPI and Income

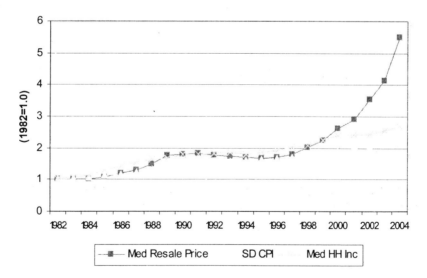

Nonresidential Construction: Analysis and Outlook

Commercial and industrial construction declined since 2000, though by a smaller amount than in other regions. Despite continuing job growth, the short-term outlook for new construction is mixed.

Three building types have provided the majority of construction spending in recent years: alterations and additions, public works, and public buildings.

Public works and public buildings spending have been, by far, the largest categories of nonresidential building in the 1990s. Public works has accounted for between $800 million and $1 billion since 1991. Public buildings accounted for another $800 million in 2002. This is the second largest category of nonresidential building.

The volume of alterations and additions has averaged $400 million since 1990.

San Diego Region Nonresidential Construction (Billions of 2003$)				
	1989	1993	2002	2003
Commercial	$1.1	$0.2	$0.4	$0.4
Industrial	0.2	0.0*	0.2	0.1
Other Nonresidential	0.1	0.1	0.2	0.2
Alterations	0.4	0.4	0.4	0.4
Public Works	0.5	0.5	0.8	0.9
Public Buildings			0.7	0.8

Source: Construction Industry Research Board
* Less than $50 million

Outlook for Future Growth

Total nonresidential building should expand in the years ahead. CCSCE projects that the fundamental determinants of construction growth—job and household gains—will remain strong in the decade ahead.

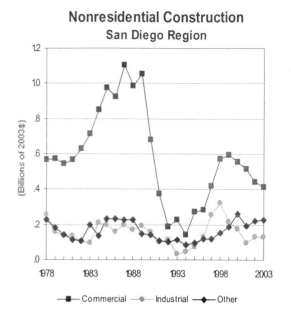

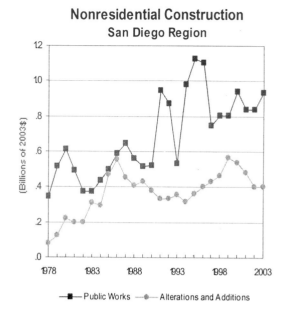

Nonresidential building should show continued growth and reach record levels in the near future. Three factors support the positive long-term outlook:

- Infrastructure spending should surge.

  Major airport and light rail expansion will augment infrastructure spending. San Diego's foreign trade growth rate is the highest in California.

- School construction, supported by new state and local bond issues, will be needed to keep pace with population growth and modernization. A major expansion of higher education facilities is planned for the decade ahead.

- Future job and population growth will also support a steady rise in spending to upgrade existing facilities.

SACRAMENTO REGION

SACRAMENTO REGION

The Bottom Line

CCSCE added two counties, Sutter and Yuba, to the definition of the Sacramento region in the 2004 edition of *California Economic Growth.* The Sacramento region definition now is the same as that used by the Sacramento Area Council of Governments (SACOG).

The Sacramento region had nearly 1 million jobs and more than 2.1 million residents in 2003, making Sacramento the smallest of California's five major economic regions.

The region retains large amounts of land for residential and industrial development. The region's economic future is very much up to local decisions, planning and investment. Growth pressures are now raising the housing, transportation and economic growth controversies previously seen mainly in the state's urban coastal regions.[1]

The Sacramento region has added jobs since 2000, despite the slowdown in government job growth. Job levels increased by 4.7% between 2000 and 2003, but

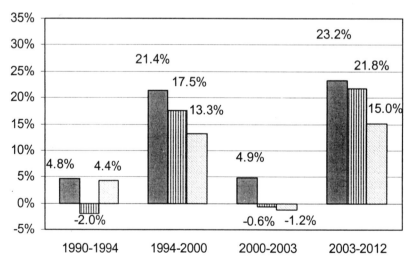

Past and Future Job Growth
Sacramento Region

■ Sacramento Region ▥ California □ United States

---

[1] The region is currently engaged in the Blueprint Project, a project for discussing regional land use and transportation choices. CCSCE prepared economic projections for the Sacramento Area Council of Governments (SACOG) to initiate the Blueprint outreach effort. CCSCE appreciates the support of SACOG, which increased our ability to analyze the regional economy. Blueprint activities can be followed at www.sacog.org.

key sectors of the region's economic base saw job losses that were offset by increases in population serving sectors. The region outpaced the state and the nation in job growth during all three recent time periods: 1990–1994, 1994–2000 and 2000–2003.

CCSCE projects that the region will again outperform the state and the nation in economic growth between 2003 and 2012. Jobs are projected to increase by 23.2%. This is above expected state (21.8%) and national (15.0%) job growth rates.

State government is the largest component of the region's economic base, especially when the professional services (legal, accounting, consulting) that relate to state government are factored in. The region has a presence in other basic industry sectors, but the future of state government activity and jobs will play a large role in determining the magnitude of growth in the region.

Housing prices have risen substantially and are now higher than in many competing western regional markets, but they still remain far lower than in the state's urban coastal markets. Housing production has increased, facilitating high levels of population growth. The region also has a competitive advantage in terms of land availability.

The region's manufacturing, professional services and state government sectors are critical to Sacramento's economic base and are facing short-term pressures. However, the region maintains competitive advantage for long-term growth in these sectors and can exercise significant control over its economic future through land use and infrastructure policies.

Income, spending and construction growth will all outpace the state and national average, driven by the region's job and population growth. Regional per capita income will remain near the national average and slightly below the statewide level.

The Region's Economic Base—Existing Status and Future Prospects

The Sacramento region possesses a number of strengths that will be the foundation for job growth in the decade ahead:

- Sacramento is the center of state government in California—a state that will add 5.5 million residents and nearly 600,000 college students by 2012. Professional service activities related to state government activities are a high-growth sector.

- The region has successfully developed a high tech complex.

- The region is a major distribution node on the I-80 corridor that serves Rocky Mountain and Midwestern markets.

- The region serves as a retail and service center for several smaller northern California county areas.

- The region has land availability and cost advantages that provide a low-cost, in-state alternative to the Los Angeles, San Francisco and San Diego regions. There has been a strong movement of people within California to the Sacramento region.

The Sacramento region economic base contains one "industry" that is much larger than all others. State Government, including general government and education activities, accounted for 107,600 jobs in 2003. Basic government jobs (state and federal) accounted for 35.3% of the region's economic base, compared to the 11.9% share statewide.

Profile of Economic Base in 2003

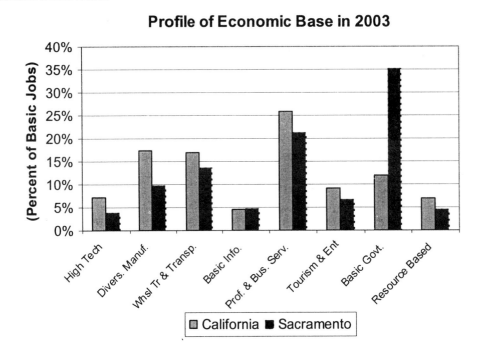

Major employers are the state government, University of California at Davis, and California State University at Sacramento.

State government and education added 16,600 jobs in the region between 1994 and 2003, but state government job levels have not risen since 2001. Higher education employment rose by 5,700 jobs to reach 26,000 in 2003. State government employment reached a high of 83,700 jobs in 2002 but lost 2,100 jobs in 2003.

Because this sector is such a large component of the region's economic base, future job trends are especially important for the region's overall potential. While the current budget deficits will probably limit near-term job growth, the substantial increases projected in state population and higher education enrollment will require higher job levels over time.

There is heated public debate in California about the appropriate number of state employees. Even before recent reductions in state government jobs, California had the lowest number of state employees relative to population among all 50 states and the District of Columbia.

In 2002 California had the equivalent of 107 full-time state employees per 10,000 residents—27% below the national average. In 2004 some state departments have had to hire additional staff in mid-year to deal with workloads that have accumulated since staffing levels were cut.

Currently, residents and policymakers are studying the recommendations of the California Performance Review about reducing employee levels in certain areas. On the other hand, there is no doubt about the substantial increase in caseloads expected throughout state government functions.

CCSCE projects an increase of 16,700 jobs in state government and education between 2003 and 2012. This will be the second-largest increase among the region's major basic industry sectors.

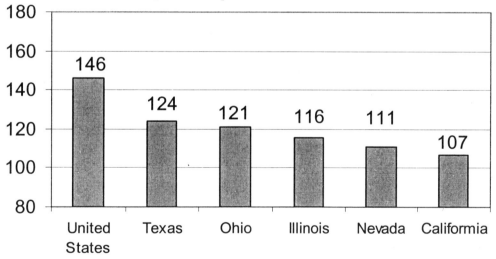

Five States with Fewest State Employees per 10,000 Population in 2002

An increasing number of professional service jobs are related to state government activities. They require firms and organizations to have an active presence in the capitol.

The Professional and Business Services sector is the fastest-growing part of the region's economic base, with 73,000 jobs in 2003. These jobs are split between legal, accounting, engineering, computer and management services. They serve the region's firms, state government and residents.

Sacramento Region
Major Sectors in Economic Base
2003
(Thousands of Jobs)

	Jobs	
High Tech Manufacturing	**13.1**	
Computer and Peripheral Equipment Mfg.		4.3
Semiconductor & Electronic Component Mfg.		5.4
Electronic Instrument Mfg.		1.6
Aerospace Product & Parts Mfg.		1.3
Pharmaceutical & Medicine Mfg.		0.4
Diversified Manufacturing	**33.4**	
Wood Product Mfg.		5.0
Fabricated Metal Product Mfg		3.7
Furniture & Related Product Mfg.		2.6
Miscellaneous Manufacturing		1.8
Food Manufacturing (excluding Preserving)		5.0
Beverage & Tobacco Product Mfg.		1.6
Printing & Related Support Activities		2.6
Plastics & Rubber Products Mfg.		1.4
Professional and Business Services	**73.0**	
Legal Services		7.4
Accounting, Tax Preparation & Bookkeeping Services		5.3
Architectural, Engineering & Related Services		8.3
Computer Systems Design & Related Services		7.3
Management, Scientific & Technical Consulting Services		5.9
Management of Companies & Enterprises		11.5
Employment Services		18.6
Information	**16.4**	
Software Publishers		1.0
Telecommunications		11.7
Wholesale Trade and Transportation	**46.8**	
Wholesale Trade		27.0
Truck Transportation		6.5
Couriers & Messengers		4.5
Tourism and Entertainment	**23.3**	
Arts, Entertainment, & Recreation		13.1
Accommodation		8.6
Government	**120.8**	
Federal Government		13.1
State Government		81.6
State Education		26.0
Resource Based	**15.6**	
Total Basic Jobs	**342.4**	

Source: EDD

The sector gained 31,100 jobs between 1994 and 2000, which accounted for over 50% of the basic industry job gain in the region. The largest gains were in employment services (temporary/contract help), which more than doubled, and in management of companies. Other gains were in architectural and computer services.

Small gains in most professional service sectors since 2000 were offset by large losses in employment services and management of companies. Professional and Business Services are projected to have the largest job growth among the region's basic industry sectors to 2012—adding 36,500 jobs above the 2003 levels.

These gains do depend, in part, on continuing growth in state government and high tech manufacturing.

| | | | | | Numerical Change | | |
Sacramento Jobs By Major Basic Industry Group 1994-2012 (Thousands)	1994	2000	2003	2012	1994-2000	2000-2003	2003-2012
High Tech Manufacturing	8.9	17.3	13.1	15.0	8.4	-4.2	1.9
Diversified Manufacturing	31.7	35.7	33.4	40.9	4.0	-2.3	7.5
Wholesale Trade & Transportation	38.4	47.2	46.8	60.5	8.8	-0.4	13.7
Basic Information	13.5	13.9	16.4	23.4	0.4	2.5	7.0
Professional & Business Services	49.8	80.9	73.0	109.5	31.1	-7.9	36.5
Tourism & Entertainment	17.8	20.5	23.3	30.6	2.7	2.8	7.3
Basic Government	116.5	119.3	120.8	138.5	2.8	1.5	17.7
Resource-Based	19.1	18.4	15.6	15.1	-0.7	-2.8	-0.5
Total Basic Jobs	**295.7**	**353.2**	**342.4**	**433.6**	**57.5**	**-10.8**	**91.2**

Source: EDD; projections — CCSCE

Wholesale Trade and Transportation sectors are the third-largest component of the Sacramento region economic base, with 46,800 jobs in 2003. Wholesale trade accounts for more than half of these jobs, and job levels have risen since 1994, driven by the gains in regional manufacturing output and the region's growing role as a distribution node on the I-80 corridor.

Based on a continuation of both of these trends, modest growth is projected. An additional 13,700 jobs are projected by 2012. This will be the third-largest numerical gain for the region's basic industry sectors.

Job growth of approximately 7,000 is projected for each of three smaller sectors—Diversified Manufacturing, Information and Tourism and Entertainment.

In 2003, there were 33,400 jobs in the region's Diversified Manufacturing sector. The largest industries in 2003 were food products and wood products (each with 5,000 jobs), followed by fabricated metal products (3,700 jobs). Diversified Manufacturing jobs have increased in the region since 1994, a positive trend, but there has been no "breakout" industry sector posting large and new growth.

In 2003, there were 13,100 High Tech Manufacturing jobs in the region. Job levels have fallen from 2000 peaks, but by less than in other regions. Intel is the largest high tech employer, with approximately 7,000 workers. It is followed by Hewlett Packard, with more than 4,000. HP job levels have fallen by 2,000 as part of HP's merger consolidation with Compaq. NEC local operations have been scaled back. Apple has 1,400-1,500 jobs with long-term plans for expansion.

The Sacramento region is still able to add significant numbers of moderately priced homes. This advantage, plus the proximity to Silicon Valley, gives Sacramento a competitive edge for high tech expansions in California. It offers the cost and quality-of-life advantages of out-of-state locations, while being located only 90 miles from Silicon Valley. Nevertheless, the potential for industry-wide job gains is limited in the long term by productivity gains that make new hiring needs quite limited. The prospects for more significant growth relate to attracting firms from other areas or getting a larger share of startups to locate in the region.

Having absorbed the loss of 15,000 defense-related jobs since 1990, the region **still managed to post significant total job gains**. The region is making some progress at having new private sector activities locate at former bases like Mather and McClellan. **These bases represent a significant opportunity for the region over the long term.** Aerojet remains a large defense related employer, with 1,300 jobs in 2003.

The Sacramento region has experienced a rising share of California's total basic jobs. The region's share rose from 4.8% in 1990 to 5.6% in 2003. The projected modest growth in state government jobs will restrain future share gains. Even so, the region is projected to have 5.8% of state basic jobs by 2012, up from the current share.

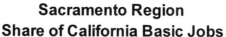

Sacramento Region
Share of California Basic Jobs

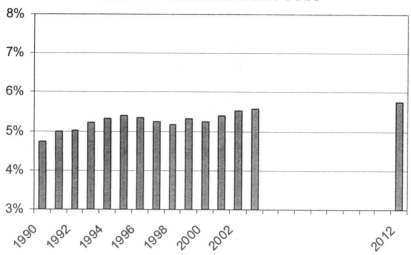

Job Projections

The Sacramento region has shown a steady increase in total jobs since 1990, outpacing the state and the nation. It has largely managed to avoid the job losses of the early '90s and also those of the recent period of state and national job losses. Total jobs grew by 27.6% between 1994 and 2003, rising from 757,400 to 966,3000. The Sacramento region growth rate was far higher than the 16.8% state job growth for the same period.

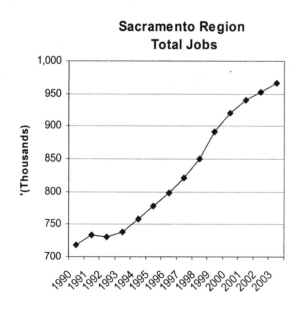

Sacramento Region
Total Jobs

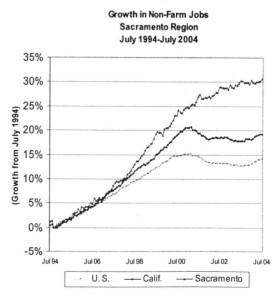

Growth in Non-Farm Jobs
Sacramento Region
July 1994-July 2004

Jobs in the region are projected to grow by 23.2% between 2003 and 2012, or by a little over 200,000 jobs. The driving factors are above-average growth in the region's economic base, fueled by Sacramento's continuing competitive attraction as a moderate-cost location to live and work within California.

	1994	2000	2003	2012	Percent Change 1994-2000	Percent Change 2000-2003	Percent Change 2003-2012
Sacramento Region	757.4	920.3	966.3	1,190.9	21.5%	5.0%	23.2%
California	13,813.1	16,232.9	16,140.5	19,659.5	17.5%	-0.6%	21.8%
United States	127,233.7	144,132.4	142,336.9	163,756.8	13.3%	-1.2%	15.0%

Sacramento Region
Total Jobs
1994-2012
(Thousands)

Source: EDD, BLS and CCSCE (Projections)

By 2012, the Sacramento region will account for 6.1% of California's total jobs, up from 6.0% in 2003, 5.7% in 2000 and 5.4% in 1994.

Jobs by Major Industry Sector

Jobs by major industry category using the new NAICS industry structure are shown on page 11-11.

The largest sector, by far, is Government, which had 236,500 jobs in 2003. The Government sector accounts for 24.5% of Sacramento region jobs, compared to 15.0% statewide.

The major difference is in the large concentration of state government employees, due to the fact that Sacramento is the state capitol.

	1994	2000	2003	2012	Numerical Change 1994-2000	Numerical Change 2000-2003	Numerical Change 2003-2012
Sacramento Region Jobs By Major Industry Group 1994-2012 (Thousands)							
Agriculture, Forestry, Fishing, Hunting	15.0	15.4	12.8	12.8	0.4	-2.6	0.0
Mining	0.8	0.8	1.0	0.8	0.0	0.2	-0.2
Construction	31.9	55.1	67.7	78.7	23.2	12.6	11.0
Manufacturing	43.7	55.2	48.5	57.4	11.5	-6.7	8.9
Wholesale Trade	21.8	25.9	27.1	33.0	4.1	1.2	5.9
Retail Trade	78.5	95.1	100.2	126.6	16.6	5.1	26.4
Transp., Warehousing & Utilities	19.0	24.5	23.0	31.8	5.5	-1.5	8.8
Information	17.9	18.8	21.8	29.2	0.9	3.0	7.4
Financial Activities	43.9	53.4	61.2	70.9	9.5	7.8	9.7
Professional & Business Services	70.0	108.2	99.2	145.4	38.2	-9.0	46.2
Educational & Health Services	64.4	75.0	85.5	120.2	10.6	10.5	34.7
Leisure & Hospitality	63.4	73.3	80.5	101.8	9.9	7.2	21.3
Other Services	22.3	27.9	29.5	38.4	5.6	1.6	8.9
Government	197.9	221.6	236.5	267.0	23.7	14.9	30.5
Self Employed	67.6	71.2	72.2	76.9	3.6	1.1	4.7
Total Jobs	757.4	920.3	966.3	1,190.9	162.9	46.1	224.6

Sources: 1990-2003 — EDD with CCSCE estimate of self-employed; 2012 — CCSCE

Sacramento Region Government Jobs (Thousands)	1990	2003	Change
Federal	31.5	14.5	-17.0
State	86.3	107.6	21.3
Government	65.4	81.6	16.2
Education	20.9	26.0	5.1
Local	75.4	114.4	39.0
Total	**193.2**	**236.5**	**43.3**

Source: EDD

The region's government jobs grew steadily, even as the region absorbed the loss of 15,000 federal civilian defense jobs resulting from base closures. State government jobs account for nearly half of the region's total government sector and 11.1% of the region's total jobs—far higher than the 2.9% share for state government jobs statewide. State government jobs grew moderately and remain the largest sector in the region's economic base. Local government jobs grew rapidly, reflecting Sacramento's rapid population growth—a trend expected to continue in the decade ahead.

The Government sector is projected to add 30,500 jobs between 2003 and 2012, split between state and local government.

Professional and Business Services posted the largest job growth between 1994 and 2000. It is projected to post the largest sector job gains (+46,200 jobs) between 2003 and 2012. With 99,200 jobs in 2003, this is the region's third-largest major industry, after Government and Retail Trade. Professional and Business Services will be the second-largest sector in 2012.

This sector, which includes legal, accounting, engineering, computer, scientific/technical and management services, now accounts for 10.3% of Sacramento jobs. While this share is below the 13.1% statewide average, Professional and Business Services is expected to be the region's fastest-growing major industry between 2003 and 2012.

Construction job levels doubled between 1994 and 2003 as the region experienced a surge of residential and public works construction. Construction accounted for 67,700 of the region's jobs in 2003. The growth in Construction job levels will continue, but on a more moderate pace, as the region already is experiencing a high level of annual construction.

Sacramento is one of the few regions in California to show a gain in manufacturing jobs since 1990. Manufacturing is still a relatively small sector in the region, with 48,500 jobs in 2003. It accounts for 5.0% of total jobs in 2003, compared with 9.6% statewide. Sacramento offers a comparatively low-cost manufacturing environment within California and should outperform the state in terms of manufacturing recovery and growth in the decade ahead.

CCSCE projects a gain of 8,900 manufacturing jobs, up 18.4% over 2003 levels.

The major population-serving sectors—Retail Trade, Financial Activities, Educational and Health Services and Leisure and Hospitality (which now includes food service)—all showed large and continuous gains in jobs. All of these sectors added jobs during both the 1994–2000 statewide high growth period **and** during the period since 2000. These three sectors are projected to add more than 80,000 jobs by 2012 and to account for more than 1/3 of the region's total job growth.

Income and Spending

The Sacramento region represents 5% of the California market. In 2003 total personal income in the Sacramento region reached $66.1 billion.

The Sacramento market is growing faster than the nation. Between 1994 and 2000 real (i.e. inflation-adjusted) income grew by 4.9% annually in the region—exceeding the national 3.7% annual growth rate. **And the Sacramento region outpaced the nation's slight income gains between 2000 and 2003.**

Because the 2004 edition of *California Economic Growth* includes Sutter and Yuba counties in the Sacramento region, **this results in a slight decline in regional per capita and average household income, as well as a slight increase in total income and spending.**

Per capita income in 2003 is estimated at **$31,213, or 1% below the national average**. The region posted small gains in both personal income and taxable sales. Along with the San Joaquin Valley, it was the only region to show positive growth since 2000. Real personal income (in 2003$) increased from $62.4 billion in 2000 to $66.1 billion in 2003. Taxable sales (in 2003$) inched up from $28.9 billion to $29.5 billion.

Sacramento Region Income and Taxable Sales 1990-2012 (2003$)				
Year	Per Capita Income	Average HH Income	Total Personal Income (Billions)	Taxable Sales (Billions)
1990	$28,297	$76,214	$45.7	$21.8
1994	$27,642	$75,039	$48.4	$21.0
2000	$32,056	$87,598	$62.4	$28.9
2003	$31,213	$88,945	$66.1	$29.5
2012	$40,373	$108,601	$103.8	$45.1
Average Annual Growth Rates				
1994-2000	2.5%	2.6%	4.3%	5.5%
2000-2003	-0.8%	0.5%	1.9%	0.8%
2003-2012	2.9%	2.2%	5.1%	4.8%
California	2.8%	2.5%	4.3%	4.0%
United States	2.9%	3.0%	3.8%	

Source: U.S. Department of Commerce; California Board of Equalization; CCSCE

Total real personal income is projected to rise by 5.1% per year in the Sacramento region between 2003 and 2012. This is well above the anticipated 3.8% annual growth nationally. The Sacramento market will be one of the fastest-growing markets, with more than one million residents in the state and nation.

Spending on taxable items will rise more slowly than income in the decade ahead. Regional spending on taxable items by households is projected to grow from $29.5 billion in 2003 to $45.1 billion in 2013 (measured in 2003$). This represents an annual spending growth gain of 4.8%—higher than the projected 4.0% annual statewide growth rate.

If the national economy produces productivity gains in the decade ahead as projected, per capita income in the region will grow by 2.9% per year and reach $40,373 in 2012 (in 2003$). This is comparable to the $40,921 per capita income projected for the nation.

Average household income in the Sacramento region was $88,945 in 2003—6% above the national average. Real average household income is projected to increase by 2.2% per year and reach $108,601 in 2012.[2]

The Sacramento region will grow faster than both the state and nation in total income and spending in the decade ahead.

---

[2] See page 5-72 for an explanation of CCSCE's measure of average household income.

Construction Activity

The value of new construction in 2003 reached the highest level in the region's history, despite the statewide economic slowdown. Private construction (residential and nonresidential combined) reached $5.8 billion; another $600 million was spent on public works, and $800 million on public buildings.

The tables and graphs below now include data for Sutter and Yuba counties.

Median home prices in the region have reached record levels of over $300,000 but remain well below prices in the Los Angeles, Bay Area and San Diego regions. Regional home prices are still competitive with a few other Western metro areas but the region's advantage over regions outside of California has largely disappeared.

Construction activity should continue to increase. The region will remain attractive to California homebuyers. Public works construction should surge as state and local governments commit funds to improving infrastructure in California.

Construction: A Large Cyclical Industry

The value of new construction activity (including public works but not public buildings) in the Sacramento region averaged $3.4 billion per year between 1978 and 2003 (measured in 2003 prices). The number of new residential units averaged 15,300. Residential and nonresidential building levels have been far above average in recent years, as shown below.[3]

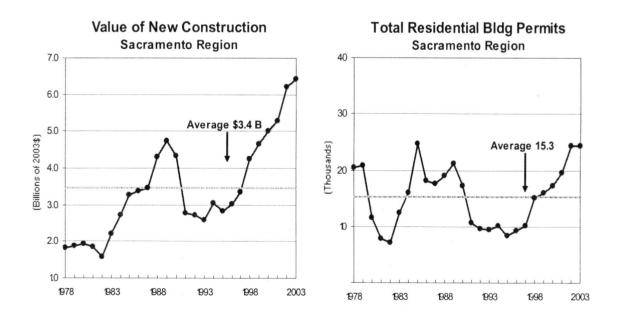

---

[3] The $6.4 billion in new construction in 2003 shown on the graph above excludes $800 billion for public buildings. The public building data is not included in the graphs because there is no consistent data prior to 1997.

Recent Construction Market Trends

The region posted record levels of new construction in 2003. Residential construction reached $4.7 billion—the highest level on record. Non-residential building remained above $1 billion, just below the all-time high.

Sacramento Region Construction Trends (Billions of 2003$)								
	New Construction				Residential Permits (Thousands)			
	1989	1993	2002	2003	1989	1993	2002	2003
El Dorado	$0.5	$0.2	$0.6	$0.7	2.2	0.8	1.9	1.9
Placer	0.9	0.6	1.7	1.5	4.7	2.1	7.2	5.3
Sacramento	2.8	1.4	3.1	3.5	13.1	5.1	12.9	13.8
Sutter			.3	.2	.2	.3	.7	1.0
Yolo	0.2	0.2	0.4	0.4	0.8	0.9	1.4	1.8
Yuba			.1	.1	.2	.3	.4	.6
Total Region	**$4.7**	**$2.6**	**$6.2**	**$6.4**	**21.2**	**9.4**	**24.4**	**24.4**

Source: Construction Industry Research Board

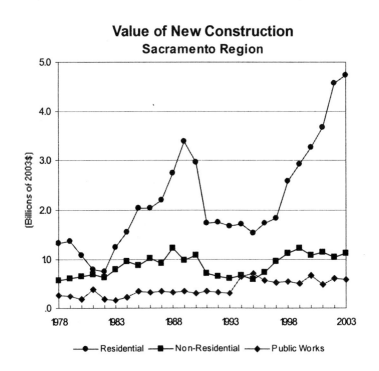

Value of New Construction
Sacramento Region

Approximately 24,400 residential units were constructed (the same as in 2002), led by building in Sacramento and Placer counties. Although Sacramento remains the largest construction market, growth pressures are pushing construction outward into El Dorado, Placer, Sutter, Yolo and Yuba.

Affordability and Household Growth: The Foundations for Housing

During the mid-1990s, affordability indices rebounded in the region. By the end of 1998, the median-priced house was affordable to more than 60% of Sacramento region households, as calculated by the California Association of Realtors. This was the highest affordability ratio in California's major regional markets.

Affordability has declined steadily since 1998 and has continued falling in 2004, reaching record low levels. Although real incomes are growing, median resale prices have increased more. Median prices have risen from $140,000 to over $300,000 during the past three years—**doubling in the midst of an economic downturn.**

Median prices in the Sacramento region are no longer below prices in most major western markets. The regional median price of $277,900 for the first quarter of 2004 compares with medians of $231,800 in Denver, $224,900 in Las Vegas, $195,100 in Portland, $148,0800 in Salt Lake City and $282,500 in Seattle.

Moreover, housing prices have been rising faster than household incomes and faster than overall price level. As shown on page 11-19, regional housing prices have surpassed the danger levels of the late 1980s with respect to income growth.

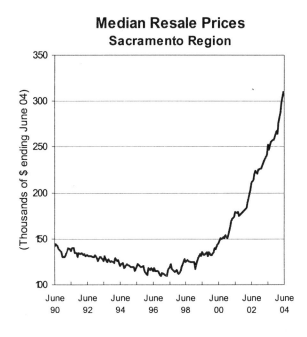

Median Resale Prices
Sacramento Region

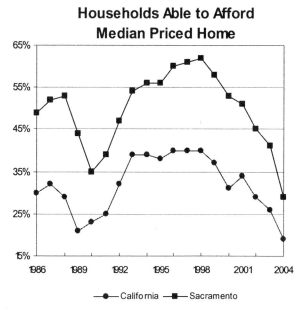

Households Able to Afford
Median Priced Home

Affordability is becoming more of a challenge in the region, and it is a challenge for lower- and middle-income families in all major regions of the state.

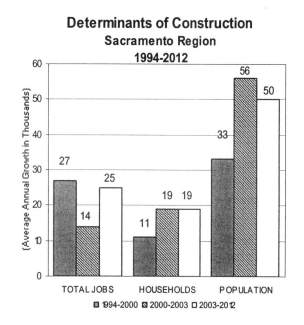

Determinants of Construction
Sacramento Region
1994-2012

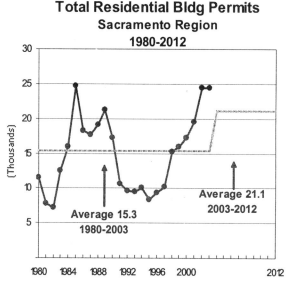

Total Residential Bldg Permits
Sacramento Region
1980-2012

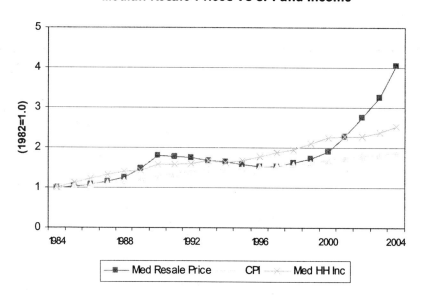

Sacramento Region
Median Resale Prices Vs CPI and Income

Job growth and demographic trends point to higher household formation in the region. Job, population, and household growth are expected to remain above the state average between 2003 and 2012. The projected annual household growth of 19,200 for 2003–2012 will support new residential construction averaging around

21,100 units per year from 2003 to 2012. The demographic projections point to a strong residential market in the Sacramento region in the years ahead.

The region is in the midst of a major and broad-based regional land use and growth-visioning project—the Blueprint Project. The focus is on organizing land use patterns to facilitate provision of needed housing while creating exciting places to live and work. The progress of the Blueprint Project can be followed on the on the website of the Sacramento Area Council of Governments (SACOG) at www.sacog.org.

Nonresidential Construction: Analysis and Outlook

Nonresidential construction, including public construction, reached $2.5 billion in 2003 including public works and public buildings. Public works ($600 million) and public buildings ($800 million) accounted for more than 50% of the region's nonresidential building in 2003.

Commercial and industrial construction leveled off with the statewide downturn. However, Sacramento remains one of the state's strongest markets for nonresidential construction growth.

Sacramento Region Nonresidential Construction (Billions of 2003$)				
	1989	**1993**	**2002**	**2003**
Commercial	$0.5	$0.3	$0.4	$0.4
Industrial	0.2	0.0 *	0.1	0.1
Other Nonresidential	0.1	0.1	0.2	0.2
Alterations/Additions	0.2	0.2	0.4	0.4
Public Works	0.4	0.3	0.6	0.6
Public Buildings			0.9	0.8

* Less than $50 million

Source: Construction Industry Research Board

Outlook for Future Growth

The following factors will support the growth of nonresidential construction in the Sacramento region:

- Job growth will exceed the state average (despite the short term budget deficit).

- State government will expand, and there are announced plans for major future state office construction.

- As a high-growth area, the region will have an above-average share of new school and transportation infrastructure. State and local bond approvals reached record levels in the November 2002 and March 2004 elections. Even higher levels of bond financing will be voted in next year.

- 4. The region will continue as a regional retail center and as a center for organizations doing business with the state government.

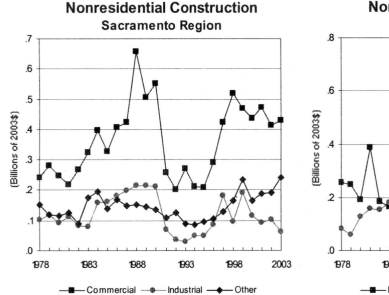

Nonresidential Construction
Sacramento Region

— Commercial — Industrial — Other

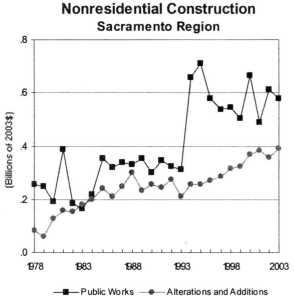

Nonresidential Construction
Sacramento Region

— Public Works — Alterations and Additions

SAN JOAQUIN VALLEY

SAN JOAQUIN VALLEY

The Bottom Line

The Valley region (Fresno, Kern, Kings, Madera, Merced, San Joaquin, Stanislaus, and Tulare counties) included approximately 1.3 million jobs and 3.6 million residents in 2003. The Valley is California's 4th- largest region in terms of jobs and 3rd-largest measured by population. The Valley economy has been less subject to cyclical swings than the economies of California's other major regions. The Valley added jobs during both the 1990–1994 and 2001 recessions.

The San Joaquin Valley has a unique economic base in California, with resource-based industries led by agriculture accounting for more than 1/3 of the region's economic base. The Valley escaped the downturns accompanying the aerospace decline in Los Angeles during the early 1990s and the high tech decline that hit the Bay Area after 2000. On the other hand, the Valley lagged behind other regions in the rapid growth period of 1994–2000, due to being largely bypassed in the growth of information and technology-related activities.

The region has been only partly successful in establishing a new economic base to offset the slow growth of farming activities. However, it has been very attractive for new residential growth and population-serving jobs. The Valley has very attractive prices for housing and industrial land, compared to other regions in the state. **Future growth will depend on the region's attraction as a residential location, but it will also require progress in attracting new basic industry jobs.**

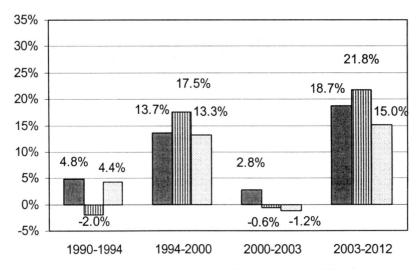

Past and Future Job Growth
San Joaquin Valley

■ San Joaquin Valley ▥ California ▢ United States

CCSCE projects that the Valley will have job growth rates above the national average between 2003 and 2012. Total jobs are projected to increase to near 1.6 million (+18.7%), outpacing the nation (+15.0%) but slightly below the state average (+21.8%).

Attractive housing prices and the availability of land have led to a surge in new housing construction. Northern Valley counties are, increasingly, an option for Bay Area commuters and housing prices are no longer nearly as affordable as they were five years ago. The northern Valley and eastern Bay Area are increasingly connected, and new jobs have moved to the I-580/680 corridors to be close to Valley housing and labor markets.

The more southern Valley counties like Fresno and Kern County still have comparatively low housing prices for many western states. Kern will probably become more connected to the Los Angeles Basin over time. The resulting growth pressures will be strongly debated in individual communities, but the location advantages will create strong market pressures for development and the incentive to do development well.

The new University of California campus in Merced County will be one clear boost to the region's economic base, and it may spawn additional higher-wage job opportunities. So far, though, no large clusters of economic activity have emerged to replace resource related job losses.

Job growth has been driven by a surge in population-serving jobs as Valley markets become large enough to support services that were previously "imported" from the coastal regions.

Per capita and average household incomes are the lowest among the state's major regions, and they will remain well below the national average to 2010. Unemployment rates are the highest among all major regions and will remain well above the state and national average.

The Region's Economic Base—Existing Status and Future Prospects

The San Joaquin Valley's economic base is still dominated by resource-based industries, as shown on page 12-4. In 2003 this sector accounted for 198,400, or 37.7%, of the region's basic jobs. Statewide, resource-based industries accounted for only 7.0% of basic jobs.

Farming is, by far, the largest single industry in the Valley's economic base, with 174,900 jobs in 2003. Farm output has remained near $27 billion for several years, and net farm income has remained near $5 billion. While California and the Valley still have the nation's largest agricultural and food products sector, it is not likely to provide significant growth in future years.

The amount of land in farming and the number of jobs related to farming are projected to decline over the next ten years. Farmland and water rights are both being sold for urban uses as agricultural productivity allows more output to be grown on less acreage.

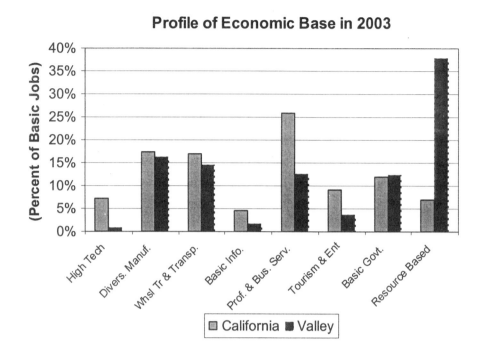

Profile of Economic Base in 2003

The other components of the Valley's resource base are mining, with 8,500 jobs (primarily related to oil activities in Kern County) and food and vegetable preserving, with 15,100 jobs in 2003. In both cases, the prospects are for continuing job declines.

Diversified Manufacturing is the second-largest economic base sector, with 86,100 jobs in 2002. The region has not lost manufacturing jobs since 1990, due to small gains in many sectors. Food manufacturing is, by far, the largest single industry. The fruit and vegetable component is included above in the resource base, but the remaining part of food manufacturing totaled 30,100 jobs in 2002—a small gain from 1990 levels.

Fabricated metal products accounted for 9,600 jobs, followed by nonmetallic minerals and machinery manufacturing (each with 5,700 jobs) and wood products (with 4,700 jobs) in 2003.

The Valley has shown a steady increase in the region's share of state Diversified Manufacturing jobs and also a slight increase in the absolute number of jobs in the sector since 1990. **The challenge for the Valley is to slowly build this base by offering access to western state markets and the Pacific Rim with lower costs than other California locations.**

CCSCE projects that the region will add more than 10,000 Diversified Manufacturing jobs by 2012, given current trends and without any major new initiatives.

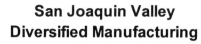

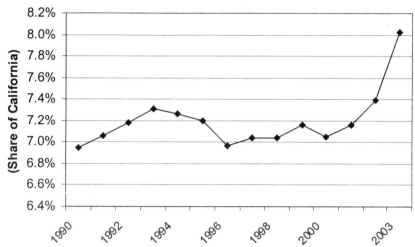

Wholesale Trade and Transportation is the third-largest basic industry sector, with 77,100 jobs in 2003. The largest component is wholesale trade, with 39,100 jobs. The fastest-growing components have been trucking (17,900 jobs in 2003) and warehousing, with 10,900 jobs.

Wholesale Trade and Transportation is projected to have the second-largest job gain among the Valley's basic industry sectors, adding 26,300 jobs by 2012. The Valley corridor is a major trucking corridor between the north and south in California, and it connects to the I-80 corridor to the east.

Professional and Business Services is the next-largest sector, with 66,400 jobs in 2003. It makes up a much smaller part of the Valley's economic base than in other regions, as shown on page 12-4. The sector accounted for 12.6% of the Valley's economic base in 2003, compared to the 26.0% statewide share. The relatively rapid growth of this sector has made less of a contribution to job growth in the Valley then elsewhere.

Professional and Business Services will contribute the largest numerical and percentage gains in basic jobs in the Valley to 2012. A gain of 33,600 jobs, or approximately 50%, is projected in this sector over the next nine years.

San Joaquin Valley
Jobs By Major Basic Industry Group
1994-2012
(Thousands)

	1994	2000	2003	2012	Numerical Change		
					1994-2000	2000-2003	2003-2012
High Tech Manufacturing	4.5	4.7	4.7	5.8	0.2	0.0	1.1
Diversified Manufacturing	81.2	88.8	86.1	98.3	7.6	-2.7	12.2
Wholesale Trade & Transportation	62.7	69.1	77.1	103.3	6.4	7.9	26.3
Basic Information	9.6	10.2	9.1	12.5	0.6	-1.1	3.4
Professional & Business Services	49.5	69.7	66.4	100.0	20.2	-3.3	33.6
Tourism & Entertainment	15.4	17.8	19.5	26.1	2.4	1.7	6.6
Basic Government	57.8	61.5	64.7	82.6	3.7	3.2	17.9
Resource-Based	209.8	229.7	198.4	180.2	19.8	-31.2	-18.3
Total Basic Jobs	490.6	551.6	526.0	608.8	61.0	-25.5	82.8

Source: EDD; projections — CCSCE

Government is the other large sector is the Valley's economic base, with 64,700 jobs in 2003 split fairly evenly between federal and state government sectors. Major government centers include the IRS services center in Fresno and major CSU campuses in Bakersfield, Fresno and CSU Stanislaus in Turlock.

The UC campus at Merced is scheduled to open soon. It will build slowly to become another major higher education center in the Valley. The campus will bring a large number of new jobs to the area by 212 and could create a set of industries affiliated with campus research.

High Tech Manufacturing and Information are also relatively small sectors in the San Joaquin Valley.

San Joaquin Valley Major Sectors in Economic Base 2003 (Thousands)		
	Jobs	
High Tech Manufacturing	4.7	
Diversified Manufacturing	86.1	
Wood Products		4.7
Nonmetallic Minerals		5.7
Fabricated Metal Products		9.6
Machinery Mfg.		5.7
Food Mfg. (excluding Preserving)		30.1
Plastics Mfg.		4.0
Professional and Business Services	66.4	
Legal Services		6.7
Accounting Services		8.2
Management of Companies		13.8
Employment Services		20.9
Information	9.1	
Telecommunications		4.9
Wholesale Trade and Transportation	77.1	
Wholesale Trade		39.1
Trucking		17.9
Warehousing & Storage		10.9
Tourism and Entertainment	19.5	
Arts, Entertainment, and Recreation		10.4
Accommodation		7.5
Government	64.7	
Federal Government		31.4
State Government		33.3
Resource Based	198.4	
Farm		174.9
Natural Resources and Mining		8.5
Fruit and Vegetable Preserving		15.1
Total Basic Jobs	526.0	

Source: EDD

The region has four major advantages that can help it overcome the negative impact of agriculture's slow growth on the region's economic base:

- The advantages of low-cost land and smaller communities. This has attracted Bay Area commuters in the northern Valley and also cost-sensitive activities such as call centers and the IRS service center.

- Location and cost advantages for distribution and transportation for north-south commerce within California serving the major coastal regions and other areas.

- Growth in state higher education enrollment, including the new UC campus at Merced. The new campus offers the possibility of startup industrial and technology developments similar to those experienced around other University of California campuses.

- The potential for new job bases connected to the region's expertise in agriculture and irrigation.

The Great Valley Center (GVC) in Modesto (www.greatvalley.org) provides an ongoing source of information and analysis of the region's economic base. GVC's hypothesis, which CCSCE supports, is that the Valley has the best chance to grow by building on existing areas of strength—rather than, for example, trying to become another Silicon Valley.

In a report titled *The Economic Future of the San Joaquin Valley*, GVC identifies six opportunity areas. One is innovative packaging of food products for consumer markets here and abroad. The example most familiar to readers is the prepackaged fresh salads now available in supermarkets.

Water irrigation technology is another small, but growing, area of possible exports. There is a center of activity around Fresno, where firms and the local colleges are cooperating to build workforce skills that support extension of the Valley's competencies in irrigation technology to other markets.

There is hope that the UC campus at Merced, along with UC Davis and other campuses, can become a center for innovative work in agricultural technology and related biotech activities.

The fourth area identified in the GVC report is the distribution and call center activities referred to above. The Valley's location and cost advantages should continue to attract a growing number of jobs in these activities.

A final two areas of opportunity are important, but a bit more speculative, from CCSCE's point of view. One target is for the Valley to compete for new light manufacturing activities, perhaps as a low-cost site for serving California, the western region and export markets. The final GVC target is for the Valley to become an Internet service center.

These are ambitious goals. The Valley's share of California's economic base has risen during both recession periods since 1990. The share fell, however, between 1994 and 2000, when the economic bases in other regions were growing rapidly.

CCSCE projects that the Valley's share of state basic jobs will remain near 8%, the same level as in 1990 and 2001. Jobs in many sectors will grow faster than the state average, but the Valley's economic base is still dominated by the resource-based sector where job losses are expected.

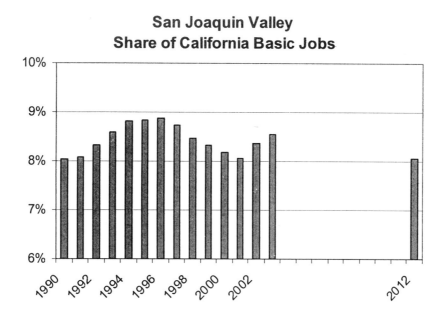

San Joaquin Valley
Share of California Basic Jobs

Job Trends by Major NAICS Industry Sector

The San Joaquin Valley has added jobs in every year since 1990. By avoiding job losses in 2001, 2002 and 2003, the Valley has pulled even with state and ahead of the nation in the rate of job growth since 1994.

San Joaquin Valley
Total Jobs

Growth in Non-Farm Jobs
San Joaquin Valley
July 1994-July 2004

Total jobs grew by 16.6% between 1994 and 2003, rising from 1,146,400 to 1,336,500. The comparable statewide job growth was 16.8%, and the national growth rate was 11.9%.

Job Projections

CCSCE projects that the Valley will grow faster than the nation between 2003 and 2012.

San Joaquin Valley Total Jobs 1994-2012 (Thousands)					Percent Change		
	1994	2000	2003	2012	1994-2000	2000-2003	2003-2012
San Joaquin Valley	1,146.4	1,302.9	1,336.5	1,586.2	13.7%	2.6%	18.7%
California	13,813.1	16,232.9	16,140.5	19,659.5	17.5%	-0.6%	21.8%
United States	127,233.7	144,132.4	142,336.9	163,756.8	13.3%	-1.2%	15.0%

Source: EDD, BLS and CCSCE (Projections)

Jobs in the region are projected to grow by 18.7% between 2003 and 2012, or by approximately 250,000 jobs. The driving factors are the region's attractive land availability and prices, and its growing proximity to the Bay Area and Southern

California regions. CCSCE's projections do assume moderate success in rebuilding the region's economic base around new industries that capitalize on the existing regional strengths.

Jobs by Major Industry Sector

San Joaquin Valley Jobs By Major Industry Group 1994-2012 (Thousands)					Numerical Change		
	1994	2000	2003	2012	1994-2000	2000-2003	2003-2012
Agriculture, Forestry, Fishing, Hunting	181.9	202.4	174.9	159.9	20.5	-27.5	-15.0
Mining	10.8	8.9	8.5	5.9	-2.0	-0.4	-2.6
Construction	41.1	58.0	69.0	82.4	16.9	11.0	13.4
Manufacturing	105.2	114.4	110.3	118.5	9.2	-4.1	8.2
Wholesale Trade	33.6	35.9	38.5	47.8	2.3	2.7	9.3
Retail Trade	114.8	126.2	132.0	165.0	11.3	5.8	33.0
Transp., Warehousing & Utilities	36.3	40.3	44.9	64.5	4.0	4.6	19.6
Information	14.4	15.3	14.2	19.9	1.0	-1.1	5.7
Financial Activities	39.4	42.0	46.6	55.6	2.6	4.6	9.0
Professional & Business Services	70.3	97.1	95.1	138.7	26.8	-2.0	43.6
Educational & Health Services	93.6	108.2	122.2	169.3	14.6	14.0	47.1
Leisure & Hospitality	73.1	84.0	89.0	111.6	10.9	5.0	22.6
Other Services	29.3	33.6	37.4	47.2	4.3	3.8	9.8
Government	207.6	238.1	252.6	296.0	30.5	14.5	43.4
Self Employed	95.1	98.2	99.6	104.1	3.0	1.4	4.5
Total Jobs	1,146.4	1,302.9	1,336.5	1,586.2	156.5	33.6	249.7

Source: 1990-2003 — EDD with CCSCE estimate of self-employed; 2012-CCSCE

Government is the largest major industry sector in terms of jobs in 2003, with 252,600 jobs, or 18.9%, of the Valley's total. Only the Sacramento region has a higher share of government jobs.

The sector has grown through both recessions, driven by a gain in local government jobs—from 141,700 in 1990 to 188,100 in 2003. State government and education jobs have increased by 50% since 1990, going from 22,500 to 33,200. The region experienced a small loss in federal government jobs as a result of base closures.

The Government sector is projected to add 43,400 jobs based on gains in local government and education and the new U.S. campus at Merced.

The Agriculture sector has the second-largest job level, with 174,900 jobs in 2003, or 13.1% of the region's job base. This is by far the highest share in California. In 1994, farm jobs accounted for 15.9% of the region's total jobs.

The table below shows the importance of farm jobs in each part of the region. One fact to notice is the sharp drop in farm jobs after 2000 while non-farm job growth continued. Farm jobs are a relatively smaller share of total wage and salary jobs in San Joaquin and Stanislaus, accounting for less than 10% of wage and salary jobs. Tulare, at 25%, has the largest share of farm jobs.

San Joaquin Valley Wage and Salary Jobs 1990-2003 (Thousands)						
	Farm			Non-Farm		
	1990	2000	2003	1990	2000	2003
Kern	29.5	48.3	403	170.7	194.1	206.8
Fresno/Madera	59.7	67.5	53.8	243.3	298.0	314.9
Kings	5.9	7.7	7.3	24.0	30.1	32.4
Merced	11.4	11.6	10.6	43.2	51.8	55.5
San Joaquin	15.6	16.7	16.5	152.7	185.8	197.6
Stanislaus	14.6	15.7	13.5	117.5	144.2	152.0
Tulare	29.5	34.9	32.9	82.4	98.2	102.8
Total Valley	**166.2**	**202.4**	**174.9**	**833.8**	**942.2**	**1.062.0**

Source: EDD

The major population-serving sectors, including Retail Trade, Educational and Health Services and Leisure and Hospitality (which now includes food services), all showed steady growth as the Valley's population grew.

These three sectors are projected to add more than 100,000 jobs by 2012, led by a 47,100 job gain in Educational and Health Services. Two factors support this substantial job growth: continuing population growth and the size of many Valley market areas, which supports specialized services that were previously obtained outside of the region. **It is this "deepening" of population-related services that has allowed job growth in the Valley to continue even in the absence of any new "breakout" basic industry sector.**

Professional and Business Services is projected to have the second-largest job gain (43,600 jobs) to 2012, among all the Valley's major industry sectors. The sector will have nearly as many jobs as Agriculture by 2012, despite having been only half as large as recently as 2000. The same "deepening" effect mentioned above for health care and retail trade is occurring in professional services, where the Valley's growing market size supports services previously purchased from outside the region.

Manufacturing jobs stayed above the 100,000 level throughout the 1990–2003 period, ending up higher in 2003 than in 1994. Manufacturing accounted for 8.3% of the Valley's total jobs in 2003, compared to 9.6% for the state as a whole. Manufacturing jobs are projected to grow by 8,200. Job growth here could be higher if the Valley is successful in creating new clusters such as water technology or agricultural/biotech innovations related to the U.C. Merced campus.

Construction job levels increased steadily since 1994, and that growth is projected to continue to 2012. Valley construction jobs are projected to double from 41,100 in 1994 to 82,400 in 2012.

The Valley has comparatively small job shares in the Information, Wholesale Trade and Other Services sectors.

Income and Spending

The San Joaquin Valley region represents 7% of the California market. In 2003 total personal income in the region reached $83.5 billion.

The Valley has the lowest per capita and average household incomes in California. It also had the lowest income growth rates in the 1990s. The region's large farm sector, together with the absence of any large high-wage sectors, is the primary reason for both trends.

Farm sales and farm income (adjusted for inflation) fell throughout the 1990s. Moreover, farm wages are among the lowest in any industry. As a result, per capita income in 2003, at $23,292, was the lowest among the major regions of California. It was virtually unchanged from 1990 levels.

Since 2000, the San Joaquin Valley has outperformed the state in terms of income growth. Two factors have supported Valley income growth: comparatively strong job growth and the immigration of higher-income residents from other regions. These factors, plus the declining share of farm activity in the region's economy, will support above-average income gains to 2012.

San Joaquin Valley Income and Taxable Sales 1990-2012 (2003$)				
	Per Capita Income	Average HH Income	Total Personal Income (Billions)	Taxable Sales (Billions)
1990	$22,364	$68,759	$61.6	$30.4
1994	$21,401	$67,302	$65.1	$28.6
2000	$23,499	$75,509	$78.0	$37.0
2003	$23,292	$77,108	$83.5	$38.6
2012	$30,924	$99,647	$132.5	$59.6
Average Annual Growth Rates				
1994-2000	1.6%	1.9%	3.1%	4.4%
2000-2003	-0.3%	0.7%	2.3%	1.5%
2003-2012	3.2%	2.9%	5.3%	4.9%
California	2.8%	2.5%	4.3%	4.0%
United States	2.9%	3.0%	3.8%	

Source: U.S. Department of Commerce; California Board of Equalization; CCSCE

Total real personal income is projected to rise by 5.3% per year in the San Joaquin Valley between 2003 and 2012. This is well above the 3.8% annual growth anticipated for the nation. With more than one million residents, the Valley region will be one of the fastest-growing markets in the state and nation.

If the national economy produces productivity gains in the decade ahead as projected, real per capita income in the region will grow by 3.2% per year, reaching $30,924 in 2012 (in 2003$). This will still be 24% below the per capita income in the nation.

Average household personal income in the San Joaquin Valley was $77,108 in 2003—8% below the national average. Average household income is projected to increase by 2.9% per year and reach $99,647 in 2012.[1]

The San Joaquin Valley will grow faster than both the state and the nation in income and spending in the decade ahead.

Spending on taxable items will rise more slowly than income in the decade ahead. Regional spending on taxable items by households is projected to grow from $38.6 billion in 2003 to $59.6 billion in 2012 (measured in 2003$). This represents an annual real spending growth gain of 4.9%—higher than the projected 4.0% annual statewide growth rate.

---

[1] See page 5-72 for an explanation of CCSCE's measure of average household income.

Construction Activity

The value of new construction in 2003 reached the highest level in the Valley's history, led by a record level of new housing permits. Private construction (residential and nonresidential combined) reached $6.4 billion; another $600 million was spent on public works and $900 million on public buildings.

Median home prices in the region have reached record levels, surging well above $200,000 in many Valley communities. Regional home prices are still competitive with other Western markets, but Valley prices are now above the national average.

Construction activity should continue to increase in the coming years. Large population growth is projected for the Valley. The region will remain attractive to California homebuyers in terms of land availability and price. Public works construction should grow as state and local governments commit funds to improving infrastructure in California.

Construction: A Large Cyclical Industry

The value of new construction activity (including public works but not public buildings) in the San Joaquin Valley averaged $3.9 billion per year between 1978 and 2003 (measured in 2003 prices).[2]

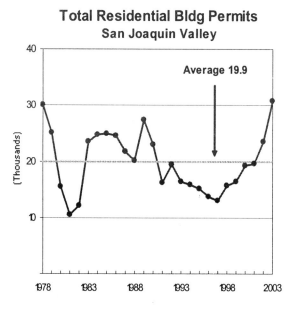

---

[2] The $7.0 billion in new construction in 2003 shown on the graph above excludes $900 million for public buildings. The public building data is not included in the graphs because there is no consistent data prior to 1997.

Recent Construction Market Trends

The region posted double-digit construction increases in 2003. Residential construction reached $4.9 billion—by far the highest level on record—as the region registered a record 30,800 residential permits. Non-residential building reached a record $1.5 billion, despite the state's slow economic growth in 2003.

San Joaquin Valley Construction Trends (Billions of 2003$)								
	New Construction				Residential Permits (Thousands)			
	1989	**1993**	**2002**	**2003**	**1989**	**1993**	**2002**	**2003**
Fresno	$1.0	$0.9	$1.2	$1.4	7.1	4.1	3.8	6.0
Kern	1.0	0.9	1.1	1.3	4.3	3.4	4.9	6.1
Kings	0.1	0.1	0.1	0.2	0.5	0.5	0.7	1.0
Madera	0.2	0.1	0.2	0.2	1.2	0.8	1.0	1.2
Merced	0.3	0.2	0.4	0.5	1.7	1.1	1.7	2.9
San Joaquin	0.9	0.7	1.1	1.9	4.2	2.6	6.3	7.0
Stanislaus	0.9	0.5	0.9	1.0	6.3	2.0	3.1	4.2
Tulare	0.4	0.3	0.4	0.5	2.0	1.8	2.0	2.4
Total Region	**$4.8**	**$3.8**	**$6.0**	**$7.0**	**27.3**	**16.4**	**23.5**	**30.8**

Source: Construction Industry Research Board

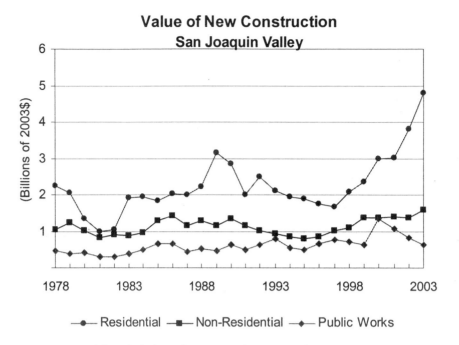

Value of New Construction
San Joaquin Valley

In recent years, residential development has accelerated in the region. There were 23,500 residential permits in 2002 and 30, 800 in 2003. Permit levels are up again in the first half of 2004. The permit trends are supported by the trend of increased domestic migration to San Joaquin Valley counties, as illustrated below.

The largest migration gains are in Fresno and Kern in the south and in San Joaquin and Stanislaus adjacent to the San Francisco Bay Area.

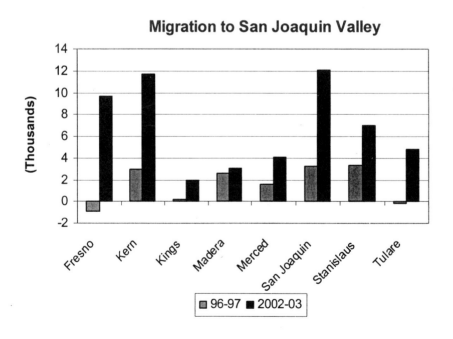

Migration to San Joaquin Valley

The southern part of the Valley is also experiencing rising construction levels that are continuing into 2003. The real value of construction is slightly above previous record levels, and housing construction is rising to record levels.

As indicated earlier in the chapter, job growth in Fresno and Kern counties has accelerated and construction levels have risen along with the job growth.

Affordability and Household Growth—the Foundations for Housing Recovery

Home prices are rising throughout the Valley. The same trends that affected California's urban regions have now spread to many San Joaquin Valley communities.

Still, Valley prices are below those in California's urban regions **and** below those in some competing markets outside the state. Moreover, affordability is high in relation to the incomes of households moving from other regions. It is also still reasonable for some existing Valley households.

Median Home Prices San Joaquin Valley		
County/City	June 03	June 04
Fresno	$159,000	$208,000
Fresno	152,000	201,000
Kern	135,000	170,000
Bakersfield	142,750	183,500
Madera	174,000	225,500
Merced	154,500	175,000
San Joaquin	257,000	300,250
Stockton	238,000	266,500
Tracy	331,100	395,000
Stanislaus	220,750	270,000
Modesto	215,000	255,000
Patterson	251,000	330,500
Tulare	128,000	155,000
Visalia	149,500	180,000

Source: California Association of Realtors

The only markets with median prices over $300,000 are in San Joaquin and Stanislaus counties. Stockton, Modesto and Patterson all have median prices above $250,000, after large increases since 2001. Tracy, which was the only Valley city with a median home price above $300,000 as recently as a year ago, now is the only city with a median price close to $400,000.

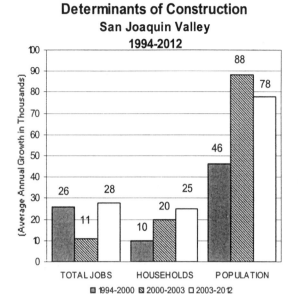

Determinants of Construction
San Joaquin Valley
1994-2012

■ 1994-2000 ◨ 2000-2003 □ 2003-2012

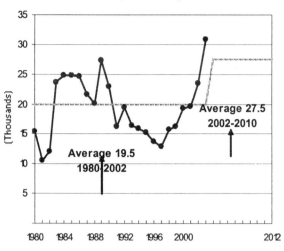

Total Residential Bldg Permits
San Joaquin Valley 1980-2012

Job growth and demographic trends point to higher household growth in the region. Job growth is projected to average 28,000 per year from 2003 to 2012. This is slightly higher than the 26,000 annual gains in the 1994–2000 period. The projected household growth of 24,900 annually for 2003 to 2012 will support new residential construction averaging around 27,500 units per year from 2003 to 2012.

Nonresidential Construction—Analysis and Outlook

Nonresidential construction reached $3.2 billion in 2003, including public works and public buildings. Public construction fell in 2003, offsetting modest gains in private nonresidential construction.

Commercial construction increased slightly to an all-time record, despite the statewide downturn. Alterations and additions also posted record building valuation in 2003. Public buildings ($0.9 billion) remained the largest category of nonresidential construction.

San Joaquin Valley Nonresidential Construction
(Billions of 2003$)

	1989	1993	2002	2003
Commercial	$0.5	$0.4	$0.5	$0.6
Industrial	0.2	0.2	0.1	0.2
Other Nonresidential	0.3	0.3	0.5	0.5
Alterations/Additions	0.3	0.3	0.4	0.4
Public Works	0.5	0.5	0.9	0.6
Public Buildings			1.0	0.9

Source: Construction Industry Research Board

Outlook for Future Growth

Three major factors will support the growth of nonresidential construction in the San Joaquin Valley.

- Job growth will exceed the state average.

- As a high-growth area, the region will have an above-average share of new school and transportation infrastructure.

- A high-speed rail project through the Valley is a potential big-ticket addition to infrastructure later in the decade.

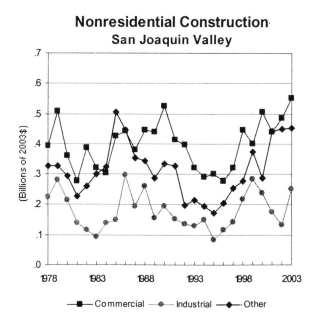

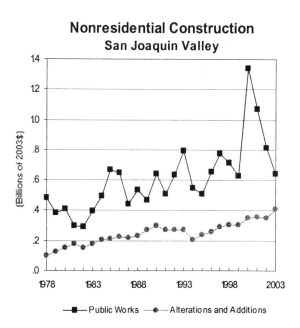

APPENDIX A

APPENDIX A

BASIC INDUSTRIES BY NAICS CATEGORIES

Farm, Natural Resources and Mining and Construction

These new NAICS categories include approximately the same number of jobs as the former SIC categories. There is considerable additional detail now available for farm and construction activities, but the job totals are similar.

The construction sector is divided into Construction of Buildings (residential and nonresidential), Heavy and Civil Engineering Construction and Specialty Trade Contractors, who provide services to firms in the other construction sectors.

Manufacturing

The Manufacturing sector is approximately the same size under NAICS as it was under the SIC structure. The NAICS Manufacturing sector had 1,857,500 jobs in 2000 while the SIC-based estimate was 1,947,800.

Publishing was removed from the Printing sector and placed in Information. Beverage manufacturing was moved from Food Products to its own separate category. Textiles were split into two categories. Medical equipment and supplies was moved from the SIC Instruments category to the NAICS Miscellaneous Manufacturing sector. Contract manufacturing was moved from SIC Management Services to the appropriate NAICS Manufacturing sector. Logging was moved to Natural Resources.

The biggest change was the creation of the Computer and Electronic Products Manufacturing sector, primarily by moving high tech sectors from the SIC Industrial Machinery (where computers were) and Electrical Equipment sector, where Communications Equipment and Electronic Components were.

This new subsector brings together those establishments engaged in the production of computers, computer peripherals, communications equipment, similar electronic products and the components for such products. The subsector was created because of the economic significance that these industries have obtained, because their rapid growth suggests that the products of these industries will become even more important to the economies of the North American countries, and because the production processes of the establishments in these industries are fundamentally different from the production processes for other machinery and equipment.

Wholesale Trade

Wholesale Trade firms were subject to significant reclassification under NAICS methodologies, as described below.

NAICS redefines the boundaries between Retail and Wholesale Trade. The new NAICS definition emphasizes what the establishment does, rather than to whom it sells. Retailers are defined as those establishments that sell merchandise (generally, without transformation) and attract customers using methods such as advertising, point-of-sale location, and display of merchandise. A store retailer has a selling place open to the public; merchandise on display or available through sales clerks; facilities for making cash or credit card transactions; and services provided to retail customers.

Wholesale establishments, on the other hand, are primarily engaged in selling or arranging the purchase or sale of (a) goods for resale, (b) capital or durable nonconsumer goods, and (c) raw and intermediate materials and supplies used in production. Wholesalers normally operate from a warehouse or office and are characterized by having little or no display of merchandise. In addition, neither the design nor the location of the premises is intended to solicit walk-in traffic. Wholesalers also do not normally use advertising directed to the general public.

The 1987 SIC defined retailers as those establishments that sold primarily to consumers, whereas wholesalers were those establishments that sold primarily to business customers.

There are now three major components of Wholesale Trade: Durable Goods, Nondurable Goods and Electronic Markets and Agents and Brokers. Currently, CCSCE classifies the Durable Goods and Electronic Market components as basic industries for the state, and the whole Wholesale Trade sector as a basic industry at the regional level.

Retail Trade

For the most part, retail subsectors under NAICS are the same as under the SIC classification. **Eating and drinking establishments (now called Food Services) have been moved to the new Leisure and Hospitality sector, so Retail Trade has fewer jobs than before.**

One new addition is Electronic Shopping and Mail Order where Internet sales activity involving consumers is included. Jobs in this sector nearly doubled from 1990 to 2000—rising from 11,600 to 22,900. They then fell to 17,300 in 2003. By any measure, the Internet activity is growing on a long-term basis, but it still represents a small portion of Retail Trade activity.

Transportation, Warehousing and Utilities

There are several significant changes and additions in the Transportation, Warehousing and Utilities sector.

The basic air, rail truck and water transportation activities have been split into a two components: direct and support. For example, air transportation now includes the carriers, and support activities for transportation now include airport operations (including food service). Because some of the previous jobs are now included in the support sector, the direct sectors for air, rail, truck and water transportation now show fewer jobs than before. In most cases, the support sector has more job growth than the direct service sector.

The sector now includes new industry segments, such as couriers and messengers and warehousing. Telecommunications and radio/TV broadcasting, which were included in the SIC Transportation, Communications and Utilities sector, have been moved to the Information sector.

Information

Perhaps the most important change in NAICS is the recognition of a new Information sector. This new sector includes those establishments that create, disseminate, or provide the means to distribute information. It also includes establishments that provide data processing services.

Industries included in this new sector are newspaper, book, and periodical publishers (previously included in the SIC manufacturing sector); software publishers (previously included in services); broadcasting and telecommunications producers and distributors (previously included with utilities and transportation); and motion picture and sound recording industries, information services and data processing services (previously included in services).

There are 34 industries in this new subsector, 20 of which are new. Some of the new industries are paging, cellular and other wireless telecommunications, and satellite telecommunications.

Financial Activities

The NAICS Financial Activities sector closely resembles the Finance, Insurance and Real Estate sector under the SIC structure. One change is the movement of rental activities (including car rentals and video and disc rentals) from Services to Financial Activities.

Professional and Business Services

There are three main segments of Professional and Business Services: 1) Professional, Scientific Technical and Management Services; 2) Management of Companies and Enterprises and 3) Administrative and Support and Waste Services.

The Professional, Scientific, Technical and Management Services category is similar to what CCSCE called professional services under the SIC classification scheme and were in the broad SIC Services category.

The Management segment is a new NAICS category and includes corporate head and regional offices and other corporate management sites. Employees were formerly included in the industry that they managed but under the NAICS structure have been moved into this new category.

Administrative and Support Services include establishments providing routine support activities for the day-to0day operations of other organizations. Major subcategories include office administrative activities, employment services and services to buildings.

Educational and Health Services

This sector is similar to the SIC sectors Educational Services and Health Services included in the broad SIC Services category.

Leisure and Hospitality

Leisure and Hospitality is a new NAICS sector combining accommodations (primarily hotels) and amusements from the SIC Services category and food service, formerly in Retail Trade.

Other Services

The NAICS Other Services sector is made up of three parts of the SIC Services sector: 1) repair and maintenance including auto repair; 2) personal and laundry services, and 3) a group of nonprofit organizations. All of these activities were formerly in the broad SIC Services category.

Government

The NAICS Government sector is similar to the SIC Government sector.

Chart A-1
California and United States
Basic Jobs by Major Category
2003
(Thousands

NAICS Code

	Diversified Manufacturing	819.0
31-321000	Wood Product Manufacturing except Sawmills	31.9
31-331000	Primary Metal Manufacturing	25.2
31-332000	Fabricated Metal Product Mfg	138.8
31-333000	Machinery Manufacturing	86.7
31-335000	Electrical Equipment and Appliance Manufacturing	36.6
31-336900	Other Transportation Equipment Manufacturing	56.0
31-337000	Furniture and Related Product Manufacturing	62.9
31-339100	Medical Equipment and Supplies Manufacturing	49.1
31-339900	Other Miscellaneous Manufacturing	42.6
32-312000	Beverage and Tobacco Product Mfg	35.7
32-313000	Textile Mills	13.0
32-314000	Textile Product Mills	17.0
32-315000	Apparel Manufacturing	89.0
32-316000	Leather and Allied Products Manufacturing	4.9
32-322000	Paper Manufacturing	30.1
32-325100	Basic Chemical Manufacturing	6.5
32-325600	Soap, Cleaning Compound and Toiletry Manufacturing	12.4
32-325900	Other Chemical Products & Preparation Manufacturing	20.7
32-326000	Plastics and Rubber Products Manufacturing	59.8
	High Tech Manufacturing	438.4
31-334100	Computer and Peripheral Equipment Manufacturing	65.5
31-334200	Communications Equipment Manufacturing	28.4
31-334300	Audio and Video Equipment Manufacturing	8.3
31-334400	Semiconductor and Electronic Component Manufacturing	108.1
31-334500	Electronic Instrument Manufacturing	107.0
31-334600	Magnetic Media Manufacturing and Reproducing	8.9
31-336400	Aerospace Product and Parts Manufacturing	73.4
32-325400	Pharmaceutical and Medicine Manufacturing	38.8
	Wholesale Trade and Transportation	766.3
41-423000	Merchant Wholesalers, Durable Goods	346.0
41-424000	Merchant Wholesalers, Nondurable Goods	233.2
41-425000	Wholesale Electronic Markets and Agents and Brokers	65.5
43-481000	Air Transportation	54.2
43-482000	Rail Transportation	12.9
43-483000	Water Transportation	4.2
43-486000	Pipeline, Scenic and Sightseeing Transportation	6.1
43-488300	Support Activities for Water Transportation	18.2
43-488900	Other Support Activities for Basic Transportation	19.3

	Information	268.6	
50-511200	Software Publishers		44.7
50-515000	Broadcasting		44.8
50-517000	Telecommunications		121.4
50-518000	Internet Serv. Providers, Web Search Portals & Data Processing		48.6
50-519000	Other Basic Information Services		9.2
	Professional and Business Services	1,596.6	
60-541100	Legal Services		138.7
60-541200	Accounting, Tax Preparation and Bookkeeping Services		103.5
60-541300	Architectural, Engineering and Related Services		149.3
60-541400	Specialized Design Services		23.0
60-541500	Computer Systems Design and Related Services		166.2
60-541600	Management, Scientific and Technical Consulting Services		111.0
60-541700	Scientific Research and Development Services		95.1
60-541800	Advertising and Related Services		60.5
60-541900	Other Professional, Scientific and Technical Services		52.1
60-550000	Management of Companies and Enterprises		255.6
60-561300	Employment Services		441.6
	Tourism and Entertainment	560.7	
50-512000	Motion Picture and Sound Recording		135.2
70-710000	Arts, Entertainment, and Recreation		233.9
70-721000	Accommodations		191.6
	Government	258.7	
90-919110	Department of Defense		58.2
90-912999	Other Federal Government		200.5
	Resource Based	472.2	
11-000000	Farm including Farm Self Employed		407.6
10-113300	Logging		2.6
10-210000	Mining		19.4
31-321100	Sawmills		7.8
32-311400	Fruit and Vegetable Preserving and Specialty		34.8

Chart A-2
California and Economic Regions
Basic Jobs by Major Category
2003
(Thousands)

NAICS Code

	Diversified Manufacturing	1,072.0
31-321000	Wood Product Manufacturing	39.6
31-327000	Nonmetallic Mineral Product Manufacturing	45.0
31-331000	Primary Metal Manufacturing	25.2
31-332000	Fabricated Metal Product Mfg	138.8
31-333000	Machinery Manufacturing	86.7
31-335000	Electrical Equipment and Appliance Manufacturing	36.6
336-3364-3366	Other Transportation Equipment	56.0
31-337000	Furniture and Related Product Manufacturing	62.9
31-339000	Miscellaneous Manufacturing	91.7
311-3114	Food Manufacturing Except Preserving	121.2
32-312000	Beverage and Tobacco Product Mfg	34.8
32-313000	Textile Mills	13.0
32-314000	Textile Product Mills	17.0
32-315000	Apparel Manufacturing	89.0
32-316000	Leather and Allied Products Manufacturing	4.9
32-322000	Paper Manufacturing	30.1
32-323000	Printing and Related Support Activities	63.9
32-324000	Petroleum and Coal Products Manufacturing	15.4
325-3254	Chemicals Exc. Pharmaceuticals	39.6
32-326000	Plastics and Rubber Products Manufacturing	59.8
	High Tech Manufacturing	438.4
31-334000	Computer and Electronic Product Manufacturing	326.1
31-336400	Aerospace Product and Parts Manufacturing	73.4
32-325400	Pharmaceutical and Medicine Manufacturing	38.8
	Wholesale Trade and Transportation	1,041.8
41-423000	Merchant Wholesalers, Durable Goods	346.0
41-424000	Merchant Wholesalers, Nondurable Goods	233.2
41-425000	Wholesale Electronic Markets and Agents & Brokers	72.2
43-481000	Air Transportation	54.2
43-482000	Rail Transportation	12.9
43-483000	Water Transportation	4.2
43-484000	Truck Transportation	109.9
43-486000	Other Transportation	6.1
43-488000	Support Activities for Transportation	75.4
43-492000	Couriers and Messengers	70.9
43-493000	Warehousing and Storage	56.8

	Information	274.5	
50-511200	Software Publishers		44.7
50-515000	Broadcasting (except Internet)		44.8
50-517000	Telecommunications		121.4
50-518000	Internet Serv. Providers, Web Search Portals & Data Processing		53.1
50-519000	Other Information Services		9.6
	Professional and Business Services	1,596.6	
60-541100	Legal Services		138.7
60-541200	Accounting, Tax Preparation and Bookkeeping Services		103.5
60-541300	Architectural, Engineering and Related Services		149.3
60-541400	Design Services		23.0
60-541500	Computer Systems Design and Related Services		166.2
60-541600	Management, Scientific and Technical Consulting Services		111.0
60-541700	Scientific Research and Development Services		95.1
60-541800	Advertising Services		60.5
60-541900	Other Professional, Scientific and Technical Services		52.1
60-550000	Management of Companies and Enterprises		255.6
60-561300	Employment Services		441.6
	Tourism and Entertainment	560.7	
50-512000	Motion Picture and Sound Recording		135.2
70-710000	Arts, Entertainment, and Recreation		233.9
70-721000	Accommodation		191.6
	Government	730.3	
90-919110	Department of Defense		58.2
90-912999	Other Federal Government		200.5
90-921611	State Government Education		210.2
90-922999	Other State Government		261.4
	Resource Based	431.8	
11-000000	Total Farm		375.0
10-000000	Natural Resources and Mining		22.0
32-311400	Fruit and Vegetable Preserving and Specialty		34.8